ANDRÉ GIDE

AND THE CODES OF HOMOTEXTUALITY

STANFORD
FRENCH AND ITALIAN
STUDIES

editor

ALPHONSE JUILLAND

editorial board

BEVERLY ALLEN

MARC BERTRAND

BRIGITTE CAZELLES

ROBERT GREER COHN

JEAN-PIERRE DUPUY

JOHN FRECCERO

RENÉ GIRARD

ROBERT HARRISON

RALPH HESTER

PAULINE NEWMAN-GORDON

JEFFREY SCHNAPP

MICHEL SERRES

CAROLYN SPRINGER

managing editor

KATARINA KIVEL

volume XLVIII

DEPARTMENT OF FRENCH AND ITALIAN
STANFORD UNIVERSITY

ANDRÉ GIDE

AND THE CODES OF HOMOTEXTUALITY

EMILY S. APTER

1987

ANMA LIBRI

Stanford French and Italian Studies is a collection of scholarly publications devoted to the study of French and Italian literature and language, culture and civilization. Occasionally it will allow itself excursions into related Romance areas.

Stanford French and Italian Studies will publish books, monographs, and collections of articles centering around a common theme, and is also open to scholars associated with academic institutions other than Stanford.

The collection is published for the Department of French and Italian, Stanford University by Anma Libri.

PREFACE

"On ne parle plus assez de Gide." This seemingly offhand comment, made by Roland Barthes in the course of an interview (1975) that subsequently appeared in *Le Grain de la voix*, points not only to a lacuna in contemporary critical theory, namely, a comprehensive study of Gide's theoretical modernism as it relates to broader issues in poststructuralism, but also to a gap in the oeuvre of Barthes himself, a work that might have been entitled: "Barthes's postmodernist Gide."[1] Barthes alludes indirectly and provocatively to this unwritten Gidean work when, in one of the interviews, he speaks of a journal that, unlike Gide, he never kept:

> Adolescent, la lecture de Gide a été très importante pour moi et, ce que j'aimais par-dessus tout, c'était son *Journal*. C'est un livre qui m'a toujours fasciné par sa structure discontinue, par son côté "patchwork" s'étendant sur plus de cinquante ans. Dans le *Journal* de Gide, tout y passe, toutes les irisations de la subjectivité: les lectures, les rencontres, les réflexions, et même les bêtises. C'est cet aspect-là qui m'a séduit et c'est ainsi que j'ai toujours envie d'écrire: par fragments. Pourquoi, me direz-vous alors, je n'écris pas un journal? C'est une tentation que

[1] Roland Barthes, *Le Grain de la voix* (Paris: Seuil, 1981), p. 213. In the context of this remark on the neglect of Gide, Barthes praises *Paludes* for its "modernité," calling for its critical rereading along with the *Journal*. The latter he acknowledges as having a special affinity with his own work in its theme of: "l'inauthenticité qui se déjoue elle-même, de l'authenticité retorse, qui n'est plus l'authenticité." In a later interview focused on the topic of the role of the intellectual (1976), Barthes refers to Gide as a powerful influence on his early career:

beaucoup d'entre nous ont, et pas seulement les écrivains. Mais cela pose le problème du "je" et de la sincérité qui était peut-être plus facile à résoudre du temps de Gide — en tous les cas que lui a bien résolu sans complexe et avec maîtrise — et qui aujourd'hui est devenu beaucoup plus difficile après les transformations de la psychanalyse et le passage du bulldozer marxiste. On ne peut pas recommencer intégralement une forme passée.[2]

Though the historical moment of the journal as literary form may well indeed be past, the "patchwork" effect of "bêtise" juxtaposed against philosophical reflection; of fragmentation and discontinuity roughly disciplined to form a combustive, unruly "book," has never been more greatly in evidence, and may be seen in Barthes's work as displaced from the aborted journal to the genre of his critical prose. Even in this displacement, Barthes may have followed Gide's example, for throughout Gide's fiction, one finds traces of this intimate patchwork, indications that portions of the *Journal* had detached themselves and drifted unerringly into the literary oeuvres: *Les Cahiers d'André Walter*, *Paludes*, *Les Nourritures terrestres*, *Les Faux-Monnayeurs* (and its accompanying *Journal*), up to the late trilogy of *récits*, *L'Ecole des femmes*, *Robert*, and *Geneviève* (the last alternately titled, like a journal, *La Confidence inachevée*).

In the choice of certain works by Gide to be singled out for close consideration in individual chapters (*Paludes*, *Les Nourritures terrestres*, *La Porte étroite*, *L'Ecole des femmes*), I was guided by a criterion that might be called, for lack of a precise term, the effect of the displaced journal. By this, I understand not so much the quality of autobiography (with its inherent claims to truth and sincerity), but rather the contrary — the negatively inscribed, artificial, essentially deceitful form of the personal. Barthes was uncharacteristically optimistic in claiming that Gide, "sans complexe et avec maîtrise," succeeded in fully resolving the problem of monological sincerity, his pre-Freudian field of operation notwithstanding. I have chosen to investigate traces of the displaced journal in terms of narrative pretenses

"Vous avez connu Gide?"

"Non, je ne l'ai pas connu. Je l'ai aperçu une fois de très loin, à la brasserie 'Lutétia': il mangeait une poire et il lisait un livre. Je ne l'ai donc pas connu; mais comme pour beaucoup d'adolescents de l'époque, il y avait mille données qui faisaient que je m'intéressais à lui."

"Par exemple?"

"Il était protestant. Il faisait du piano. Il parlait du désir. Il écrivait." (Barthes, p. 246)

---

[2] Barthes, p. 305.

of sincerity; revealing, wherever appropriate, the negative value of Gide's confessional "false coin" as it emerges in the broken, circular, fragmentary structures of his style.

Following Derrida, de Man, Deleuze and Spivak, I have also been well served by Nietzsche's speculations "On Truth and Falsity in their Ultramoral Sense":

> What, therefore, is truth? A mobile army of metaphors, metonymies, anthropomorphisms; ...truths are illusions of which one has forgotten that they *are* illusions, ...coins which have their obverse effaced and now are no longer of account as coins but merely as metal.[3]

Derrida ("La Mythologie blanche") and de Man ("Rhetoric of Tropes: [Nietzsche]"), have both made use of this passage as a point of disembarkation for the theory of rhetorical "usure," of what de Man characterizes as that "degradation of metaphor" that merits condemnation "because it forgets the un-truth, the lie that the metaphor was in the first place."[4] Their discovery of a rhetoric of philosophy in Nietzsche's projected philosophy of rhetoric urges extension of the critique of linguistic fakery to the conceits of narrative and rhetorical simulacra invented by Gide. Gide, it must be said, deflates the suspense of such an endeavor by performing much of this critique himself.

My response to the dilemma of Gide's awareness of the "original error" within every figure of speech and narrative device has been to sidestep the philosophical ramifications of a full-scale deconstruction of Gidean narratology in favor of a series of close readings designed to reveal ways in which Gide's writings (particularly his "oeuvres de jeunesse") anticipate recent developments in the interpretation of rhetorical negation from Blanchot to Kristeva. At the same time, in the progression of chapters, which themselves move through Gide's writings selectively and more or less chronologically, I have attempted to preserve a sense of the narrative constituted by the modern history of the sign: first, as it was defined by the Symbolist movement; second, by Gide as both writer and critic; and third, by Barthes himself, whose conception of the evolution and erasure of signification remains, in my mind, among the most sophisticated and accessible of poststructuralist analyses.

[3] "On Truth and Falsity in Their Ultramoral Sense," ed. Oscar Levy (New York, 1964), 2:174, as cited by Gayatri Chakravorty Spivak, "Translator's Preface," in Jacques Derrida, *Of Grammatology* (Baltimore: Johns Hopkins University Press, 1974), p. xxii.
[4] Paul de Man, *Allegories of Reading* (New Haven: Yale University Press, 1979), p. 111.

There is, of course, another reason for reading Gide *with* Barthes, for daring the ridiculous by envisioning a work entitled: *Gide, lecteur de Roland Barthes*! In addition to the uncanny complementarity of their literary projects— Gide's experiments in theoretical fiction, Barthes's transformation of theory into an iconoclastic form of "writing"— there is also the coincidence of their intellectual trajectories. Both move in their literary careers from the genres of post-Symbolist, degree zero classicism to the rhetorical codes governing "the lover's discourse," or what we have called "homotextuality." In the dialectic between askesis and affirmation, litotes and hyperbole, aestheticized, Platonic love and the literal, immediate eroticism of the textual body, a poetics of gender may be traced that establishes profound affinities between the two authors. Chapters II, and III each deal with aspects of this homotextual poetics, from the homoeroticism accentuated by Gide's rewriting of the Narcissus myth to the patterns of "male bonding" structuring the sophistic altercations in *Paludes*. Following these readings, an attempt is made in Chapter IV to define homotextuality as a theoretical construct in the context of Gide's explicit politics of gender from *Les Nourritures terrestres* to *Corydon*. I am, of course, aware that there is no way systematically to define the term. In using it, I have been conscious of its value as a kind of omnibus signifier referring to dimensions of the relationship between Greek codes of ideal love and what the early sexologist Edward Carpenter would characterize as a "homosocial" epistemology, to displacements and indeterminacies of narrative voice and gender, and to the fluctuating semiosis of a sexually suggestive textual silence.

ACKNOWLEDGEMENTS

I would like to acknowledge the consistent support and guidance of my former teachers at Princeton University: Victor Brombert, Albert Sonnenfeld, and Ralph Freedman. I would also like to thank Michael Riffaterre of Columbia University, Gérard Genette of the Ecole des Hautes Etudes in Paris, and George Pistorius and Mark Taylor of Williams College for their useful suggestions and stimulating discussions on the themes of this study.

For his invaluable criticism, incisive editorial comments and personal encouragement, I wish to recognize the efforts of Professor Robert Greer Cohn of Stanford University.

A special debt of gratitude must be expressed to Francis Oakley, President of Williams College and to John Reichert, Dean of Faculty, for their help in providing assistance from Williams College for several trips to France, research expenses, and a publishing subsidy. I also thank them for intellectual encouragement and exchange.

The intial research for this book was supported by a discretionary grant from Princeton University and a year-long fellowship from the French Ministry of Foreign Affairs for work at the Ecole Normale Supérieure.

Finally, I would like to express my deep appreciation for their help with production of the manuscript to Eileen Sahady, Donna Chenail, and especially Peggy Bryant.

Paris, 1985

For Anthony Vidler

CONTENTS

I. Barthes's Gide: The Style of Writing
without style   1

II. Emptying Out the Symbolist Sign: Narcissus
or the Insufficient Symbol   13

III. Not's Knots: Denial and Difference in *Paludes*   44

IV. Homotextual Counter-Codes: The Hyperbolic
Discourse of *Les Nourritures terrestres*   74

V. The Etiology of the Unspoken: Negation
and Gender in the *Récits*   105

Selected Bibliography   151

Index   159

I

BARTHES'S GIDE

THE STYLE OF WRITING WITHOUT STYLE

The early works of André Gide have held an uncertain place in literary history and interpretation somewhere between the residues of late Symbolism and the first tentative experiments in modernism. Critics have tended to dismiss them as overly precious "oeuvres de jeunesse," preludes to the major writings that scarcely merit close reading. Germaine Brée, writing in the 1950s, considered *Le Traité du Narcisse*, *Le Voyage d'Urien* and *La Tentative amoureuse* (all published prior to 1895) to be minor works, simple "variations on a theme":

> Il s'agit, par de savantes variations sur un thème, de s'approprier les techniques littéraires d'un cercle "éminement ésotérique et cénaculaire". Ces trois oeuvres consciemment élaborées dans l'esprit et le ton "symbolistes", sont de charmantes fantaisies littéraires dont la création n'a point coûté de grands efforts à Gide.[1]

A.G. Lehmann, in his classic study *The Symbolist Aesthetic in France*, accorded *Le Traité du Narcisse* a more positive pedigree when he situated it at the crux of a new aesthetic development of the 1890s. For Lehmann, *Le Traité* demarcated a shift away from the "pastiche idealism" and mystification of poetic imagination in vogue among so many of Mallarmé's disciples, and towards a genre of theoretical fiction that explored the philosophical underpinnings of language and symbolic form.[2] However, he too was unconcerned with a detailed analysis of the individual text. It was not until Jean Delay's pioneering

[1] Germaine Brée, *André Gide: l'insaisissable protée* (Paris: Société d'Edition Les Belles Lettres 1953), p. 41.
[2] A.G. Lehmann, *The Symbolist Aesthetic in France* (Oxford: Blackwell, 1968), p. 47.

psychobiography, *La Jeunesse d'André Gide*, that the early works were examined in depth as the textual expression of onanism and repressed homoeroticism, and tropes of extenuation, anxiety, paroxysm and melancholia were read as variants of the Romantic *Schaudern*, in turn associated with psychosexual neuroses.

Delay's sophistication as a reader of Gide's early texts paved the way for their critical re-evaluation. Christian Angelet's recent book, *Symbolisme et invention formelle dans les premiers écrits d'André Gide* devotes careful attention to such themes as the myth of Narcissus as the *summa* of all myths (or mythology at the mirror stage); the positive status of absence or nothing; and the role of *Paludes* in fomenting a transition from Symbolism to modernity. But while Angelet's explication of Gide's early writings provides an incisive overview of their formal structures and intellectual influences, a less historicized and more philosophical approach to Symbolist aesthetics would perhaps yield further dimensions of Gide's rhetoric, and reveal a thematic repertoire that would situate him as neither entirely Symbolist nor completely modernist but rather as writer who is peculiarly susceptible to interpretation as a post-Symbolist, and especially so if read from a postmodernist perspective.

Certainly the preponderance of a flat, understated language in Gide's early writing together with a classical subordination and hierarchy of word to phrase, phrase to page, and page to work (a formula which Gide most likely adapted from Paul Bourget and evidence of what Brée has called his "tired Neoplatonism") would seem to warrant the classification of these works as "post" rather than prototypically Symbolist. Conversely, the themes of the self-effacing author or autocritical text coupled with the techniques of generic pastiche, self-quotation and the decomposition of narrative into lapidary fragments (most notably in *Les Nourritures terrestres*) signal the importance of Gide's "oeuvres de jeunesse" for the theory and practice of postmodernism.

The post-Symbolist Gide and his postmodernist interpretation are not, in fact, so very far apart from each other. Both, it can be argued, constitute responses to what might be seen as a "crisis of writing" which occurred during the last decade of the nineteenth-century, a crisis precipitated by Mallarmé whose writing exalted the ontology of the word in terms of its ability to gesture towards its own metaphysical limits. Mallarmé limned a linguistic border at which signs collapsed into silence, leaving only a polluting semantic trace of their former appearance. Whether it is the smoke that curls in serpentine directions from the pipe, the vibrations of the air and resettling of dust after the flick of the fan, the wild gesticulations of the actor or clown miming the missing texts of verbal representation, or the enigmatic blotches of ink spilled on the pristine page, his poems and critical fragments point to that Nietzschean moment in the history of literature— somewhere between afternoon and twilight— where "happy" unself-critical writing is no longer possible. It is that moment which a generation of critics in the twentieth century— Blanchot, Barthes and Derrida in particular— would take as their eternal present, but which Gide and his contemporaries soon came to distrust because it inevitably condemned them to a romantic nostalgia for what had been lost.

At the outset of his career, Gide was faced with two formidable options imposed by prior tradition: the rhetorically saturated conventions of Symbolism in poetry, and the monolithic legacy of Realism in fiction. He could of course choose to be derivative of one using the preferred genre of the other and indeed, his first work, *Les Cahiers d'André Walter*, with its soaring flights of mood and masturbatory expirations, perfectly exemplifies Symbolist lyricism in a fictional mode. However, as *Le Traité du Narcisse* reveals upon close inspection, the late Romantic vein of Symbolism with which *André Walter* was imbued, was soon to be rejected; its cloying hyperboles relegated to the backroom of juvenalia. This left a return to Realism, a logical choice for a fledgling author whose talents lay with fiction. The paradigms offered by the great masters of Realist narrative from Stendhal to Maupassant prescribed the depiction of historical panoramas and a descriptive mode that privileged accumulation of the empirical particulars of social reality. But where the nineteenth-century Realists could plunder an historical epoch replete with tableaus of an entire society in heretical ferment, Gide's immediate world was restricted to the rarefied ambiance of the literary socius. Within the depoliticized intellectual circles to which he himself belonged, his own social text was necessarily conjugated with the texts of conversation and debate which constructed ideological opinion for the intelligentsia. In this context, even the option of assimilating Realist and Naturalist descriptive techniques within a Symbolist setting had already been achieved with brilliant "élan" in J.K. Huysmans' *A Rebours*.

Inevitably, Gide's response to social realism favored ironic parody over respectful imitation. Resurrecting the *sôtie*, a medieval genre of black humor which he redefined in a modern context as "ironique et critique," he indirectly attacked the implicit seriousness of the nineteenth-century family chronicle which was so often accompanied by a catalogue of urban miseries. In the triad of texts that comprised the *sôtie* oeuvre, *Paludes* (1895), *Le Prométhée mal enchaîné* (1899) and *Les Caves du Vatican* (1914), he revitalized the Socratic and Menippean origins of the carnivalesque, employing all the conventions of "banquet discourse" to parrot the self-indulgent banter of Parisian literati. He also satirized the Realist fidelity to repugnant detail by means of grotesque pastiche, inverting their inversion of the Romantic aesthetics of the Sublime and the Beautiful with gratuitous, historically decontextualized renditions of the Ugly and Low.

Gide's answer to the Symbolist sign, with its nihilistic, radically narcissistic referential function was in certain respects even more complex than his answer to social realism, for it involved the very mark or signature for which he would earn the esteem of his readers — namely, the evolution of his personal style. Gide came to be known as the master of modern classicism; the simplicity and clarity of his diction was held up as a model worthy of emulation, his poetic economy revered as exemplary of that supreme value of classical aesthetics, the art of understatement or litotes. "Le classicisme," Gide wrote in 1919, "tend tout entier vers la litote" and with this pronouncement, he commemorated the orientation of an entire modern "écriture" towards the theory and practice of a single figure of speech.[3]

Gide came to litotes through his distaste for the salient features of Symbolist style: the tendency of a writer such as Gautier (who he attacked in his preface to *Les Fleurs du mal*) towards hyperbole, amplification, lyrical outburst and metaphorical excess. A severe Protestant upbringing had left him, moreover, with a moralistic bent to his character to which one can partially attribute his criticism of the amoral, self-reflexive doctrine of *l'art pour l'art*. However, as we shall attempt to show, the question of a style, after Mallarmé, was not to be easily resolved through simple recourse to the classical tradition. Reference, signification, the laws of genre and the status of the symbol itself had undergone revisionist critique within the Symbolist movement and one could no longer manipulate the instruments of literature without addressing the invisible quotation marks which hovered around their appearance on the page.

The self-consciousness and anxiety which the question of style provoked for the post-Symbolist generation is evinced in Gide's writings by innumerable authorial interventions: glosses, commentaries, footnotes, inserted narratives, prefaces, prologues, epilogues and

[3] André Gide, "Billets à Angèle," *Incidences* (Paris: Gallimard, 1924), p. 40.

postscripts, in short, an endless proliferation of disruptive devices that signal the parenthetical presence of a critical reader. More than in the later *récits* where a classically conservative elegance seems to prevail with relative tranquillity, the early works bear witness to a tumultuous "scene of writing" where the thrust towards stylistic purism is continually stymied by metacritical digressions and didactic interruptions. The overall effect of these deflationary conceits is to alert the reader to what might be called a "negative writing," a writing which challenges its own formal structures at every turn, a writing that chisels away at the reader's acceptance of a literary apparatus, a writing which avails itself, whenever possible, of the figures of negation, whether they be simple negative markers (such as "ne... pas") or complex tropes of signification (such as litotes, diminution, irony and preterition).

* * *

The ramified grammatical constructions and rhetorical codes which constitute Gide's negative writing find their contemporary analogue in critical theory in the poststructuralist stylistics of Roland Barthes. Barthes's ludic operations on the organic body of the phrase (his dismemberment of *a priori* concepts, his puns, his detachment of prefixes and suffixes from their lexical roots, his distortion of ordinary syntax through diacritical invention and neologism) paralleled on a formal level Gide's equally transgressive treatment of narrative. More importantly however, Barthes's concern with the norms of classicism and his inquiries into the problem of stylistic economy led him to a definition of negative writing that he characterized as "le degré zéro de l'écriture."

Barthes's own career began, significantly enough, with an article published in 1942 in *Existences: Journal du Sanatorium des Etudiants de France* while he was recuperating from tuberculosis. Entitled "Notes sur André Gide et son *Journal*," the essay focused on Gide's "coquetterie de l'uniforme" by which he referred to Gide's consummate ability to say the most with the least, that is, to adhere to the classical rule of litotes by stating what was essential in simple, commonplace language.[4] That Barthes's first article was on Gide, that this article on Gide contained the germs of his own future research on the litotic nature of classicism, and that his style in the article mimics the posturing of Gide's own stylistic posturing to which he gave reign in his

---

[4] Roland Barthes, "Notes sur André Gide et son *Journal*," *Existences* 27 (July 1942). The article has been republished in the *Bulletin des Amis d'André Gide* 67 (July 1985).

celebrated *Journal*, reveals some of the profound "liens de parenté" between the two authors. Barthes himself acknowledged his debt to Gide in his own pastiche of the journalistic form—his mock autobiography *Roland Barthes par Roland Barthes*. Here, he intersected his posture as a writer with Gide's through the conceit of two diagonal geographical lines, lines which trace the *Abgrund* or "native ground" on which Gide gave symbolic birth to Barthes. Writing about himself alternately in the first and third person, Barthes described Gide's "influence" (a term which he of course problematized) as follows:

> ...A l'histoire des sources, il faudrait substituer l'histoire des figures: l'origine de l'oeuvre, ce n'est pas la première influence, c'est la première posture: on copie un rôle, puis, par métonymie, un art: je commence à reproduire celui que je voudrais être...
>
> L'un de ses premiers articles (1942) portait sur le *Journal* de Gide; l'écriture d'un autre ("En Grèce", 1944) était visiblement imitée des *Nourritures terrestres*. Et Gide a eu une grande place dans ses lectures de jeunesse: croisé d'Alsace et de Gascogne, en diagonale, comme l'autre le fut de Normandie et de Languedoc, protestant, ayant le goût des "lettres" et jouant du piano, sans compter le reste, comment ne se serait-il pas reconnu, désiré dans cet écrivain, l'*Abgrund* gidien, l'inaltérable gidien, forme encore dans ma tête un grouillement têtu. Gide est ma langue originelle, mon *Ursuppe*, ma soupe littéraire.[5]

As mother's milk is to the child, so Gide's "literary soup" is to Barthes; it is the substance that nourished him in his infancy as a writer and the matrix which fostered his acquisition of language or "langue *mater*nelle."[6]

Gide appeared again in a table which Barthes sketched charting his literary career in phases; each group of his works coordinated with a significant "intertext" and ranged under a particular "genre." Using his own personal nomenclature for the genres, Barthes saw his latest work in terms of "moralité,"—here with Nietzsche in parentheses as the intertext,—having passed through other genres, such as "textualité," "sémiologie" and "mythologie sociale." The origins of all these genres, however, is no genre at all, but simply marked as "l'envie

[5] Roland Barthes, *Roland Barthes par Roland Barthes* (Paris: Seuil, 1975), p. 103.
[6] See Philippe Roger, *Roland Barthes, roman* (Paris: Grasset, 1986). For a fuller interpretation of how the Gidean "Ursuppe" nourished Barthes's ontologico-metaphysical and mystical penchant, see pages 320-25. For an elaboration of Barthes's mimetic posturing, informed on the one hand by what Barthes describes as the "oscillation" of Sollers, and on the other hand by the "Hésitation" of Gide, see pages 315-17.

d'écrire" and bracketed. For this entry it is Gide who stands as the intertext, similarly bracketed. No work of Barthes himself is cited to complement this elided origin.

This suppression of Gide's tangible legacy can be read in two ways: either his function as intertext was so continual and all-encompassing that there is no single work that bears his imprint, but rather an entire corpus that attests to its dialogical relation to Gide, or, that Barthes, in an act of killing his literary forbears, was refusing Gide any more than an honorable mention. A third alternative, however, might be seen in Barthes's choice of Gide as his paradigmatic "écrivain sans style" in *Le Degré zéro*. In the opening essay of this work, Barthes offered up a poetic, quasi-mystical discursus on the essence of style. His alluring projection of style as private ritual, splendid prison, solitary reverie, transparent embellishment, historical transcendence and secret cabal with the flesh is posed against a concept of art or artifice, a kind of "artisanal craft" that specializes only in rewriting what others have already written: "Le type même de l'écrivain sans style," Barthes wrote, "c'est Gide, dont la manière artisanale exploite le plaisir moderne d'un certain éthos classique."[7] Here, Gide is placed not with writers, but with musicians like Saint-Saëns, who based his art on a reworking of Bach, or Poulenc, who "rewrote" Schubert. Gide is thus withdrawn from the canon of the great stylists—Hugo, Rimbaud and Char— who, natural, organic writers, are above literature and outside history and society.

Such an exclusion seems brutal. Was it a pejorative act? Or was Barthes, by removing Gide from the sanctuary of style, reserving him for a role which, within his own theoretical purview, was superior to that of the pure stylist? Perhaps a clue lies in the argument that high style "n'est nullement le produit d'un choix, d'une réflexion sur la Littérature," that is, a self-reflexive, self-conscious recasting of literary antecedent, but rather an independent silhouette etched in a historical vacuum (*DZ* 12). This would explain Barthes's interpretation of Gide as the writer "par excellence" whose "exploitation of modern pleasure" is predicated on "a certain classical ethos" and thus the result of a parasitical relation to previous tradition. If, at first sight, the connotations attached to this characterization of Gide appear negative, they are neutralized when one recalls the theoretical framework within which Barthes himself worked, a framework which

---

[7] Roland Barthes, *Le Degré zéro de l'écriture* (Paris: Seuil, 1972), p. 13. All further references to this work will appear in the text abbreviated *DZ*.

presupposes the profoundly citational, secondary, predatory nature of all modern writing. Given this context, Gide's status is reversed: barred from the title of "last stylist," he goes on to acquire the prestigious rank of "first non-stylist" or preeminent "writer" in the modern sense with which Barthes endued this avocation.

According to this analysis, Barthes's Gide, defined as the archetypal "writer without style," occupies a crucial position in the development of twentieth-century criticism, in semiotics, psychoanalytical interpretation, poststructuralist and deconstruction, particularly as explored and practiced by Barthes. There is just one problem with Barthes's formulation, however, for clearly Gide *did* have a style, one which was alluded to and continues to be alluded to by each generation. The question then becomes: What is the style of writing without style? Where are its roots and of what is it comprised? These questions will be the point of departure for our study, and will inform our investigation of Gide's negative writing.

*   *   *

Barthes himself traced the appearance of negative writing to the purification and rhetorical codification of the French language in the 1650s. Its principal characteristics included: "une technique," that is, an ensemble of rules and recipes designed to convince or persuade the auditor/reader, "un enseignement," or system of institutionalized interpersonal relationships (between the rhetorician and his pupils), "une science," or protoscience that specialized in the analysis of linguistic effects in terms of their classification and definition as logical operations, "une morale," or body of ethical prescriptive norms and codes of conduct, "une pratique sociale," which refers to the political power structures implicit in the use of rhetoric by its practitioners, and "une pratique ludique" or anti-rhetoric that derides its noble model through irony, erotic or obscene allusion, parodic games and so on.[8] According to Barthes, this structuration of a national language in the classical period punctuates the historical moment in which writing acquires "une sorte de négativité, un horizon qui sépare ce qui est défendu et ce qui est permis, sans plus s'interroger sur les origines ou sur les justifications de ce tabou" (*DZ* 41). It is this unquestioned ethics of linguistic protocol whose "negativity" is posited in a repressive tendency to constrain poetic *inventio* so as to nurture the systematic,

[8] Roland Barthes, "L'Ancienne Rhétorique," *Communications* 16 (1970).

relational laws governing linguistic usage and rhetorical economy, that emerges as the cutting edge of classical aesthetic doctrine. Happy in its hegemony until 1848 (the year of the bourgeois revolution in France and the moment, in the history of aesthetic norms, when the Romantic credo of the mixture of genres gained academic respectability), this classical doctrine is gradually displaced by an increasing pluralism of literary forms accompanied by what Barthes describes as "a problem of justification":

> ...Or, on a vu que, vers 1850, il commence à se poser à la Littérature un problème de justification: l'écriture va se chercher des alibis; et précisément parce qu'une ombre de doute commence à lever sur son usage, toute une classe d'écrivains soucieux d'assumer à fond la responsabilité de la tradition va substituer à la valeur-usage de l'écriture, une valeur-travail. (*DZ* 46)

This "valeur-travail," worn like a badge or special insignia by an exclusive brotherhood whose members include, in Barthes's view: Gautier ("maître impeccable des Belles-Lettres"), Flaubert ("rodant ses phrases à Croisset"), Valéry ("dans sa chambre au petit matin") and Gide ("debout devant son pupitre comme devant un établi"), surfaces as the modern equivalent of the "valeur-usage" of the classicists (*DZ* 47). Both groups exhibit a common commitment to "une préciosité de la concision," but where the masters of neoclassical tragedy concentrated their talents on distilling the mannered refinements of imitation and verisimilitude (following the dictates of Aristotle and Plato with respect to the representation of nature), the moderns propose a naturalistic work ethic that boasts long hours dedicated to the honing and perfecting of form (*DZ* 47).

Barthes leaves on one side the precise nature of this form, implying only that it consists in an endless reworking of writing itself. It is, however, within Barthes's image of the bourgeois artist as a tireless craftsman who treats style as a raw material that must be shaped and reduced to a minimal essence, that we might begin to decode Gide's cryptic remark that "Le classicisme tend tout entier vers la litote."

The classical definition of litotes is most succinctly given by Fontanier, summarizing two centuries of traditional usage:

> La *Litote*, qu'on appelle autrement *Diminution* et qui n'est guère, au fond, qu'une espèce particulière de *Métalepse, au lieu d'affirmer une chose, nie absolument la chose contraire, ou la diminue plus ou moins, dans la vue même*

de donner plus d'énergie et de poids à l'affirmation positive qu'elle déguise.[9] (Fontanier's emphases)

Fontanier thus moves beyond the etymological definition of litotes which refers to that which is small, smooth and simple, to link it with a cluster of litotic figures including diminution, metalepsis (or indirection) and negative affirmation (as in the substitution of "I do not deny..." for "I concede..."). His paradigmatic examples of litotes return it to its origin in French classicism, among them a phrase from *Le Cid* cited by subsequent rhetoricians (Littré, Quillot, Morier) where Chimène replies to Rodrigue's impassioned query regarding her affection for him with "Va... je ne te hais point." In the context of the tragedy, the beauty of this phrase stems from the fact that it constitutes a grossly understated expression of her feelings. Forbidden by the moral strictures of her "devoir" and the linguistic laws of classical decorum and propriety to reveal her true sentiments, yet unwilling to sacrifice avowal altogether, Chimène resolves the dilemma by finding the most discreet and diminutive form of affirmation possible— an affirmation couched in a double negative (haïr plus "ne... point"). This minimal utterance produces the maximum effect— a less which says more— by virtue of the absent subtexts with which it is surrounded. Chimène succeeds in communicating the significance of her utterance not through the words themselves, which out of context might suggest thst she is only mildly interested in Rodrigue or even contemptuous of him, but rather because her phrase refers to an unstated referent— her passion— which only a subtle interpreter is capable of divining. In this sense, her use of litotes, though pleasing to the classical audience because of its modest ingenuity, involves a dangerous game, for it relies, like irony, on a formula that deceives insofar as it fails to say what it really means. It is precisely this dangerous aspect of the figure, its versatility as a weapon of verbal warfare or hidden motives, that prompts the rhetorician Morier to issue an injunction against its over-liberal deployment: "la litote... doit être maniée avec prudence; mieux vaut n'y recourir que rarement" and causes the philosopher Jankélévitch to condemn its false or self-serving possibilities: "La litote qui rapetisse ou minimise l'égo en vue d'un intérêt égoïste n'est pas une ironie, mais une fraude et une mesquinerie sordide."[10]

---

[9] Pierre Fontanier, *Les Figures du discours* (Paris: Flammarion, 1977), p. 133.
[10] Respectively, Henri Morier, *Dictionnaire de poétique et de rhétorique* (Paris: PUF, 1861), and Vladimir Jankélévitch, *L'Ironie* (Paris: Flammarion, 1964), p. 85.

If litotes is potentially so incendiary a trope, then why did Gide accord it such a privileged status, identifying it with a modern classicism which he himself fostered both through his own writings and the aesthetic tenets propounded in *La Nouvelle Revue Française*?[11] A partial answer may be found in the negative performative power embedded in litotic writing. Its reliance on grammatical forms that endow subdued, self-effacing language with an unsettling affective charge was the ideal instrument for a writer who sought to discredit the hyperbolic affectations of Symbolism without relinquishing Symbolism's sophistication of formal invention. Its kinship with irony, or with a family of tropes (such as preterition, periphrasis, ellipsis, zeugma, asteism, anacoluthon, etc.) all of which deliver their message by evoking an absent text that must be inferred from context and tone, provided a perfect means of satirizing the dagger-sharp innuendos and precious circumlocutions of Symbolist dialogue. Its capacity to dissimulate an intended meaning that the user has a vested interest in revealing indirectly offered a way of promulgating a homosexual counter-code that negates heterosexual norms without recourse to crude or explicit formulations. Finally, its conduciveness to a cerebral, analytical, intellectual style suited Gide's project of rewriting classical mythology in a mode that negated the fashionable, avant-garde treatment of myth by modernists such as Cocteau, Picasso and Stravinsky.

Each of these dimensions of a stylistically litotic writing emerges in the early works of Gide, which, in turn, reveal a negative agenda hidden in their midst. Whether it is the struggle against Symbolist lyricism evinced as a will to metaphorical impoverishment in *Le Traité du Narcisse*, or the attack on Symbolist solipsism as an existential stance in *Paludes*, or the critique of the Romantic authorial self as represented in *Les Nourritures terrestres*, or the affirmation of modern classicism through the denigration of modernist rivals; in all of these examples, a negative logic can be discerned. Coinciding with this diverse array of polemically instrumentalized modes of negation, is an equally litotic trajectory, evolving as Gide's oeuvre unfolds, delineating an aesthetics of stylistic minimalism that displays its aporias, apertures, and tiny flaws like precious gems rescued by the jeweler's artisanal skill.

Gide devised a host of techniques to reduce his texts to this state of sobriety. Sometimes, as in *Le Traité du Narcisse*, he fashioned a

---

[11] For a full discussion of NRFian classicism see Auguste Anglès's exemplary work, *André Gide et le premier groupe de la Nouvelle Revue Française* (Paris: Gallimard, 1978). See also my article, "Writing without Style: The Role of Litotes in Gide's Concept of Modern Classicism," *French Review* (October 1983).

void—a mirror or archetypal crystal—that reflected "en abyme" an endlessly elusive text of the self. At other times, as in *Paludes*, he devised a calculus of difference and degree that charted the path of the signifier as it deferred its meaning and deposited a residue of absent reference. Alternatively, in *Les Nourritures terrestres*, he combined the classical art of the maxim, a self-enclosed, irreducible genre, with a "homotextual" asceticism and in his later *récits*— *L'Immoraliste*, *La Symphonie pastorale*, *La Porte étroite* and *L'Ecole des femmes*— he refined a vocabulary of non-articulations—the gaps, pauses, silences and suppressions which normally serve only to round out verbal exchange between characters in a work of fiction.

These multifarious definitions of negative writing, some the result of revisionist polemic addressed to immediate issues in aesthetics and sexual politics, others distilled through laborious formalist technique, flourished in a cultural climate of moral relativism chilled by the not so distant winds of Romantic irony. Gide's style of writing without style cannot be removed from the ethos in which it took root; it owes much of its impetus and contour to the "fin-de-siècle" nihilism that prevailed as he began his career as a writer. Though he succeeded in taking his distance from the Symbolist movement, his endeavors to invent a post-Symbolist sign were not, as *Le Traité du Narcisse* records, without affirmations of a Mallarméan presence. Indeed, Gide's reaction to the excesses of Symbolism were precisely that: more a criticism of the epigones— Parnassians (Heredia, Banville, Leconte de Lisle), and Decadents (Gautier, Régnier, Louÿs)— than of Mallarmé himself, who remained for Gide "un maître assez dangereux."[12]

[12] In 1909, taking up the counter-attack against two of Mallarmé's detractors (Jean-Marc Bernard and following him, Léon Bocquet) both of whom accused Mallarmé of poetic "impuissance," Gide wrote in the *Nouvelle Revue Française* (February 1909), p. 292:

> Sans doute il est fâcheux que ces vers compromettants soient de telle tenue, de telle beauté, de telle noblesse, de tel poids, d'un accent jusqu'alors si neuf, que le cerveau dans lequel ils ont enfoncé leur éblouissement glacé s'en souvienne malgré lui désormais, et que leur insolite sonorité se prolonge à travers le bruit abondant de maints autres poètes fussent-ils chantres de la Joie, de la Vie, de Fécondité. Mais qu'importe à M. Bernard Bocquet?
>
> Je ne me poserai point en défenseur d'une cause que je ne peux faire mienne car je tiens Mallarmé pour un maître assez dangereux...

II

(EMPTYING OUT THE SYMBOLIST SIGN)

NARCISSUS OR THE INSUFFICIENT SYMBOL

> L'éclosion des êtres est-elle permanente dans
> l'immensité comme dans la petitesse?
>> (Baudelaire, *Sur mes contemporains:*
>> *Victor Hugo*)

The parenthetic subtitle of *Le Traité du Narcisse* (1891) remained throughout repeated publications *Théorie du symbole* and as such it has guided critics towards an understanding of the work as a commentary on the theory and practice of Symbolism. However, the "symbol" of which Gide speaks might in fact be more accurately characterized, not as the implement of Symbolist aesthetics from Baudelaire to Mallarmé, but as a post-Symbolist sign, that, in Gide's definition, emerges as a litotic critique of its overblown predecessor. This post-Symbolist sign manifests itself in a rhetoric that might be qualified as "insufficiently" Symbolist, with its erasure of adjectives that adumbrate or embellish seen as indicative of a general propensity towards condensation and attenuation. Alternatively, it may be construed in the *Traité*'s attention to the theory of signification, which, though it reveals an undeniable affinity with the metalinguistic idioms of Mallarmé, seeks nonetheless to surpass them by restoring an ethical dimension to such decadent icons as the flower, the mirror, the crystal or the figure of Narcissus himself.

These figures appear, but under the sign of negation: the flower is registered as an absence: "il n'y a plus de berge, ni de source, plus de métamorphose et plus de fleur mirée"; the mirror is featured as "une glace sans tain," and the crystal appears as a recalcitrant archetype typifying a frozen, formal ideal of paradise, intrinsically identified with a classically static work of art. Narcissus himself is introduced as the sole occupant of a landscape as denuded, contourless and metaphysically barren as a neoclassical stage set. He is a belated Narcissus; a Narcisse born after the great age of Ovid's *Metamorphoses*, where, mesmerized by the image of his own beauty reflected in the water, he became transformed into a flower. Here, there is no allusion to his physical perfection; on the contrary, he is portrayed as the faded, gray subject of a monochrome sketch ("les grisailles").

Juxtaposed discordantly with the style of the *Traité* is its generic character, which seems to anticipate a postmodern work of art in its heterogeneous quotation of multiple literary forms. The question of the status of a treatise that doubles as a rewriting of a myth is provoked by the full title and extended into the prologue and epilogue which frame this scant ten-page work. A metacritical gloss that challenges the value of the interior text opens and closes the *Traité*. The prologue begins: "Les livres ne sont peut-être pas une chose bien nécessaire; quelques mythes d'abord suffisaient" and the epilogue echoes with: "Ce traité n'est peut-être pas quelque chose de bien nécessaire. Quelques mythes d'abord suffisaient."[1] These cynical commentaries suggest that all postmythic writing, including the *Traité*, is an inferior form of literature because it is superfluous. Myths, by having already stated what needed to be said, accede to the privileged standard of what is referred to at the end of the prologue as "déjà dit," — "said already." Parasitical tautologies, books and treatises alike are thus doomed to oversufficiency.

The negative inscription of the *Traité* by its author announces the anti-Narcissistic narcissism, or self-effacing coquetry, of the twentieth-century writer vis-à-vis his own text, — a paradigm best exemplified by Barthes in his rumination on "the death of the author"; in his citation of an unflattering critic ("Délicieux essayiste, favori des adolescents intelligents, collectionneur d'avant-gardes, Roland Barthes égrène des souvenirs qui n'en sont pas sur le ton de la plus brillante conversation de salon..."), or in his own mythically self-shattering *Roland Barthes*.[2] More specifically, this pose of prefatorial negation raises the question of why the author should be compelled to rewrite the myth

---

[1] André Gide, *Le Traité du Narcisse*, in *Romans, récits et sôties* (Paris: Gallimard, 1958), respectively pp. 3, 12. All further references to this edition of the work will appear in the text abbreviated *TN*.

[2] Roland Barthes, *Le Bruissement de la langue* (Paris: Seuil, 1984), p. 394.

of Narcissus in treatise form if the myth had indeed sufficed all along. In resolving this question, two levels of analysis impose themselves — that of the treatise's content, its ostensible proto or post-Symbolist doctrine, and that of the rhetoric of content, that is, the aesthetic arguments embedded in its linguistic and narrative structures.

As far as the first level is concerned, the *Traité* emerges as a polemic that deploys the myth of Narcissus as a vehicle for an attack on "l'art pour l'art." By reformulating the Platonic theory of imitation, with its emphasis on the existence of *a priori* Truth behind the formal representation of an Idea, Gide attempted to restore the notion of a fixed or absolute referent, and even more precisely, a referent with a *moral value* to the philosophy of artistic form. Although this appears surprising in a young author with such manifestly Decadent leanings (Pierre Louÿs, Barbey d'Aurevilly, J.K. Huysmans and Maurice Maeterlinck were among those whose influence was recorded in the *Journal* of 1890-1891), there is no doubt that the *Traité* sets itself apart from the work of those esthetes who favored an ethically relative concept of the artistic sign.

On the second level, namely the story which is recounted by the rhetoric of the *Traité*, a less didactic position unfolds. Here, one descries an effort to distill a classical style, one that is still heavily influenced by the Symbolist vernacular (with its highly wrought syntax and ultra-literary themes) yet gravitating towards a flatter, more impersonal tone; a less catholic diction and a predilection for intellectual rigor over and against sheer beauty. The effect of this double agenda — moral referentiality and the redefinition of classicism (or what might otherwise be called "Symbolist classicism") — is to strengthen the position of aesthetic argument within literary discourse to the point where literature is almost completely transformed into philosophy and philosophy seems to concern itself exclusively with the eroded status of literature.

The Traité *as Anti-Symbolist Manifesto*

From the very beginning of the *Traité*, the notion of the book is given strikingly didactic considerations, with the book's function as a mere "amplification" of myth ("les livres ont amplifié les mythes") held up as evidence of its gratuitousness as a medium of expression. It must be remembered, however, that in 1891, Gide's demystification of the book implied a polemical thrust or motive that could easily have been construed by his Symbolist readers as a veiled critique of Mallarmé, whose own reification of the book (most obvious in his posthumous masterwork published under the title *Le Livre*) emerged in *Variations sur un sujet — VI. Le Livre, instrument spirituel*.[3]

Though published in July 1895, some three years after the *Traité*, but summarizing ideas which Mallarmé had no doubt shared previously with members of his coterie, this essay guaranteed the absolute primacy of the book with authoritative pronouncements such as: "tout, au monde, existe pour aboutir à un livre," and "Un journal reste le point de départ; la littérature s'y décharge à souhait."[4] Using the text as a source of imagery that adequately describes itself, he paid homage to each part of its anatomy: its cover, its fold, its pages, its typography. He also imbued these references to the palpable, material aspect of the text with a religious resonance, a resonance derived from language evoking intense states of spiritual exaltation. "Je me réjouis," he wrote, "si l'air, en passant, entr'ouvre et, au hasard, anime, d'aspects, l'extérieur du livre" (*OC* 378). Here, the opening of a book evokes mystical, religious ecstasy:

> Le pliage est, vis-à-vis de la feuille imprimée grande, un indice, quasi-religieux: qui ne frappe pas autant que son tassement, en épaisseur, offrant le minuscule tombeau, certes, de l'âme. (*OC* 379)

As a "tomb of the soul," the book is worshipped like the Bible for its hermetic message and its "precious secrets" of the spirit ("intervention du pliage où le rythme, initiale cause qu'une feuille fermée, contienne un secret, le silence y demeure, précieux et des signes

---

[3] Gide's debt to Mallarmé's lexicon of the metaphysics of the book extends far beyond the repetition of the word "livre" and its variants or component parts. It encompasses a much broader vocabulary of thought and imagination including specific words and sonoric signifiers typical of Mallarmé's writing such as "pensée, idée, dé," and so on. In an illuminating appendix to his book *Towards the Poetry of Mallarmé* (Berkeley: University of California Press, 1965) devoted to "the significance of letters in Mallarmé's oeuvre, Robert Greer Cohn notes the prevalence of the sound "é" particularly in the words cited above. It is perhaps no accident that not only are these very words frequently reiterated by Gide throughout the treatise, but so too is this favored Mallarméan sound (as in the word *Traité*). One assumes that this borrowing is quite self-conscious on Gide's part, but occasionally, one wonders whether the borrowings were solely in one direction. There is a striking instance in the *Traité* where the Apocalypse is partially blamed on a dice-thrower: "parce qu'un joueur de dés n'avait pas arrêté son vain geste." Published four years before *Un Coup de dés*, the *Traité* seems here to have anticipated Mallarmé's most famous poem.

[4] Stéphane Mallarmé, *Variations sur un sujet*, in *Oeuvres complètes*, ed. Henri Mondor (Paris: Gallimard, 1945), pp. 378, 379. All further references to this work will appear in the text abbreviated *OC*.

évocatoires succèdent...."), encoded like hieroglyphs in the interplay of black and white on the printed page (*OC* 379). These cryptic signs, Mallarmé suggests, are a "miraculous" medium whose transcription into print is comparable to a sacred "rite": "Approchant d'un rite de la composition typographique" (*OC* 380). The transcendental aura, fostered by words such as "quasireligieux," "tombeau de l'âme," "miracle," "rite," and later, "un sacrifice dont saigna la tranche rouge des anciens tômes" or "divin bouquin," serves to hypostatize the book, to fetishize it as a votive object, thereby assuring its unconditional value as a source of spiritual plenitude (*OC* 380-81).

In the beginning of *Le Traité*, a similar conflation of the textual and transcendental occurs, but with the hallowed sign of the book (initially corrupted by the pluralization, "les livres"), now replaced by myth. It is myths that support the entire edifice of religion, and it is mythical "hieroglyphs" which attract the veneration of the masses and elicit the services of the "priests." Hieroglyphs are worshipped as a hieratic prewriting, the prestige of which accrues from a superior claim to *origins*. Due to their preeminent anteriority, these mythical signs, though opaque, function like transcendental signifieds or "God-terms" from which all language is derived and to which all future words refer back. Accordingly, the myth, as the generic counterpart of the mythical sign or hieroglyph, occupies a privileged position in the hierarchy of literary genres. In contradistinction to subsequent genres, it embodies the perfect adequation of truth in its condensed representation of Ideas. The abbreviated version of the myth of Narcissus, in the introductory passages of the *Traité*, might be read as an example of the attempt to approximate this norm of adequation inherent in the originary genre:

> Narcisse était parfaitement beau, — et c'est pourquoi il était chaste; il dédaignait les Nymphes—parce qu'il était amoureux de lui-même. Aucun souffle ne troublait la source, où, tranquille et penché, tout le jour il contemplait son image... (*TN* 3, italicized in the text)

This diminutive text provides a clue to the enigma of why myths alone are "suffisant," by demonstrating how less is more, or at least adequate to its Idea. Each phrase is perfunctory and informative, declarative and unadorned like the shorthand of a synopsis. The story's details are elided rather than elaborated through unbeleaguered references to conventional motifs of the Narcissus *topos*: beauty, autoeroticism, the conceit of the reflecting pool, the disappointment of the nymph Echo, whose love is unrequited. Its narrative tense is the gnomic past — a time which is forever freshly actual, exempt from the tarnishing nuances of history. Its author is effaced and its narrator anonymous, so that the myth appears as a neutral carrier of pure ideas devoid of the prejudices of a speaking subject. These advantages account for the myth's durability, monumentality, universality and supremacy in the hierarchy of literary archetypes implied by the *Traité*.

By elevating the myth above the book, Gide inverted the paradigm offered by Mallarmé, while at the same time assimilating the metaphysical attributes that Mallarmé ascribed to the book into his concept of myth. Unlike Mallarmé's pages, which are firmly secured to the book's binding, Gide's become unloosed from the "livre du mystère" (despite the fact that it is protected by the "philosophical shade" of Ygdrasil the Norse Tree of Life). Here, the sudden agitation of a violent storm causes the leaves of the book to become unfettered and disseminated in the wind:

> L'arbre Ygdrasil flétri chancelle et craque; ses feuilles où jouaient les brises, frissonnantes et recroquevillées, se révulsent dans la bourrasque qui se lève et les emporte au loin, — vers l'inconnu d'un ciel nocturne et vers de hasardeux parages, où fuit l'éparpillement aussi des pages arrachées au grand livre sacré qui s'effeuille. (*TN* 6)

This apocalyptic destruction of the book can be interpreted as a rejection of both the Judeo-Christian and the Symbolist Bible, with their common pretensions to an authoritative, divinatory word. It is a rejection foreshadowing the incendiary exhortation in the preface to *Les Nourritures terrestres*: "et quand tu m'auras lu, jette ce livre, — et sors," obliquely inveighing against the Symbolist acceptance of the word for its own sake.

As an attack on the reification of the book, the *Traité* must therefore be distinguished from the partisan Symbolist pamphlet that it was and continues to be considered. A more accurate nomenclature would be aesthetic manifesto, but this too would have to be qualified, for it is a manifesto which, by assimilating the myth of Narcissus into its ideational framework, transforms it into a critical myth, or more specifically, a myth that examines, the process of symbolization. In this sense, the subtitle *Théorie du symbole* becomes consonant with the project of rewriting the myth of Narcissus. Together they constitute a generic hybrid which Gide implies is the only available option left to the myth-maker in a postmythic age. Resigned to the "burden of the past" and to the futility of trying to recapture the lost status of original myth, the writer settles for second best—a flawed reproduction of the ancillary model that is as relevant and faithful to the tenor of the modern epoch as Greek mythology was to its own time. This rationale, recalling Barthes's image of Gide as an artist who exploits the classical ethos through quotation, conforms to a litotic logic of understatement. Advocating the substitution of a modern genre which, though it falls below or "under" the standard of "sufficiency" represented by the ancient genre, is nonetheless "enough"; it outlines a last resort for the artist who inhabits a fallen world of literary forms.

One of the most striking ways in which Gide modifies the structure of conventional myth is by inserting a bulky Footnote into the *Traité*. Footnotes are appropriate to an academic or didactic mode of exposition and not strictly speaking to myths. The effect of the Footnote, and such a long one at that, is to alienate the reader from the immediacy of the Narcissus story even more radically than did the *Traité*'s prefatory discursus on the relationship between myths and books. Its axiomatic structure and aggressive separation from the main body of the text prompts readers to treat it as the sole pretext for the entire treatise, a bias encouraged by Gide himself. In an *avertissement* ultimately excised from the final publication he wrote:

> (Je préviens le lecteur que j'ai écrit tout ce traité pour deux notes Plutôt à seule fin de les encadrer et de les faire comme nécessaires— Plutôt que de les passer, je préférais donc qu'il ne lise qu'elles,—le reste, ennuyeux, n'en est que la sauce.)[5]

As Robidoux points out, an echo of this sentiment can be discovered in the intial published version of the Footnote itself:

> C'est là ce que je voudrais dire. J'y reviendrai toute ma vie; je vois là toute la morale, et je crois que tout s'y ramène. Je ne veux que l'indiquer ici, en une note; aussi bien, en ce mince traité, craindrais-je d'en faire éclater l'étroit cadre.[6]

Though this passage was deleted from all editions after 1912, it helps to explain why the critical attention of Gide's first readers was focused

---

[5] André Gide, "Fragments autographes" (Collections de Mme Catherine Gide). Cited by Réjean Robidoux, *Le Traité du Narcisse (Théorie du Symbole) d'André Gide* (Ottawa: Editions de l'Université d'Ottawa, 1978), p. 76.

[6] André Gide, *Le Traité du Narcisse* (Paris: Librairie de l'Art Indépendant, 1892), p. 5. Cited by Robidoux, p. 77.

on the Footnote and intimates the extent to which Gide calculated and committed himself to a dynamic tension between intrinsic and extrinsic texts. The Footnote acts as a critical commentary, resuming and passing moral judgement on seminal motifs of the *Traité*. Treating as suspect an attitude of ironic detachment towards form (despite the use of formalistic distancing devices, such as citation, in the principal diegesis), the Footnote seems to argue for a reauthentication of the decadent symbol through the reinstatement of "true," morally enracinated signs.

Though the Footnote and the primary text appear virtually at odds, with the former a condemnation of the aesthetic practices of the latter, they nonetheless share the Narcissus *topos*: the Footnote admonishes the artist against becoming infatuated with the surface appearance of his own creation just as the main narrative recounts the unhappy plight of a young man fixated on his own reflection. Viewed as a single, integral entity, the outer frame and inner mimetic centerpiece exemplify a structure which Gide christened the "mise en abyme." In portions of his early *Journal*, he developed this idea as a literary corollary of the blason or heraldic emblem. The "mise en abyme" plays a crucial role in the *Traité* because it provides a paradigm of textual reflexivity — of the text looking at itself, or taking account of its own capacity to symbolize. This is precisely what is implied by a myth that doubles as a theory of the symbol. Just as Narcisse achieves self-consciousness through self-replication (ascertaining that his mirror is both identical and different), so the text of the *Traité* projects the cognizance of its own mimetic status as a symbolic form through the replication of itself "en abyme."

The "mise en abyme" as a "mise en oeuvre" of a Theory of the Symbol

In 1891, Gide wrote to Valéry: "Je lis une plaquette de Hello sur le style. Et j'étudie le blason! C'est admirable. Jamais je n'avais regardé ça."[7] Valéry responded by sending him a discouragingly difficult heraldic motto to decipher, but Gide, undaunted, continued to speculate on its implications for literary theory and practice. Shortly after a trip to Holland where he studied the Dutch masters with enthusiasm, Gide assembled an eclectic assortment of texts and paintings whose common property was the "procédé du blason." In his *Journal* of 1893, he wrote:

[7] Letter of November 1891, *Correspondance: D'André Gide et de Paul Valéry, 1889-1939*, ed. Robert Mallet (Paris: Gallimard, 1955), p. 138.

J'aime assez qu'en une oeuvre d'art on retrouve ainsi transposé, à l'échelle des personnages, le sujet même de cette oeuvre. Rien ne l'éclaire mieux et n'établit plus sûrement toutes les proportions de l'ensemble. Ainsi, dans tels tableaux de Memling ou de Quentin Metzys, un petit miroir convexe et sombre reflète, à son tour, l'intérieur de la pièce où se joue la scène peinte. Ainsi, dans le tableau des *Ménines* de Velasquez (mais un peu différemment). Enfin, en littérature, dans *Hamlet*, la scène de la comédie; et ailleurs dans bien d'autres pièces. Dans *Wilhelm Meister*, les scènes de marionnettes ou de fête au château. Dans *La Chute de la Maison Usher*, la lecture que l'on fait à Roderick, etc. Aucun de ces exemples n'est absolument juste. Ce qui le serait beaucoup plus, ce qui dirait mieux ce que j'ai voulu dans mes *Cahiers*, dans mon *Narcisse* et dans *La Tentative*, c'est la comparaison avec ce procédé du blason qui consiste, dans le premier, à en mettre un second "en abyme."[8]

In its figuration of the "abyme," the blason belongs to a family of symbolic insignia including the *impresa* ("symbole composé en principe d'une image et d'une sentence, et servant à exprimer une règle de vie ou un programme personnel de son porteur"); the *Concetto* (defined as the *means* of expressing a concept as distinct from the concept itself); the medieval *Emblem*, and the ancient *Hieroglyph*.[9] What distinguishes these special insignia from any other symbol or conventional sign is their capacity to reflect, in their very structure, the mediation of an idea by form, and the instrumental role of the subject as author or observer in this dialectical process. Whether it is a convex mirror which refracts, like a prism, the reciprocal gaze between the painter's eye, the eyes of his model, and those of the painting's viewer, or a story within a story, which, through self-reflexive duplication, heightens the reader's awareness of his own implication in the process of fiction-making, these "abyssal" signs possess a unique claim to self-representation. It was precisely this ability to symbolize its own symbolic procedures— its own *techné*— that attracted Gide to "le *procédé* du blason" (as opposed to just simply "le blason"). His conviction that the *means* by which an idea is rendered intelligible should be included as part of the work of art, though apparently an extremely modern notion, can in fact be traced to a tradition that, revived in the Renaissance, derives ultimately from Aristotle's response to the Platonic doctrine of the symbol. As Robert Klein summarizes this classical debate in his treatment of the Renaissance *imprese*:

[8] André Gide, *Journal* I (1889-1939) (Paris: Gallimard, 1948), p. 41. All further references to this work will appear in the text abbreviated *J*.

[9] Robert Klein, "La Théorie de l'expression figurée dans les traités italiens sur les *imprese*, 1555-1612," *La Forme et l'intelligible* (Paris: Gallimard, 1970), p. 125.

Représenter une idée par une figure qui "participe" à l'universalité et à l'idéalité de son objet est, comme on sait, la fonction propre du symbole, telle que l'ont conçue les néo-platoniciens de la Renaissance: signe magique ou expressif, charme évocateur, incarnation ou reflet de l'Archétype, présence atténuée de l'intelligible, "ombre" ou préparation de l'intuition mystique. A cette richesse du platonisme et des courants qui s'en réclament, l'aristotélisme ne pouvait opposer, dit-on, que le signe conventionnel ou l'allégorie comme simple étiquette et "définition illustrée". Mais Aristote offrait en réalité, par sa conception du rapport entre la pensée et l'expression, entre l'idée et sa réalisation dans l'oeuvre, un autre moyen d'approfondir le sens des images d'idées. On peut les envisager sous deux aspects, dont la complémentarité est bien caractéristique du péripatétisme: l'expression imite les articulations de la pensée, qui sont celles de la chose, et autorise par là une logique des imprese; d'autre part, l'invention et la représentation recréent le concept dans la matière sensible et ce procès fonde, non une esthétique, mais un *techné*: une science de l'impresa-art.[10]

By reviving and adapting the blason to modern narrative, Gide might be perceived as the heir of the Renaissance Neoplatonists. Like them, he valued the incantatory, "magical or expressive" heraldic sign, capitalizing on its power to bring the referent or idea for which it stands to life. In this sense, his concern with the blason foreshadows his later commitment to rhetorical and narrative forms which are "alive"; in direct association with the ideas or referents which they represent; uncorrupted by "dead" or supernumerary adornment. But, like Aristotle, Gide also relished a formal technique that would reveal "expression imitating the articulations of thought" and the way in which "invention and representation re-create the concept within sensible matter." Accordingly, he wove these precepts into his definition of the "psychological novel":

Un homme en colère raconte une histoire; voilà le sujet d'un livre. Un homme racontant une histoire ne suffit pas; il faut que ce soit un homme en colère, et qu'il y ait un constant rapport entre la colère de cet homme et l'histoire racontée. (*J* 41)

This definition hinges upon yet another theoretical principle which emphasizes how a sign, such as the blason, is converted into a narrative figure that also operates as a theory of the symbol. In a journal entry from 1893, Gide characterized this principle as textual "retroactivity"— a dynamic, transitive relationship between subject

10 Klein, pp. 135-36.

and object. The text, he suggests, acts on and transforms the subject ("J'ai voulu indiquer, dans cette, *Tentative amoureuse*, l'influence du livre sur celui qui l'écrit, et pendant cette écriture même"), just as the subject animates the objects which he perceives, then imagines, and then represents in the text:

> ...Nulle action sur une chose, sans rétroaction de cette chose sur le sujet agissant. C'est cette réciprocité que j'ai voulu indiquer; non plus dans les rapports avec les autres, mais avec soi-même. Le sujet agissant, c'est soi; la chose rétroagissante, c'est un sujet qu'on imagine. C'est donc une méthode d'action sur soi-même, indirecte, que j'ai donné là; et c'est tout simplement un conte. (*J* 40)

Whether through the portrayal of the relation between form and idea, or subject and object, Gide sought to represent consciousness itself, caught off guard in the act of creating a symbol. The emblematic device of the "mise en abyme" captures this moment because, like a chamber of mirrors, it reproduces the image of the subject perceiving the image (of himself) which he has formed. It also depicts symbolization as a narrative process through the concept of multiple frames: in the outermost frame, Narcisse struggles to see himself, and while gazing into a Heraclitean stream, dreams of Adam. The second frame, demarcated by a separate section, is situated in Narcisse's dream of Paradise and features Adam obsessed, like Narcisse, by the desire to contemplate himself. His autoeroticism brings about the destruction of Paradise; a scene that provides a tertiary frame encapsulating the Footnote. Finally, the Footnote encloses a portrait of the artist who, like his predecessors Narcisse and Adam, is punished for the sin of preferring an idealized self-portrait over and against a rigorous depiction of Truth.

These successive frames act like a telescopic lens magnifying the themes of the *Traité* through each repetition. The Footnote, like the "motto" traditionally placed at the heart of a noble escutcheon, contains the most condensed and miniaturized form of these themes. Though it constitutes the smallest, most pithy expression of the aesthetic manifesto within, as Gide put it, "ce mince traité," it is paradoxically the largest, most inclusive and expansive version of the myth, for it is here that the aesthetic effect of self-reflection (essential to all symbols according to Gide) is most explicitly subjected to moral scrutiny and redefined as a problem of self-preference or Narcissism. The Footnote "en abyme" renders what appears typographically to

be marginal or of inferior importance, the most crucial portion of the
Traité.

The Footnote as Moral Parable

According to Robidoux, the Footnote qualifies as "the least Symbolist
or Mallarméan and the most typically Gidean portion of the treatise."[11]
He cites in this regard Albert-Marie Schmidt's opinion that the note
exemplifies, par excellence, "le côté protestant, un peu prêcheur de
l'oeuvre."[12] The explanation for these judgements lies perhaps in the
fact that the Footnote possesses an explicitly moral tone which differs
distinctly from the voice that prevails in the rest of the *Traité*. Graft-
ing Schopenhauer's Neoplatonic theory of subjective detachment
(based on the concept of the "Genius" whose sublimely indifferent,
wholly objective "Will" enables him to divine and express the "Idea")
onto a Calvinist ethics of individual self-sacrifice, the Footnote projects a sinister subtext whose full explication relies on the intertext
of Gide's journal.

   Gide's advocacy in the Footnote of the artist's subordination to
Truth-embodying symbols can be unravelled in the rather terrifying
series of assaults on the authorial self recorded in the *Journal* of 1890.
Written in tandem with the *Traité*, the *Journal* recounts the tale of a
moral, spiritual and aesthetic crisis which Gide experienced during
this period. The story begins in March, with Gide's despair over the
difficulty of writing a sequel to *André Walter* (tentatively entitled *Allain*).
He wrote: "J'ai la tête encombrée de mon oeuvre; elle se demène dans
ma tête; je ne peux plus lire, non plus écrire; elle s'interpose toujours
entre le livre et mes yeux. C'est une inquiétude d'esprit intolérable"
(*J* 16). Gide's "intolerable uneasiness," when obstructed by a writing
block, carries the initial symptoms of an infectious privation
culminating, by November, in a temporary lapse of identity: "Je ne
suis même plus. Perdu, du jour où j'ai commencé mon livre..." (*J*
18). The long, arid periods preceding creative production are experienced as an illness during which the only work possible consists
of skeletal schemes or normative outlines for a future work. The
scheme reads like a tablet of negative commandments that are consummately exigent towards the writer. Under the upper-case title
"MORALE," the scheme unfolds as follows:

[11] My translated paraphrase of Robidoux, p. 76.
[12] Albert-Marie Schmidt, *La Littérature symboliste (1870-1900)* (Paris: PUF, 1960) as
cited by Robidoux, p. 76.

Premier point: Nécessité d'une morale.

2. Une morale consiste à hiérarchiser les choses et à se servir des moindres pour obtenir les principales. C'est une stratégie idéale.

3. Ne jamais perdre de vue le but. Ne jamais préférer le moyen.

4. Se considérer soi-même comme un moyen; donc ne jamais se préférer au but choisi, à l'oeuvre.

(Ici lacune, où se pose la question du choix de l'oeuvre et du libre choix de cette oeuvre. Pour manifester. Mais encore... Peut-on choisir?)

Songer à son salut: égoïsme.

Le héros ne doit même pas songer à son salut. Il s'est *volontairement* et *fatalement* dévoué, jusqu'à la damnation pour les autres; pour manifester. (*J* 18)

These commandments, rendered emphatically negative by the reiterated imperative "Ne jamais...", underscore the cryptic mandate of "manifestation" and the necessity of purging the work of art of the author's hubris. These are also the principal dicta of the Footnote which begins by postulating that:

Les Vérités demeurent derrière les Formes — Symboles. Tout phénomène est le Symbole d'une Vérité. Son seul devoir est qu'il le manifeste. Son seul péché: qu'il se préfère.

Nous vivons pour manifester. Les règles de la morale et de l'esthétique sont les mêmes: toute oeuvre qui ne manifeste pas est inutile et par cela même, mauvaise. Tout homme qui ne manifeste pas est inutile et mauvais. (*TN* 8)

The ethical dimension of this doctrine of manifestation is further elaborated in terms of "the moral question" which the artist must confront:

La question morale pour l'artiste, n'est pas que l'Idée qu'il manifeste soit plus ou moins morale et utile au grand nombre; la question est qu'il la manifeste bien. — Car tout doit être manifesté, même les plus funestes choses: "Malheur à celui par qui le scandale arrive," mais "Il faut que le scandale arrive." (*TN* 8-9)

Here, there appears to be a logical contradiction, for on the one hand, the note seems to argue for the unilateral, indiscriminate, uninhibited "manifestation" of all truths, even at the risk of creating scandal. This is the interpretative stress placed on the Pauline quotation: "Malheur à celui par qui le scandale arrive," mais "Il faut que le scandale arrive." On the other hand, the note validates only that which is "manifested well," suggesting an unexpected concern with the formal appearance of truth, a selective standard towards the mode of representation which in turn affirms a tacit affinity with the Symbolist attention to the surface of signifiers. On which side does the argument of the Footnote stand, promiscuous manifestation or continent formalism?

In his recent study of Gide's *Journal*, entitled *L'Ecriture du jour*, Eric Marty circumvents this dialectical tension by reversing the hierarchy of surface and depth in a phenomenological treatment of the Gidean manifestation. According to his interpretation, what is manifested at any one moment is simply an interior state of mind. Thus the *Journal*, as Narcissus paradigm, becomes the reflection of shifting psychic *topoi*, changes in mood and daily tribulations. As Marty notes, Gide even imagines the transformation of the reflective surface of Narcisse's pool as a frozen mirror for the use of a metaphorical skater[13]:

> Patinage. Glace où l'on n'a pas encore patiné. Ne se distingue pas de l'eau—perfide—on croirait glisser sur l'eau même—le soleil éclairant la glace, qui fait miroir—et l'on s'y voit—de sorte que, par la vitesse et l'inclinaison du corps, en tournant combinées, je me semblais comme me coucher dans le vide et me regardais de très près, penché sur ce reflet, comme Narcisse. (*J* 103)

Following the system of existential "patinage," the reflection of Narcissus in the ice should be construed as an indication of the absolute relativity of the manifestation, thus undermining the moralism implied in the Footnote. But just when phenomenological relativism seems to triumph, both in the vagaries of Narcisse's gaze and, by extension, in the egocentric projections of Gide's *Journal*, it is suddenly condemned as an expression of *vanitas*. The hubris of the subject's Christ-like illusion of "walking on the water" is dispelled: Christ becomes Narcissus staring into the void. The punishment for relativism emerges then as the sacrifice of Narcissism, a concept reiterated in the Footnote in terms of the artist's relation to his work: "L'artiste et l'homme, vraiment homme, qui vit pour quelque chose, doit avoir d'avance fait le sacrifice de soi-même. Toute sa vie n'est qu'un acheminement vers cela" (*TN* 9).

[13] Eric Marty, *L'Ecriture du jour* (Paris: Seuil, 1985), pp. 260-61. Marty cites Gide's fascination with mirrors in a journal entry of October 18, 1907, where Gide describes his experience of gazing not at his work but at his own reflection in a mirror (cf. *André Walter*), thus displacing Narcissism in the text to a Narcissism of the writer momentarily preoccupied with his writing position, but denied solace in a self-reflective art. Paradoxically, then, the antidote to textual Narcissism is writer's Narcissism.

Whereas in the Footnote, the actual nature of the artist's self-sacrifice to a higher esthetico-moral ideal is never adumbrated, in the *Journal*, especially those entries concurrent or immediately post-dating the *Traité*, the story is continued. The negative vein of self-critique is developed into a writing credo that exerts progressively puritanical constraints on daily life. Penitent resolutions such as the following accrue: "Je recommence à écrire. C'est par lâcheté morale que je me suis interrompu. Je devrais, par hygiène, me forcer à écrire chaque jour quelques lignes" (*J* 22). At the end of the *Journal* of 1891, this resolution is strengthened into a categorical imperative which is litotic through double negation, and which insists that the artist "not be able not to write": "Et pour la vie entière de l'artiste, il faut que sa vocation soit irrésistible, qu'il ne puisse pas ne pas écrire (je voudrais qu'il se résiste à lui-même d'abord, qu'il en souffre)" (*J* 28). Here the exacting requisites of writing appear contigent upon the repression of physical well-being. Though such repression is temporarily revoked (during the period of Gide's homosexual initiation in North Africa under the tutelage of Oscar Wilde), it returns in full force at the end of 1893 and is recorded in a section of the *Journal* published under the title *Feuillets*. Again, we witness a return to moralistic tables prescribing a cruel regimen of self-deprivation. Material comforts are reduced to a minimum; the author's room resembles a monastic cell:

> Dans ma chambre, un lit bas; un peu d'espace, un meuble de bois avec large planche horizontale à hauteur d'appui; une petite table carrée; une chaise dure. J'imagine couché; compose en marchant; écris debout; recopie assis. (*J* 48)

He proscribes all but the modicum of food and sleep ("Peu de manger... Ne pas trop dormir") and perhaps most disturbing of all, like Alissa in *La Porte étroite*, he bans the aesthetic succor afforded by good books, good music and fine art:

> Lectures d'oeuvres médiocres ou mauvaises;
>
> ...
>
> Ne jamais chercher à s'entraîner au moment même par la lecture ni par la musique; ou bien choisir un auteur ancien et ne lire (mais pieusement) que quelques lignes.
>
> ...
>
> Dans la chambre de travail, pas d'oeuvres d'art, ou très peu, et de très graves: (pas de Botticelli) Masaccio, Michel-Ange, l'*Ecole d'Athènes* de Raphaël; mais plutôt quelques portraits ou quelques masques: de Dante, de Pascal, de Leopardi; la photographie de Balzac, de... (*J* 49)

This disciplinary regime, designed to render life "nasty, brutish and short" embodies a sinister death-wish if followed to its logical conclusion. Denied physical and spiritual nourishment, the author must die, replaced perhaps by the modern scriptor devoted to impersonal public works. The sacrifice of the author, only alluded to in the Footnote, is in the *Feuillets* quintessentially expressed by the writer's ultimate proscription: "Pas d'autres livres que des dictionnaires." Roland Barthes would confirm the death of the author in similar terms:

> ...succédant à l'Auteur, le scripteur n'a plus en lui passions, humeurs, sentiments, impressions, mais cet immense dictionnaire où il puise une écriture qui ne peut connaître aucun arrêt: la vie ne fait jamais qu'imiter le livre, et ce livre lui-même n'est qu'un tissu de signes, imitation perdue, infiniment reculée.[14]

The effacement of the artist's ego, a common motif in both the Footnote and the *Journal*, points to this Barthesian concept of the text as a depersonalized catalogue of quotations whose ultimate point of reference has been permanently lost. It is a concept that corresponds to an ideal of purified, abstracted prose; of writing that is mythical by virtue of its freedom from the myth of an authorial signature. The authorial self must be atrophied, rendered abject, and governed by a rigid code of conduct that enables it to imitate, in its quotidian rituals, the passion-depleted contents of a dictionary. Set in the context of the *Journal*, the Footnote can be interpreted as an anti-Narcissus parable morally condemning artistic self-love and aesthetically condoning the death of the author. It is also a litotic parable insofar as it proposes the reduction of art to "manifestation," the reduction of "manifestations" to "symbols," the reduction of "symbols" to "truths" and finally, the reduction of those who purport to represent truths — artists, writers — to faceless ciphers.

The Typology of Inadequacy

The figure of the pitifully inadequate hero typifies the Gidean Narcissus, who, unable to distinguish the boundaries between self and exterior world in this "paysage sans lignes," is depicted at the outset yearning unsuccessfully for a mirror. The riverbank at which he stops is only a dim outline, "Un cadre brut," that designates an empty void rather than a liquid looking glass:

[14] Barthes, *Le Bruissement de la langue*, p. 65.

Simples bords, comme un cadre brut où s'enchâsse l'eau, comme une
glace sans tain; où rien ne se verrait derrière; où derrière, le vide ennui s'éploierait. Un morne, un léthargique canal, un presque horizontal miroir; et rien ne distinguerait de l'ambiance incolorée cette eau
terne, si l'on ne sentait qu'elle coule. (*TN* 3)

The mirror, turned on a horizontal angle away from the subject and
"lacking silver" denies rather than affirms the identity of the troubled
observer. It images only an existential abyss — "le vide ennui" — which
peers out from under its transparent surface. It is the very same void
that haunts Narcissus from within, motivating his search for reflection.

Narcissus, identified with the myth of the empty self, correlates
semiotically to the figure of negation. A mythological character whose
persona has been depleted, Narcissus complements the prose style
of the *Traité* which is metaphorically impoverished; as limpid and col-
orless as the "morne" and "léthargique canal." Both character and prose
style can be interpreted as constituent components of a typology of
inadequacy that in turn can be seen as the response of the *Traité* to
the problem of its own negativity; its status as a flawed and fundamentally gratuitous literary genre. It attempts to salvage some vestige of
value in the following ways:

1. It exposes and "kills" the *Superfluous Author*.
2. It purports to make a virtue out of deficiency and deviance by
generating sympathy for the *Inadequate Hero*.
3. It undertakes the conversion of inadequacy or "too little" into
"sufficiency" or "enough" by developing a rhetoric of insufficiency based
on the *Inadequate Sign*.

We have already examined the process by which the author is
enfeebled and effaced, and we have begun to analyze a similar predica-
ment in the portrayal of the unselfconscious Narcissus, a contradiction in terms since the name "Narcissus" is synonymous with absorbed
self-contemplation. Confronted with the spectre of his own non-
presence in the Heraclitean stream, Narcisse takes recourse to reverie,
conjuring forth in his dream a vision of Paradise — a frozen tableau
composed of "first forms" at the center of which is the "first man."
Like Narcisse, Adam is afflicted by the desire for self-knowledge and
unlike the other forms in Paradise, he refuses to content himself with
simple "manifestation," or pure, non-self-reflexive being. His interior
lament echoes that of Narcisse, but is imbued with erotic innuendos
unavailable to his double. Where Narcisse modestly aspires only to
perceive himself, Adam links this desire with the urge to "affirm his

power." For him, ignorance of one's appearance is tantamount to impotence:

> Tout se joue pour lui, il le sait, — mais lui-même... — mais lui-même
> il ne se voit pas. Que lui fait dès lors tout le reste? ah! se voir! — Certes
> il est puissant, puisqu'il crée et que le monde entier se suspend après
> son regard, — mais que sait-il de sa puissance, tant qu'elle reste
> inaffirmée? (*TN* 6)

Adam's longing to test his strength by obtaining visible proof of his existence challenges the complacency of Paradise, which rests on the assumption that "prouver était inutile." His obsession with a male "other," simultaneously alike (the same sex) yet different (the effect of alienation from one's own image) also suggests a form of auto-eroticism which doubles as homo-eroticism. This paradigm is implicit in the psychosexual definition of Narcissism as a complex that describes both onanism and homosexuality. Displacing his fixation on his own phallus to the phallus of other men, the Narcissist seeks to satisfy his desire for self-as-other. In the *Traité*, Adam enacts this complex by seizing a branch of the Tree of Life (recalling medieval woodcuts representing Adam lying horizontally with the tree protruding from his body like a giant phallus). The sexual connotations of Adam's gesture are reinforced by the reaction of the Tree: its body opens ("une imperceptible fissure d'abord"), it emits a cry ("strident siffle"), it sways, cracks, trembles, convulses and scatters its symbolic seed (the leaves of the Book of Mystery) (*TN* 6). As in the Bible, Adam pays for his transgression. Whereas before he was a unitary being, sufficient unto himself by virtue of remaining ignorant of his ontological separation from Paradise, now he must suffer the ravages of division. In a grotesque parody of the birth of Eve and the advent of heterosexuality (which doubles as a rewriting of Plato's myth of the Androgyne whose division into two explains, according to Aristophanes in the *Symposium*, the origin of the sexes), Adam pays for the crime of self-preference with the loss of self-sufficiency:

> Et l'Homme épouvanté, androgyne qui se dédouble, a pleuré
> d'angoisse et d'horreur, sentant, avec un sexe neuf, sourdre en lui l'in-
> quiet désir pour cette moitié de lui presque pareille, cette femme tout
> à coup surgie, là, qu'il embrasse, dont il voudrait se ressaisir, — cette
> femme qui dans l'aveugle effort de recréer à travers soi l'être parfait
> et d'arrêter là cette engeance, fera s'agiter en son sein l'inconnu d'une
> race nouvelle, et bientôt poussera dans le temps un autre être, incomplet
> encore et qui ne se suffira pas. (*TN* 6)

Adam's internal bifurcation produces man and another half, a half which, though it resembles him ("presque pareille"), is nonetheless sexually different, thereby reversing the Narcissus model (sexually the same, yet perceived as distinct from self). This mirror punishment, which relies on the adverse effects of a margin of difference (inherent in the "presque" of "presque pareille"), blocks the future integration of the sexes implied in the figure of the androgyne. From now on, Adam's progeny, like his Platonic forbears, will be stunted, fragmented, incomplete, and constantly in quest of their "other halves." Difference will mark future generations like a quantity subtracted from their prelapserian status as singular, self-sufficient egos.

Adam's race, doomed to the repetition of difference, becomes haunted by nostalgia for its lost plenitude: "Triste race qui te disperseras sur cette terre de crépuscule et de prières! le souvenir du Paradis perdu viendra désoler tes extases, du Paradis que tu rechercheras partout" (*TN* 7). The priests and the poets make a prodigious effort to recover and reassemble the pages of the divine book (disseminated to the winds after Adam's destruction of their shelter) in the hopes of recuperating the means of returning to Eden, but their endeavor is to no avail. Paradise, according to the pontifications of the narrator, can be rebuilt only temporarily ("Le Paradis est toujours à refaire; il n'est point en quelque lointaine Thulé" [*TN* 7]). Present in "each thing" like a "grain of salt" or "the archetypal structure of a crystal," it vanishes as soon as these "things" are brought together in a collective. As an ensemble, "things" become no longer content to simply "be." Galvanized by the narcissistic desire to attain preeminence as "first forms," they compete with their fellows, and in the process are morally tarnished — "salie, gauchie, et qui ne se satisfait pas" (*TN* 7).

The sullied forms of Adam's world spell out the fate of its morally tainted inhabitants for whom there is no alternative but to resign to permanent imperfection. Within these negative strictures, however, there is the possibility of converting Adam's "deviancy," his weakness for a male double, into a positive virtue. The clue to effecting this conversion derives from the citation in the Footnote: "Malheur à celui par qui le scandale arrive," mais "Il faut que le scandale arrive." This dictum posits the *necessity* of scandal despite the fact that it wreaks misfortune, and suggests that Adam's daring "manifestation" of homoerotic desire was worth the forfeiture of Paradise.

The transformation of erotic "weakness" into moral strength was certainly one of Gide's preferred themes, primarily because it suited his defense of homosexuality. According to the argument in *Corydon*, the homosexual's sacrifice of social acceptance (the result of publicly avowing one's sexual preferences) was comparable to a heroic act, a plea for society's outcasts and marginals and a testimony to the rights of individuals who refuse to conform. However, as Walter Benjamin pointed out, though Gide elevated his cause by embracing the plight of the oppressed in all its manifestations, it was the discrimination against homosexuals which concerned him the most:

> Si Gide, dans toute son oeuvre, s'est tourné vers maintes formes de faiblesse, si, dans son étude sur Dostoïevski, qui est à beaucoup d'égards un portrait de l'auteur par lui-même, il réserve une place centrale à la faiblesse comme "insatisfaction de la chair," "inquiétude," "anomalie," la seule à laquelle il revienne toujours et qui mérite un extrême intérêt est la faiblesse de l'homme pour l'homme.[15]

The valorization of difference as a courageous deviation from the norm only reinforces the homosexual version of the Fall, so clearly suggested by Adam's advances towards the phallic Tree of Life and Narcisse's retribution for attempting to achieve the "baiser impossible":

> Narcisse cependant contemple de la rive cette vision qu'un désir amoureux transfigure; il rêve. Narcisse solitaire et puéril s'éprend de la fragile image; il se penche, avec un besoin de caresse, pour étancher sa soif d'amour, sur la rivière. (*TN* 10)

Though Narcisse is fully prepared to succumb to this fragile male other, possession of the image is ultimately thwarted by the brutal realization that self is other.

> Il se penche et, soudain, voici que cette fantasmagorie disparaît; sur la rivière il ne voit plus que deux lèvres au-devant des siennes, qui se tendent, deux yeux, les siens, qui le regardent. Il comprend que c'est lui, — qu'il est seul — et qu'il s'éprend de son visage...
> Il se relève alors, un peu; le visage s'écarte. La surface de l'eau, comme déjà, se diapre et la vision reparaît. Mais Narcisse se dit que le baiser est impossible, — il ne faut pas désirer une image; un geste pour la posséder la déchire. Il est seul. — Que faire? Contempler. (*TN* 10)

In a transformation of the classical version of the Narcissus legend, Gide's Narcisse takes cognizance of his own myth — of a self defined through the realization that it is enamored of itself. As the giant lips

[15] Walter Benjamin, "André Gide et ses nouveaux adversaires," *Oeuvres* II, tr. Maurice de Gandillac (Paris: Denoël, 1971), 213.

approach and the eyes in the water return the gaze with reciprocal intensity, the illusion of the other is dispelled. Narcisse's outstretched arms fall to his side as he recognizes the futility of his longing, but rather than renounce the beautiful "fantasmagorie" altogether, he becomes a "symbol" of the post-Symbolist sign — the figure of an absent figure, of de-eroticized, aesthetically mediated Narcissism.

The Rhetoric of Insufficiency

The struggle between desire and renunciation, enacted within the drama of Narcissistic sublimation, is in the style of the *Traité* echoed by a parallel struggle between over and understatement. And even as Narcisse is compelled to resign himself to the renunciation of desire, so in the text Gide develops a rhetoric of insufficiency predicated on the "inadequate sign." Images that were delicately cultivated in Symbolist art — the flower, the mirror and the crystal — are in the *Traité* negated, reduced, or bracketed as emblems of an irretrievable perfection. The language is puritanically minimalist rather than poetically expressive, though occasionally lyrical transports succeed in traversing the boundaries of restraint.

The origins of Gide's rhetoric of insufficiency can be traced in part to his discovery of classical mythology under the guidance of Paul Valéry. As a Symbolist acolyte, Gide was closer to Valéry and Valéry's transmission of Mallarmé than to Mallarmé himself, whose treatment of mythological subjects (as in *L'Après-midi d'un faune*, subtitled an "eclogue," or *A Hélène*, his translation of a prose poem by Poe that dimly evokes the Trojan heroine, or his abbreviated profiles of Greek deities and heroes in *Les Dieux antiques*) tended to exalt myths for their occult associations and "natural" proverbial wisdom: "en même temps... dotés d'une beauté et d'une vérité merveilleuses" (*OC* 1164). Valéry placed "truth" before "beauty," and philosophical truth before "marvellous," verity in his approach to mythology; however, like Mallarmé, he also extended the parameters of myth into language. In his "Préface à Monsieur Teste," he called for "une Chimère de la mythologie intellectuelle... l'emploi, sinon, la création, d'un langage forcé, parfois énergiquement abstrait," thereby implying that mythology should be "intellectual" and indissociable from disciplined "abstract" language.[16]

It was Valéry who acted as Gide's principal mentor during the early years of his literary formation and it was also to Valéry that Gide

[16] Paul Valéry, *Monsieur Teste* (Paris: Gallimard, 1946), p. 12.

dedicated *Le Traité du Narcisse*, complementing the former's previous dedication to him of the early version of his poem *Narcisse parle* (1890), and consecrating a quasi-mystical moment in their friendship when both had sat and conversed in the cemetery of Montpellier. Here, they had come across the putative grave of the poet Edward Young's daughter, whose epitaph read: "Narcissae placandis manibus." Valéry translated these words ("pour apaiser les mânes de Narcissa") and used them as an epigram to *Narcisse parle*.[17] Gide, for his part, commemorated their meeting in *Les Nourritures terrestres*: ("A Montpellier, le Jardin botanique... Je me souviens qu'avec Ambroise, un soir, comme aux jardins d'Academus, nous nous assîmes sur une tombe ancienne, qui est tout entourée de cyprès; et nous causions lentement en mâchant des pétales de roses").[18] Several critics, most notably Jean Delay and Robert Mallet, have cited this episode as proof of the profound impact that Valéry and Gide had upon each other. Réjean Robidoux even goes so far as to attribute the supreme status eventually accorded the Narcissus myth in the Symbolist pantheon to the concurrent experiments with the *topos* by Valéry and Gide:

> On a dit que Narcisse, figure privilégiée de l'idéalisme, est le seul mythe qu'ait renové, sinon inventé, le symbolisme. L'affirmation est juste, et il y aura certes lieu d'y revenir; mais il paraît non moins certain qu'avant le *Narcisse parle* de Valéry et le traité de Gide cet esprit de toute une époque n'a pas encore cristallisé dans une mise en oeuvre expresse de ce mythe, alors que, tout de suite après, apparaîtront les *Narcisse* les plus divers.[19]

Valéry and Gide, perhaps more than Mallarmé, seemed to have taken the ancient sense of the Narcissus legend quite literally. They accommodated the psychoanalytical paradigm of Narcissism, or self-love, to the narrative structure of a parable about the relationship between the author and his text, capitalizing on the figure of the writer taken in and seduced by the reflection of himself in the mirror of his prose.[20] They also developed, in the midst of Symbolism, an independent and to some degree anti-Symbolist stance towards the stylistic

[17] Paul Valéry, *Narcisse Parle, Album de vers anciens 1890-1900* (Paris: Cahiers des Amis des Livres, 1920), no pagination.

[18] Gide, *Les Nourritures terrestres*, p. 179.

[19] Robidoux, pp. 20-21.

[20] The fine distinction that I am making here between Mallarmé's treatment of the Narcissus *topos* and that of Gide and Valéry becomes difficult to maintain in the face of a poem such as *Hérodiade*, where the specular iconography of mirrors, jewels, glass,

rendering of myths through the clarity and concision of their own writing. These qualities astonished Gide's closest and most faithful critic — his cousin and wife-to-be Madeleine Rondeaux. She was struck by the serendipitous evidence of a stylistic shift in what was only Gide's second publication and moreover, a work which followed so soon after the emotive *Cahiers d'André Walter*. According to Jean Delay:

> Lorsqu'elle lut *Le Traité du Narcisse*, en juin 1892, Madeleine Rondeaux fut surprise et effrayée du changement qu'il manifestait. Elle admira la qualité de ce "devoir de rhétorique artistique" et y sentit la naissante maturité d'un écrivain épris du classicisme: "Si il [*sic*] y a un mois tu m'avais dit comme ce matin: Je suis au fond tellement classique!" j'aurais ri et parlé de vaste imagination. Mais non, maintenant je dis "peut-être." Le sentiment m'en était venu en avançant dans *Narcisse* — en étant sensible à la justesse des proportions, à la parfaite eurythmie de l'ensemble.[21]

In her rhetorically sensitive reading of her companion's work, Madeleine perceived what few critics have ever discerned — a classical, measured, almost mathematical use of language. One might attempt to characterize this use of language more specifically in terms of six distinct yet interrelated types of signs, all of which are "inadequate" insofar as they serve to denude the text of figurative embellishment. They include: *opaque signs*, which resist decipherment or block interpretation; *abstract signs*, which privilege the concept or epistemé over poetic color and shape; *quantitative signs*, which connote cold, purely intellectual calculation; *negative signs*, which gesture towards a metaphysical nihilism; *redundant signs*, which valorize repetition and depreciate variety of expression; and *reductive signs*, which posit a textual value of "degree zero."

The opaque sign can be most readily identified in terms of a cluster of arcane, hermetic allusions with sources as diverse as the Bible, the *Eddas*, classical philosophy, gnosticism and German Romanticism. Through the superimposition of archetypes, the *Traité* encodes a congeries of cultural hieroglyphs. The story of Genesis is collapsed into a Scandinavian myth of origins in which Ygdrasil is featured as the

reflected light and virginal narcissism lends itself to similar analogies between text and authors.

[21] Jean Delay, *La Jeunesse d'André Gide*, II, *D'André Walter à André Gide* (1890-1895) (Paris: Gallimard, 1957), 126. Delay quotes from Madeleine's letter to Gide, June 17, 1892.

support of the universe (a myth which, as Christian Angelet has surmised, Gide may have borrowed either from Leconte de Lisle's *Poèmes
barbares*, or from Carlyle's description of the *Eddas*, in turn resumed
by Taine in his *Histoire de la littérature anglaise*).[22] Adam and Narcissus
are assimilated into one figure (a precedent for which Otto Rank and
others discovered in the Neoplatonic and gnostic traditions whereby
Adam's fall from grace is attributed to the sin of self-infatuation), and
the representation of Eden, composed of a triad of hypostasized
allegoremes — the logarithmic tree (Number), the book of Mystery
(Letter) and the shadows of the leaves (possibly evoking the union
of Geometry and Literature in Philosophy) — can be read as a syn-
cretic trilogy (or "triple logos"), connoting alternately the Pythagorean
triangle, the Platonic unity of Idea, Appearance and Representation,
or the Holy Trinity.[23] These highly imbricated allusions complement
vocatives of praise such as "Hypostase de l'Élohim, suppôt de la
Divinité!" or elliptical formulations such as "S'il était, ou s'il n'était
pas, que nous importe? mais il était tel, s'il était," which conspire to
give the text a Kabbalistic or biblical aura. Studded with the great
enigmas of world religion, the *Traité* emerges as a provocation to
hermeneutical decipherment. Indeed it is the interpretive perplex that
is posed from the very beginning as an opaque sign in the guise of
an inscrutable "fable" of "hiéroglyphe":

> Le peuple s'étonnait à l'apparence des fables et *sans comprehendre* il adorait;
> les prêtres attentifs, penchés sur la profondeur des images, pénétraient
> lentement l'intime sens du hiéroglyphe. Puis *on a voulu expliquer*;... (*TN*
> 3; my italics)

The failure of the masses to comprehend the fables together with their
desire for explication for the hieroglyphs underscores the mystery and
inaccessibility of these signs, and indeed legitimates the entire enterprise of writing books and treatises as a response to the "people's" de-
mand for exegesis.

Just as the "people" are baffled by their votive objects, so Narcisse
is baffled by the undulations of the water at which he stares in the

---

[22] Christian Angelet, *Symbolisme et invention formelle dans les premiers écrits d'André Gide*,
Romanica Gandensia 19 (Ghent, 1982), p. 20. Angelet's analysis of *Le Traité du Narcisse* is particularly strong in its discussion of Schopenhauer's influence on the esthetico-
moral ideas in Gide's early works or, alternatively, in its interpretation of where and
how Gide might be said to have misread the German philosophers.
[23] Angelet, p. 21 (for reference to Otto Rank's analysis of the conflation of Adam
and Narcissus).

hopes of descrying his own image: "Narcisse regarde émerveillé; — *mais ne comprend pas bien*, car l'une et l'autre se balancent, si son âme guide le flot, ou si c'est le flot qui la guide" (*TN* 4; my italics). Here, the mysterious flood tide frustrates the possibility of self-knowledge and renders Narcisse as obtuse an observer, as his double Adam: "Mais, spectateur obligé, toujours, d'un spectacle où il n'a d'autre rôle que celui de regarder toujours, il se lasse. (...) A force de les contempler, *il ne se distingue plus de ces choses: ne pas savoir* où l'on s'arrête — ne pas savoir jusqu'où l'on va!" (*TN* 6; my italics). Here the opaque sign consists of Adam's own body, as occluded to him as the "appearances" of "first forms" to the Scholar. "Le Savant," another variation of the frustrated seer, is barred by his inductive method from intuiting the nature of true "first forms": "Mais, ces formes premières, le Savant les recherche, par une induction lente et peureuse, et, désireux de certitude, *Il se défend de deviner* (*TN* 9; my italics). These inadequate readers are all confounded by the spectacle of objects that elude interpretation. The most striking figure for such objects is the "stagnant miroir," which, as we have already noted, emerges in the text as defective a glass reflecting "nothing" ("le rien") in the form of an opaque surface. Its antonym, the crystal, is distinguished by contrast as an airy structure composed of "*transparent*," "*revelatory*" words. What they reveal, however, is never disclosed, thereby rendering them equally opaque to the reader.

Related to the opaque sign is the pure *abstraction*, a semantic form which is familar as a philosophical value or ideological concept (as in the slogan "Liberté, Egalité, Fraternité"). Like many of Mallarmé's works, the *Traité* possesses an analytical lexicon comprised of technical and critical terms, among them: "Prétexte, induction, deviner, symbole, pensée, idée, innombrables exemples, théorie, doctrine, les règles, l'esthétique, la morale" and even "ce traité." These terms are distinguished by their reference to textual rather than to concrete or material objects. Together with philosophical principles ("les Vérités, le bien, le mal"), they function as an antimetaphorical force, as the antithesis of visually descriptive figures of speech, or as the agents of the text's "retroactive" inscription of its own reading and writing. Illustrative of Gide's theory of the symbol which records and exposes its symbolic devices, the analytical lexicon names its own metacritical underpinnings. This autoreferential dimension, though it may in its own way constitute a highly rarefied poetry of epistemology and criticism, serves for the most part to depoetize the literary work and thus to lead it further away from literature and closer to philosophy.

Perhaps the strongest expression of abstraction lies in the linguistic terminology of numerical values and mathematical functions. This terminology prevails throughout in a dry, *quantitative* language indicating number, size, proportion, dimension, and comparative relation: identity and difference, equality, less and more, degree and dimension, singularity and complexity, condensation and diversification, sufficiency and insufficiency, nothing versus all. The concept of pure number is frequently evoked in reference to the perfection of Paradise. The Tree of Life which stands at its center and whose roots extend to all of Creation, is described as "L'arbre logarithmique"—a logos that posits the fixed or base number against which all things are proportionally measured. This absolute standard of numerical value (anticipating Mallarmé's hypostasized evocation of "LE NOMBRE" in *Un Coup de dés*), surfaces in expressions such as: "Jardin des Idées! où les formes, rhythmiques et sûres, révélaient sans effort leur nombre"; or, "Tout était parfait comme un nombre et se scandait parfaitement," or again, "et quand il a perçu, visionnaire, l'Idée, l'intime Nombre harmonieux de son Être" (*TN* 5, 9, 10). In all of these examples, the numerical standard applies to the constituent components of Paradise, each of which embodies a "visionary ratio" of balance and harmony.

Paradise, distinguished by relations of equality and reciprocity, is mirrored on a microcosmic level in the internal structure of each of its parts. By contrast, the post-lapserian world is defined by dissymmetry and competitive difference. For example, prior to his fall, Adam is described as "unique" and "encore insexué." Afterwards, he is divided into two parts, each of which strives against the other to repossess its missing half. Since neither half succeeds, the gloomy prospect for the human race is permanent schism and struggle for advantage.

Adam's transition from a unisexual to a bisexual being parallels the radical transition from singularity to plurality that occurs when the Book of Mystery—a single entity— is transformed into scattered pages.[24] The reverse motion occurs when Adam's "sad race" disperses

[24] Robert Greer Cohn, in his *Mallarmé's Masterwork: New Findings* (The Hague: Monton, 1966), cites a passage from Baudelaire's formulations of numerical mysticism on Mallarmé's language (and by implication the appropriation of this same language by Gide), but also shows the extent to which Gide's dialectical paradigms of singularity and infinity appear to be rooted in what Cohn characterizes as a "cosmic-erotic" Symbolist imagery. Baudelaire wrote: "Comment le père 'un' a-t-il pu engendrer la dualité et s'est-il enfin métamorphosé en une population innombrable de nombres? Mystère! La totalité infinie de nombres doit-elle ou peut-elle se concentrer de nouveau dans l'unité originelle? Mystère!"

over the earth in the hopes of regathering the Book's contents into a single unit. This dialectic between diversification and condensation recurs with such monotonous frequency (tears accumulate into streams which evaporate, only to produce clouds which then shed drops of rain, reflected images are broken apart into multiple, random particles of light, only to be reformed when the wavelets die down), that the text often seems to resemble a cosmic flow chart. This quantitative configuration of the cosmos is also prevalent in the text's movement between all ("tout") and nothing ("rien"), or, to put it more mathematically, between infinity and zero. Phrases beginning with "tout" abound: "Toutes choses sont dites déjà"; "Tout s'y cristallisait"; "Tout s'efforce vers sa forme perdue"; "tout est à refaire, à refaire éternellement" (*TN* 3, 5). Used primarily as an indefinite pronoun rather than as an adjective, the word "tout" signals un unquantifiable sum that gestures towards an ineffable superlative dimension. Its opposite pole, "rien," functions in a similar fashion, but also exudes a special aura as one of Mallarmé's preferred "mots clefs." Mallarmé imbued the term with a paradoxical fullness—the potential plenitude of an as yet unstated poetic inspiration. By contrast, Gide's use of the pronoun is deflationary ("rien que le seul Narcisse") or at best unspecific: "Tout demeurait immobile, car rien ne souhaitait d'être mieux." This trivialization of a word that carried such inflated connotations in the Symbolist lexicon foreshadows Gide's outright parody of Mallarméan absences and silences in *Le Voyage d'Urien* (1892). In this work, aporias surface as the vague objectives of a burlesque quest: the "voyage d'Urien" becomes the "voyage du rien"—of nothing—towards "quelque chose d'autre," that is, towards a "something else" which is never disclosed or discovered. This figuration of the void furnishes the fundamental irony of the text: "L'ironie consist d'abord," so Christian Angelet has argued, "à donner du corps à des riens." Though in the *Traité*, this irony is less overtly apparent, the repetition of the pronoun "rien" contributes, nonetheless, to the emptying out of the Symbolist sign.

"Tout" and "rien" both represent the total levelling of difference. Unlike other quantitative designations that depict Judgement and Thought in terms of the weighing and balancing of values or the calculation of difference and degree, these pronouns negate intellectual comparison and are therefore "cosmic" or transcendental concepts. By including such concepts in its rhetoric of quantity, the *Traité* depicts a mathematical allegory of the mind governed by symbols of reason's borders. All or nothing, both an "n'th degree," or degree zero, describe the outer limits of language beyond which reason fails to travel. In this sense, they express the sheer *negation* of thought, or intellectual nihilism. The nihilistic current that runs throughout the *Traité* is further reinforced on a linguistic level by the heavy use of specific grammatical indices of negation. As in the phrase: "Il n'y a plus de berge ni de source; plus de mêtamorphose et plus de fleur mirée," negative markers ("ne... plus... ni"), expunge the visual associations attached to images such as "slope, spring and flower." Like a refined form of preterition (a figure which says what it is not going to say), these negatives disavow what has been affirmed. Here, they deaden the pictorial field of metaphor that has just been evoked.

Another effective means of restricting figuration is through *redundancy*: specifically, the repetition of flat, uninteresting words, or phrases devoid of imagery. "Répéter à l'excès," Roland Barthes maintained in *Le Plaisir du texte*, "c'est entrer dans la perte, dans le zéro du signifié."[25] Perhaps the most bankrupt signifier in any language is the word "thing," and it is not surprisingly the most frequently reiterated in the *Traité*. It appears approximately sixteen times, tied only with the equally innocuous word "form." Often the terms are used interchangeably or in rapid sequence within successive passages, generating an unrelieved litany of vacuous utterances. Phrases such as "Toujours les mêmes formes passent"; "Comme le temps ne fuit que par la fuite des choses, chaque chose s'accroche et se crispe"; Le Poète... déscend profondément au coeur des choses"; "il sait redonner une forme éternelle, *sa* Forme véritable enfin," are heavy freight for a text as abbreviated and highly wrought as the *Traité* (*TN* 4, 9, 10). If a "message" can be deduced from this flagrantly monotonous repetition (strengthened by the plethora of verbs containing the prefix "re," as in: "recommencer, refaire, recueillir, revêtir, refleurir, recristalliser"), then it consists of the argument that "less is more"; that is, that the least metaphorically saturated words are worth repeating the maximum number of times, or, alternatively, that the less stylistic variety, the more the reader will focus on the esthetico-moral ideas.

This argument may appear unconvincing, but it is completely in line with the puritanical bent of the *Traité*'s ideology of the symbol, the artist, and the work of art. Based on the unchallenged premise that *reduction* increases the value of the aesthetic subject or object, the text perseveres towards an ideal of stylistic minimalism. The most

[25] Roland Barthes, *Le Plaisir du texte* (Paris: Seuil, 1973), p. 67.

apparent depiction of this ideal occurs in Paradise. Small in scale, a paragon of smoothly running, self-reliant order, it exemplifies the Deist utopia of a clockmaker's creation. Like a cosmological machine — an astrolobe, planisphere or timepiece — Paradise "operates" according to abstract laws but remains as fixed and immobile as a classical monument: "Tout demeurait immobile, car rien ne souhaîtait d'être mieux. La calme gravitation opérait seule lentement la révolution de l'ensemble" (*TN* 5).

Classicism in a musical mode is explicitly evoked by the comparison of Paradise to a "pastoral symphony":

> Eden! où les brises mélodieuses ondulaient en courbes prévues; où le ciel étalait l'azur sur la pelouse symétrique; où les oiseaux étaient couleur du temps et les papillons sur les fleurs faisaient des harmonies providentielles; où la rose était rose parce que la cétoine était verte, qui venait c'est pourquoi s'y poser. Tout était parfait comme un nombre et se scandait normalement; un accord émanait du rapport des lignes; sur le jardin planait une constante symphonie. (*TN* 5)

This synaesthetic description illustrates many of the principles of classicism which Gide later defined in his critical writings. The absence of extraneous detail recalls a formulation developed in his *Feuillets* (1892-1893): "Dès que l'idée d'une oeuvre a pris corps, j'entends: dès que cette oeuvre s'organise, l'élaboration ne consiste guère qu'à supprimer tout ce qui est inutile à son *organisme*" (*J* 49; Gide's italics). The rhythm and compositionsl rigor of the ensemble connotes Platonic principles of artistic beauty (purity of line; simple, abstract shapes; metrical discipline; and the preeminence of structural laws) all of which are suggested by Gide's dictum (in *Feuillets*) that: "L'idée de l'oeuvre, c'est sa composition." The form of Paradise is also illustrative of a theory of classical subordination and hierarchy which Gide would later elaborate in an Appendix to *Incidences* (1919) entitled "Réponse à une enquête de la Renaissance sur le classicisme":

> La perfection classique implique, non point certes une suppression de l'individu (peu s'en faut que je ne dise: au contraire) mais la soumission de l'individu, sa subordination, et celle du mot dans la phrase, de la phrase dans la page, de la page dans l'oeuvre. C'est la mise en évidence d'une hiérarchie.[26]

[26] André Gide, "Réponse à une enquête sur le classicisme," *Incidences* (Paris: Gallimard, 1924), p. 219. Marcel Muller has pointed out to me that Nietzsche advanced a similar formulation which he in turn seems to have borrowed from Paul Bourget. In *La Nouvelle Revue* of November 15, 1881, Bourget wrote: "L'organisme

"Hierarchy" is certainly "evident" in Paradise, "où l'Idée refleurit en sa pureté supérieure;... où *l'orgueil du mot ne supplante pas* la Pensée" (*TN* 10; my italics). Moreover, it resembles the "mise en abyme," which also depends on the subordination of part to whole, and on the capactiy of each part to function as a whole (container and contained). The fact that this metonymic structure is common to *both* the classical norm and the narrative paradigm implies that the "mise en abyme" constitutes an expression of Gide's classicism, and further, that classicism is deeply embedded in his concept of the work of art whether on a narrative or stylistic level. Indeed, classicism emerges as the umbrella term or *summa* of all the myriad versions of the inadequate sign that comprise what we have called the rhetoric of insufficiency. The fact that it surfaces so strongly during the author's ostensibly Symbolist phase is somewhat perplexing (as evinced by Madeleine Rondeaux's reaction); however, as his later work indicates, it was to become the preferred stylistic mode.

The *Traité* attests to Gide's discovery of classicism as an alternative to the intensely personal style of *Les Cahiers d'André Walter*. The first

social... entre en décadence aussitôt que la vie individuelle s'est exagérée sous l'influence du bien-être acquis et de l'hérédité. Cette même loi gouverne le développement et la décadence de cet autre organisme qui est le langage. Un style de décadence est celui où l'unité du livre se décompose pour laisser la place à l'indépendance de la page, où la page se décompose pour laisser la place à l'indépendance de la phrase, et la phrase pour laisser la place à l'indépendance du mot. Les exemples foisonnent dans la littérature actuelle qui démontrent cette féconde vérité" (cited by J. Kamerbeek, "Style de Décadence," *Revue de Littérature Comparée* [April 1965], p. 268).

Nietzsche's version of this hierarchical theory of decadence appeared in a letter of 1884-85 addressed to the musician Dr. Carl Fuchs: "Die rhytmische Zweideutigkeit, so dass man nicht mehr weiss und wissen soll, ob etwas Schwanz oder Kopf ist, ist ohne allen Zweifel ein Kunstmittel mit dem wunderbare Wirkungen erreicht werden können: der "Tristan" ist reich daran, — als Symptom einer ganzen Kunst ist und bleibt sie trotzdem das Zeichen der Auflösung. Der Theil wird Herr über das Ganze, die Phrase über die Melodie, der Augenblick über die Zeit (auch das tempo), das Pathos über das Ethos (Charakter, Stil, oder wie es heissen soll—), schliesslich auch der *esprit* über den "Sinn". Verzeihung! was ich wahrzunehmen glaube, ist eine Veranderung der Perspektive: man sieht das Einzelne viel zu scharf, man sieht das Ganze viel zu stumpf, — und man hat den *Willen* zu dieser Optik in der Musik, vor Allem man hat das *Talent* dazu! Das aber ist décadence" (also cited by Kamerbeek, p. 274).

It is interesting to note that the hierarchical paradigm of *decadence* common to Bourget and Nietzsche, with its emphasis on the independence of part from whole, reappears in the Gidean *classical* norm but in reverse. The syntactic similarity of his formulation to Bourget's and Nietzsche's provides convincing evidence for the supposition that these theories of decadence were the sources of his theory of classicism.

person pronoun, which before unburdened itself over-generously with confessions of adolescent frustration and soul-searching reflections on the plight of the writer, is sharply curtailed and depersonalized in the *Traité*. Ebullient, exclamatory utterances such as: "Ah! ne pas pouvoir se voir! Un miroir! un miroir! un miroir! un miroir!" are brutally undercut by dry, sparsely inflected passages (*TN* 3). When, in Part II, a hyperbolic account of the Apocalypse is rendered, the mood is gradually deflated by the voice of a didactic commentator:

> Car la faute est toujours la même et qui reperd toujours le Paradis: l'individu qui songe à soi tandis que la Passion s'ordonne, et, comparse orgueilleux, ne se subordonne pas. (*TN* 8)

The didactic Gide and the classical Gide were to become intimate associates in Gide's rewriting of mythology and the *Traité* can be read as the record of a pact made between them which was to endure. Though the prose forms that resulted from this pact would vary considerably, they can all be traced back to the *Traité* in at least three respects: the deflation of Symbolist hyperbole is accorded a positive value and "le degré zéro" emerges as the preeminent stylistic fiction, Gide's rereading of myth (Narcissus, Prometheus, Oedipus or Theseus) becomes inseparable from the aesthetic redefinition of modern classicism as it relates to language, and philosophical argument is allowed to contaminate literary codes to the point where literature recedes into its own theory. What remains of the myth of Narcissus is paradoxically (because of her absence in Gide's version) little more than Echo, who is carried over into *Paludes* in the form of the "réplique," that "stichomythic" and continually deferred origin of social discourse. Barthes's interpretation of the Narcissus legend would only confirm and theoretically "echo" its Gidean antecedent:

> ...dans la scène, je colle à ce qui vient d'être dit. Le sujet (divisé et cependant commun) de la scène énonce par distiques: c'est la stichomythie, modèle archaïque de toutes les scènes du monde...
>
> Chaque argument (chaque vers du distique) est choisi de telle sorte qu'il soit symétrique et pour ainsi dire égal à son frère, et cependant augmenté d'un supplément de protestation: bref d'une *surenchère*. Cette surenchère n'est jamais rien d'autre que le cri du Narcisse: *Et moi! Eh moi!* (Barthes's emphasis)[27]

[27] Roland Barthes, *Fragments d'un discours amoureux* (Paris: Seuil, 1977), p. 245.

III

NOT'S KNOTS

DENIAL AND DIFFERENCE IN *PALUDES*

> L'amitié mondaine est épidémique: tout le monde s'attrape, comme une maladie. Supposez maintenant que je lâche dans ce réseau un sujet douloureux, avide de maintenir avec son autre un espace étanche, pur (non touché), consacré; les activités du réseau, son trafic d'informations, ses engouements, ses initiatives, seront reçues comme autant de dangers. Et, au milieu de cette petite société, à la fois village ethnologique et comédie de boulevard, structure parentale et imbroglio comique, se tient l'Informateur, qui s'affaire et *dit tout à tout le monde*.
>
> (Roland Barthes, *Fragments d'un discours amoureux*)

If, at one moment in his *Fragments d'un discours amoureux*, Barthes casually embroiders the elocutionary cliché "faire une scène" with a fresh adaptation of the Narcissus myth, at another point in the text he offers a précis of *Paludes* that in its turn provides a critical framework for deconstructing the work's rhetoric of "mondanité," especially as it pertains to the Symbolists. From the very title, which poses itself in marshy darkness ("ordure") against the Symbolist meadow of flowers and light ("verdure"), to the fatuous dialogue of literary circles which could hardly be a more direct caricature of the Symbolist soirée, to the persistently deadpan, paratactic style of the writing, *Paludes* emerges as Gide's most genial attempt to construct a multistoried negation of the literary and social codes of Symbolism.

Written, as scholars have often noted, during his sojourn in 1894 in an isolated mountain village in the Jura, *Paludes* exudes the "parfum de mort" permeating this way-station of cure.[1] Assimilated to

---

[1] Gide used this expression in a passage of *Si le grain ne meurt* cited by Jean-Jacques Thierry in his bibliographical notes to *Paludes*, included in the Pléiade edition: *Romans,*

the stultifying, rarefied atmosphere of the Parisian salon, the fatal odor releases a poisonous intellectual fever which innoculates its literary population against life. *Paludes* — connoting a malarial swamp — designates a disease of the overly civilized, that is, writing. Its symptoms are discernible in the narrator's distaste for immediate experience and corresponding predilection for a textual mode that reveals its parasitical relation to established literary genres and clichés. The narrator of *Paludes* dines on a Symbolist menu, starting with a "potage" seasoned according to the taste of Huysmans and ending with a liqueur flavored by Oscar Wilde. Nourished thus, by a surfeit of rich linguistic food and drink, he produces a text that at one level travesties the figures of Symbolist overstatement and synaesthesia. On another, the narrator employs Symbolism's own conventions of scientific verisimilitude — the Realism of Huysmans — to portray relentlessly what has become, for Gide, the "ennui" of Symbolism. As Colette's husband Willy (perhaps himself one of the cast of characters) intimated in his reading of the work's photographic fidelity to the epic boredom of the milieu which it represents:

> *Paludes*, c'est proprement, avant tout, et peut-être uniquement un livre héroïque. Beaucoup de gens s'ennuient, tous les hommes s'ennuient — et M. André Gide s'ennuie. Photographier cet ennui, le rendre avec tant de vérité, tant de gris, tant de langueur, qu'il prenne le lecteur à la gorge, qu'il l'étreigne et qu'il l'étrangle, qu'il lui donne l'horreur — et mieux — la conscience de son ennui, voilà le but du livre...[2]

In its true-to-life depiction of existential torpor, *Paludes* thus qualifies as a Realist text, but one whose social frivolity shamelessly undercuts the high seriousness of its nineteenth-century precedent. Deprived of their social and didactic ramifications and subordinated to the depiction of artistic paralysis, the techniques of Realist description are obliquely ridiculed even as they are deployed.

If the Symbolist trope and the Realist genre constitute raw material for travesty and pastiche, so too does the conceit of the author-hero. Identifiable in Romantic literature as a fictional narrator who acts as the agent of textual irony (exposing, as in Rousseau's *Confessions*, the persuasive, deceptive powers of literary artifice), the author-hero

récits et sôties (Paris: Gallimard, 1958), pp. 1471-72. All further references to *Paludes* will be to this edition and will appear in the text abbreviated *P*.

[2] Cited by Claude Martin, in *La Maturité d'André Gide: de 'Paludes' à 'L'Immoraliste' (1895-1902)* (Paris: Klincksieck, 1977), p. 69.

emerges in *Paludes* as doubly ironic, an *eiron* of the Romantic *eiron*. Not only does he unveil his hidden status as the author of *Paludes*, but he also presents himself as the critic of a work that has no content, or, alternatively, that flaunts its lack of content as a substitute for the lack. Textual impotence combines with sexual impotence in order to make of this work a paradigm, no longer of an anti-Symbolist treatise but of a rather original aesthetic of literary sublimation, an aesthetic predicated on styleless style, and the negative economy of textual production.

Rhetorical Parody and Pastiche

If one begins to isolate and distinguish the myriad voices embedded in *Paludes*, one becomes aware of the extent to which this text approximates a kind of "tour de force" in literary ventriloquism. Close to what Mikhail Bakhtin has called narrative "heteroglossia" (the convergence of multiple discouses and genres) or to what Michel Foucault has referred to as "hétérotopies" or the "hétéroclite," the narrative practice of *Paludes* exemplifies a technique of simultaneous and superimposed pastiche. Like a palimpsest, the clichés and conventions of Barrèsian nativism can be discovered beneath a sarcastically oversaturated rhetoric of Symbolism in its turn overlaid by the ironic imitation of Naturalist and Realist description. Foucault, commenting on the disturbing laughter provoked by a text by Borges, offers a vivid characterization of this elusive counterfeit writing. "Hétérotopies," he claims,

> inquiètent, sans doute parce qu'elles minent secrètement le langage, parce qu'elles empêchent de nommer ceci et cela, parce qu'elles ruinent d'avance la 'syntaxe', et pas seulement celle qui construit les phrases...
>
> ...les hétérotopies... dessèchent le propos, arrêtent les mots sur eux-mêmes, contestent, dès sa racine, toute possibilité de grammaire; elles dénouent les mythes et frappent de stérilité le lyrisme des phrases.[3]

According to Foucault, heterotopias "dessicate" and "immobilize" the living phrase because of their bottomless and multidirectional referentiality. Who can identify to what referent a phrase that concurrently quotes its own style while parodying another points? The loss of a clear destination or place (*topos*) leads, Foucault would seem to imply, to the loss of clear stylistic classification, to the hollowing out or

[3] Michel Foucault, *Les Mots et les choses* (Paris: Gallimard, 1966), pp. 9-10.

hybridization of genres, and the bankruptcy, complete ironization, or permanent dissemination of the sign.

One form of heterotopia that can be seen as a kind of "deep structural" punning or autopastiche consists of the representation of Symbolism as symbolic of its own making. That *Paludes* invites interpretation as a parody of a Symbolist creation myth is evinced by its overall structure, its obsessive reenactment of difficult beginnings, and its implicit parody of the symbolists *as writers*. Baudelaire labored for a lifetime in order to produce a slender volume of poems that would stand as the perfect *summa* of literary creation and Mallarmé, as his letters to Cazalis reflect throughout, suffered intense and protracted periods of literary sterility in order to reap an equally modest harvest of poetry and prose. The stereotype of the author as one who toils with Herculean endurance to distill an ideal work of art, never shrinking from honing and revising an original version or starting again from degree zero, pervaded the literary ethos of the 1890s. In *Paludes* (the writing of which requires six days like the Biblical Creation of the world), the story of Genesis is told and retold as the painful birth of a literary text. Adamic man is featured as a shepherd-author who navigates his way through the viscous deltas of marsh poetics. Like Noah, he is portrayed arranging figures of speech—primordial flora and fauna—into "lines" organized in turn into paragraphs that float like makeshift arks on stagnant pools of ink or become moored on the banks of white paper.

These rites of writing are carefully recorded in the narrator's description of his determination to "re-commence" or "re-undertake" the arduous task of composing *Paludes*. The raw tabloid of a work in progress, *Paludes* transparently reveals the as yet unformed foetus of a whole or completed text. Elison, excision or the loss of a word or thought are registered as part of an internal drama of arrested textual development. In phrases such as "je repris la plume; je biffai tout cela," or "Je ne sais plus ce que je voulais dire... ah! tant pis; j'ai mal à la tête... Non, la pensée serait perdue,—perdue..." the Romantic *topos* of the work's organic gestation is ironically reversed, with the text presented as a monster; its growth stunted by the writer's inhibitions (*P* 108-26). In addition to representing the fissures in the text or the impasse obstructing the flow of literary inspiration, the narrative also evokes a range of intimate, self-conscious moments in the process of rhetorical decision making. With the justification of a caesura: "Je sais ce qui vous étonne: c'est la césure," or the capture of a passing phrase: "Tiens! une phrase! notons cela," the Symbolist writer's metacritical poetics of rhetorical invention are inadvertently pastiched (*P* 142, 126). So too is his infatuation and ultimate inebriation with his own metaphors:

> ...— Ne pas pouvoir se faire entendre... C'est pourtant vrai, cela que je leur dis — puisque j'en souffre. — Est-ce que j'en souffre? — Ma parole! à de certains moments, je ne comprends plus du tout ni ce que je veux ni à qui j'en veux; — il me semble alors que je me débats contre mes propres fantômes et que je... Mon Dieu! mon Dieu, c'est là vraiment chose pesante, et la pensée d'autrui est plus inerte encore que la matière. Il semble que chaque idée, dès qu'on la touche, vous châtie; elles ressemblent à ces goules de nuit qui s'installent sur vos épaules, se nourissent de vous et pèsent d'autant plus qu'elles vous ont rendu faible... A présent que j'ai commencé de chercher les équivalents des pensées, pour les rendre aux autres plus claires — je ne peux cesser; rétrospections; voilà des métaphores ridicules;... (*P* 125-26)

Plagued by a phantom vampire who drains the writer of his artistic energy, dazed by the exigencies of communication, and exhausted by the search for equivalencies in language for thoughts, the narrator mimics the private anguish of the Symbolist author whose propensity for serpentine, allusive chains of association and arcane or rococo figures of speech, lead him into a maze of unintelligible "métaphores ridicules" from which there is no easy exit.

The Symbolist creation, *Paludes* implies, is flawed by its indulgence of excessive tropes. Allowed to multiply and migrate, undisciplined by the classical dictates of clarity and restraint, figures of speech become grotesque contortions of poetic consciousness. As Wolfgang Holdheim has pointed out, often the effect of this rhetorical extravagance is concentrated in a single word or phrase, thereby aggravating the attrition of meaning which Foucault ascribed to the heterotopia:

> "Au lieu de mon bol de lait, pour varier, je pris un peu de tisane," André reports one morning, and he echoes that statement the next day. To his friend Hubert, the perpetually agitated man of action, he explains that "on ne sort des cités que par des moyens énergiques, des express." A little later, referring to his intention of telling Angèle that her room is too small, he specifies: "j'emploierai même le mot *exigu*." Obviously this terminology is too emphatic for the contents. But in all these cases, overstatement has a special structure and is not merely an exaggerated expression of an ordinary state of affairs. The emphasis is not sustained but localized in a word or two ("pour varier," "des

moyens énergiques," "même"), after which the formulation pointedly falls back into an appropriate banality.[4]

Holdheim identifies overstatement as one of the crucial techniques of *Paludes*'s satirical effect but neglects to note that in addition to signaling the banality behind the narrator's pretensions to sophistication, *Paludes*'s overstatement parodies the language of exaggeration in a Symbolist context. Language's surplus, its "plus que CELA," is presented as a deficit measuring what Symbolism fails to deliver on the level of meaningful content. The Symbolist writer, mired in the marsh of inflated language, stagnates like the narrator and his amanuensis (Tityre) in their respective *Paludes*. The word "paludes" is itself an overstatement in the sense that it is a trope (a euphemism for marsh or mud-flat) on a trope (with "marais" a euphemism for anus or excrement).[5] Both the literary work and the mud-flat connote a liminal territory — linguistic chaos and geomorphic sludge — from which are born, respectively, the Rabelaisian rhetoric of obscenity and invective, and originary biological forms.

Though Gide reserved his outright parody of tropisms for a later *sôtie* (*Les Caves du Vatican*), he nonetheless festooned *Paludes* with descriptions of natural organic life: from the flora and fauna of public gardens to the marine microcosms encased in a household fishbowl. Here, too, there is a kind of interior punning or pastiche on the relationship between the literal depiction of nature and the conceits of Naturalist writing. The classification and stratification of society which Flaubert, Zola, Maupassant or the Goncourts were thought to have rigorously applied to literature, are turned as a system back on to their "roots" in botanical taxonomy. Thus we find the plant world divided into social classes mirroring the classes of French fin-de-siècle society. The "aristoloche," as its name implies, emerges as an emblem of the aristocratic, highly strung, "mondain" character-type just as Huysmans' variegated, rarefied, hot-house flower stands in for Des Esseintes in *A Rebours* or Proust's "orchidée" designates Charlus, erotically fertilized by the "bourdon" (Jupien) in *A la recherche du temps*

[4] Wolfgang Holdheim, *Theory and Practice of the Novel: A Study on André Gide* (Geneva, 1968), p. 172.

[5] For the association between "marais" and "anus" in relation to the medieval sôtie, see Ida Nelson, *La Sottie sans souci. Essai d'interprétation homosexuelle* (Paris: Bibliothèque du XVe siècle XXIX, 1977). As cited by Bertrand Fillaudeau, *L'Univers ludique d'André Gide: les sôties* (Paris: Corti, 1985) pp. 143-44.

perdu. The "Jardin des Plantes," featured as the home of upper-class display flowers such as the "aristoloche," is balanced on the opposite side of the social spectrum by the paludal marsh itself, which harbors plebian "plantes utiles"—"des bourraches, des guimauves efficaces et des centaurées très amères" (*P* 129). These ungainly, medicinal flora, described in minute detail and cautioned against for their poisonous contents, suggest a jibe at Naturalist writing, where attention to repugnant detail often lead to a kind of poetics of the Ugly.

Paludes is the haven for a pernicious species of water-fowl—"des sarcelles, un gibier peccamineux"—which Tityre, the narrator's fictional double, is fond of eating (*P* 101). Frequent ingestion of the bird gives rise to swamp fever, a malady which, it turns out, bears a close resemblance to sexual excess ("peccamineux" derives from *peccare*, "to sin," "pécher"). Like its coinhabitants, the "vers de vase" (a pun on "verses of the chamber-pot" and the biblical "worm" or serpent), the "sarcelles" act as the agents of a post-lapserian, subterranean society, free from sexual constraints. Moss and algae "make depth with shadow," and waterweeds lovingly offer air bubbles for the larvae to breathe. The language used to describe these activities mimics the extreme preciosity of diction, used by some of the more decadent Symbolists, Huysmans in particular:

> Un air presque tiède soufflait; au-dessus de l'eau, de frêles gramens se penchaient que firent ployer des insectes. Une poussée germinative disjoignait les marges de pierres; un peu d'eau s'enfuyait, humectait les racines. Des mousses, jusqu'au fond descendues, faisaient une profondeur avec l'ombre: des algues glauques retenaient des bulles d'air pour la respiration des larves. (*P* 104)

Tityre's stagnation in the marsh, his "morbid rootedness" (as Weinberg has described it), in this sluggish country of algae, fungus, worms and insects, satirizes the sedentary life of the Symbolist as well as Virgil's nostalgia for a preeminently organic mode of life where men are firmly "enracinated" in Arcadia. This satire anticipates Gide's altercation with Maurice Barrès over *Les Déracinés*, which he pointedly mocked in his second *sôtie*, *Le Prométhée mal enchaîné* (1899). In a bibliographical note to his analysis of "L'Histoire de Tityre" in *Le Prométhée*, Kurt Weinberg conjectures that the word "marais" is a possible pun on the name "Maurras," Barrès' fellow proponent of nativistic, nationalistic literature.[6] Barrès, as is well known, argued that a plant

6   Kurt Weinberg, *On Gide's 'Prométhée'* (Princeton: Princeton University Press, 1972), p. 139.

when uprooted from its native soil and transplanted to foreign territory, will sicken and die. His story of a provincial, talented young writer whose demise is the result of the nefarious influence of Parisian cosmopolitanism, bolstered its message with this botanical analogy. Gide, whose knowledge of botany was superior, contested Barrès' thesis by demonstrating that transplanted hybrids prove to be the hardier plants. Those which remain "enracinés," over-cared for like Tityre's oak, become drained of their vitality and eventually perish. Though *Paludes* (1895) precedes the publication of *Les Déracinés* (1897), it nevertheless succeeds in deprecating the vogue of provincialism already popularized by Barrès and others during the 1890s, while at the same time satirizing the Symbolist conceit in which the work of art is habitually compared to an exotic, fragile flower.

The parodic effect of multiple pastiche is compounded still further by abrupt shifts in genre and the collage of literary citations. The trappings of a personal diary or journal are, for example, ruthlessly undermined by the intrusion of discontinuous dialogue, morsels of doggeral, glosses and commentaries, and etymologies of abstruse, academic terms. Quotations from Virgil's *Eclogues* and Mallarmé's *Don du poème* and *Brise Marine* are interspersed with citations from a tertiary *Paludes* in turn pulled out like the lining of a pocket and worked back into a scene as part of a public reading. Indeed, as Bertrand Fillaudeau has pointed out, Mallarmé's celebrated rejuvenation of language through syntactic dislocation is absurdly abstracted, as phrases from his poems are misquoted, shuffled and whimsically recathected. Of the erroneous citation (acknowledged as such): "*Nous partirons! je sens que des oiseaux sont ivres!* Angèle! c'est un vers de Monsieur Mallarmé!— je le cite assez mal—il est au singulier"... (*P* 136), Fillaudeau remarks: "Ici, il y a non seulement changement de personne mais aussi collage de deux fractions de vers, éloignées dans *Brise Marine*: vers 2— Fuir! là-bas fuir! Je sens que des oiseaux sont ivres vers 9— Je partirai! Steamer balançant ta mâture." He also inventories additional Mallarméan borrowings: the motif of sterility from *Azur*, the recurrent image of the window from *Fenêtres*, "la nuit d'Idumée" (transposed into Hubert's night of hunting in the mountains of Idumée) from *Don du poème*, and, from the same poem, several references to "Palmes!" and an evocation of the "lampe angélique" from which, Fillaudeau surmises, the name "Angèle" is derived.[7] Misquotation, mock-plagiarism and the corruption of canonic poetic masterpieces when combined

[7] Fillaudeau, pp. 184-85.

with the mixture of discourses, approximates what Geoffrey Hartman, in his discussion of Derrida's notion of "dessemination" and its affinities with the poetic practice of Christopher Smart, associates with the "age of bastardy" in writing:

> That he (Smart) pairs a biblical figure with a common plant, and a proper name with a multiplying mouthful, is a miraculous cast of the tongue. It is wit as Jean Paul, or Freud, understood it, 'wild pairings without a priest.' If there is a priest, it is the author — whose authority, however, is put in question by such promiscuous yokings.[8]

The proximity of Smart's bastard writing to Gide's redefinition of a "bastard genre," — the *sôtie* — may be demonstrated by a closer look at the evolution of this narrative type and its specific instrumentation by Gide.

The Sôtie *as Negative Novel*

Paludes, as many critics have observed, is a self-conscious revival of the medieval *sôtie*, used by Gide at once to parody all the grotesqueries of Realism from Zola to Huysmans, and at the same time to establish an ironic version of the genre; one that will reveal its equivocal position between Symbolism and modernism by means of a host of negative affirmations that comprise the text's ontology: its status as a book, the place of its narrator-author, and its technical strategies.

Defined as "un genre bâtard situé à la joncture des récits et du roman," the *sôtie* is a synonym in French for "sottise, niaiserie, propos léger."[9] It appeared at the end of the fifteenth century, according to Weinberg, as the possible outgrowth of the ecclesiastic fools' revels (*festum stultorum, fatuorum* or *follorum*) and flourished under Louis XII as a form of religious satire that ridiculed the unpopular politics of the King and Pope Julius II. Most famous was the Abbé Gringoire's *Sottie contre Pape Jules II*, in which the author played the allegorical role of the Church in fool's motley. "Related to the morality play," Weinberg maintains:

> the sôtie illustrated the Renaissance idea of the fool's freedom. Cryptically clad in the fool's motley, dangerous and unpleasant truths could be boldly expressed with impunity. The sôtie was founded on the Pauline

[8] Geoffrey H. Hartman, *Saving the Text* (Baltimore: Johns Hopkins University Press, 1981), p. 48.

[9] *Grand Larousse encyclopédique du XXème siècle* (Paris: Larousse, 1967).

concept of this world as a realm of foolishness [Rom. 1:22] where the faithful are "fools for Christ's sake" but "wise in Christ."[10]

Weinberg follows the definition offered by Lanson in his *Histoire de la littérature française* (1894). "Les sots," were "les célébrants de la *fête des fous*," of which "le principe réside en l'idée d'un monde renversé qui exprimerait en la grossissant, la folie du monde réel."[11]

Gide's version of the *sôtie* in *Paludes* follows Lanson's emphasis on the parody of a real situation insofar as its dramatis personae are modeled on actual Symbolist contemporaries and its dialogue anchored in the topical issues undoubtedly debated in literary circles of the time. However, his reprise of the term took on a modern connotation when, shortly after publishing his third *sôtie*—*Les Caves du Vatican*—he wrote in his *Journal*: "*Sôties, récits*, je n'ai jusqu'à présent écrit que des livres ironiques et critiques."[12] This definition raises the question of whether *Paludes* qualifies as a *sôtie* simply because it is "ironical and critical." Weinberg argues persuasively that it does because "what was decisive here was not the genre in itself but rather a prevalent mood and tendency within a narrative which assumes the role of highly grotesque farce, an ironical mystery play that derides itself."[13] One might argue here that although Weinberg's emphasis on the text's autoderision seems highly appropriate, it underestimates the extent to which *Paludes*'s irony conforms to the generic traditions of the *sôtie*. Like Rabelais's *Gargantua* and *Pantagruel*, works which may be seen as most clearly typifying the Renaissance conventions of grotesque realism and carnivalesque black humor, *Paludes* adopts a transgressive attitude towards linguistic protocol, particularly in its use of what Bakhtin has called "banquet discourse," defined as possessing "special privileges" such as "the right to a certain license, ease and familiarity, to a certain frankness, to eccentricity, ambivalence, that is, the combination in one discourse of praise and abuse, of the serious and comic."[14]

Examples of this discourse, further ramified by Bakhtin as a pluralistic confluence of narrative voices, can be traced throughout

---

[10] Weinberg, p. 24.

[11] Gustave Lanson, *Histoire de la littérature française* (Paris: Hachette, 1951), p. 213.

[12] André Gide, *Journal, I (1889-1939)* (Paris: Gallimard, 1948), p. 437. All further references to this work will appear in the text abbreviated *J*.

[13] Weinberg, p. 23. For a broader discussion of this problem, see Fillaudeau, pp. 27-58, 95-97.

[14] Mikhail Bakhtin, *Problems of Dostoevsky's Poetics*, tr. Caryl Emerson (Minneapolis: University of Minnesota Press, 1984), p. 120.

the banquet scene in *Paludes*, a scene recalling Plato's *Symposium* (as well as the Last Supper) in which a coterie of skilled rhetoricians, including Socrates and his beautiful protegé Alcibiades, participate in a debate on the nature of love. In *Paludes*, the banquet emerges as a kind of mock-Platonic, polyphonic dialogue that travesties its distinguished classical counterpart through the absurdity and illogicality of the arguments. Instead of Plato's muscular sophists, we find an assembly of effete, fin-de-siècle salonists — among them — Alexandre, a voyeuristic philosopher, Evariste, a critic, Barnabé, a moralist, and a host of innocuous hangers-on (Hildebrant, Ildevert, Patras, Philoxenus and Isidore) — all of whom engage in a series of discursive encounters arriving "nulle part."[15] Though the element of what Weinberg refers to as "grotesque farce" is here directed against literary codes and cliques rather than political, social or religious institutions (as in the Renaissance carnivalesque or the grotesque realism of Zola or Huysmans) it has the same effect of turning them upside down. The anti-utopia of the fool's kingdom parallels the anti-utopia of marsh heuristics, with gratuitous digression and whimsical paranomasia displacing the conventions of classical symposia, as well as the norms of the nineteenth century novel.

It was Gide's commitment to the refutation of the novel that may have provided the crucial motive for his revival of the *sôtie*. In July 1914, he wrote: "Pourquoi j'appelle ce livre (*Les Caves du Vatican*) *sôtie*? Pourquoi *récits* les trois précédents? Pour bien marquer que ce ne sont pas là des *romans*" (*J* 437; Gide's italics). Here significantly enough, Gide chose not to stress those aspects of the *sôtie* which would obviously oppose it to the novel: its political performative power, its aura as theatrical spectacle, or its living tie to folk culture. Instead, he underscored the *sôtie*'s ability to represent a narrative counter-code or negative novel, distinguished by its ironic emplotment of the novel's generic demise. Gide's rejection of the novel in 1914 echoed the negative programme of the book that he had articulated most explicitly in his "Postface pour la deuxième édition de *Paludes* et pour annoncer *Les Nourritures terrestres*" (1895):

[15] Claude Martin has identified a number of these eponymous Symbolist colleagues: Hubert as Pierre Louÿs, Tancrède as Léon-Paul Fargue, Hermogène as Henri de Regnier. Certainly there is no doubt that *Paludes* qualifies as a roman à clef, which, in addition to caricaturing the intellectual mannerisms of various literary figures of the day, also travesties the sectarian differences and diverging doctrines within the schools of Symbolist thought (whence the epigraphe "*Dic cur sic* [L'autre école...])." For further elaboration, see Claude Martin's note 18, p. 61, and Fillaudeau's section on "les jeux anthroponymiques," pp. 144-57.

J'aime aussi que chaque livre porte en lui, mais cachée, sa propre réfutation et ne s'assoie pas sur l'idée, de peur qu'on n'en voie l'autre face. J'aime qu'il porte en lui de quoi se nier, se supprimer lui-même; qu'il soit un tout si clos qu'on ne puisse le supprimer que tout entier, qu'il ne laisse après lui pas de déchets, de résidus, pas de cendres, soit comme ces compositions chimiques, agglomérats, juxtapositions d'é-quipotences si parfaites qu'elles se maintiennent en équilibre et tran-quilles, mais qu'une plus fervente étincelle va pouvoir à l'instant réduire, supprimer, au moins pour nos yeux, en une disparition volatile, en gaz subtil.[16]

Here, negativity is positively inscribed as a principle of critical self-contradiction. The work that embodies its own antithesis — its own "hidden refutation," "denial" or "suppression" — is a work alive dialec-tically, capable of arguing with itself or participating in its own inter-pretative critique with the reader. The dynamism of this antithetical force is compared to a spark igniting a chemical compound that up until now, like the classical work of art or conventional narrative, has maintained its equilibrium. Though the great tradition of the book will be destroyed by flame, its trace, characterized as "volatile" and "subtle" will compensate the loss.

Gide's theory of the self-negating text is apparent in the idiom of withering, mocking remarks directed by the narrator at his own work in progress, but it surfaces even more clearly as a figure of textual absence, an absence describing the plotless web of disjointed fragments that circle aimlessly through and around each other, articulating *Paludes*'s lack of center or central theme. Following a much stymied beginning, *Paludes* drags slowly towards its conclusion with the an-nouncement of a new project's commencement, a work to be entitled *Polders*, the Dutch term for a piece of low-lying land that has been reclaimed through a system of dikes from the sea, and the antonym of *Paludes* which connotes an uncivilized, malarial swamp. This non-ending is followed by a large blank space crowned by "a table of remarkable phrases from *Paludes*," one of which is starred and refers to a note on the bottom of the page exhorting the reader to fill in the gap. The gap can be interpreted as a sign of the total abdication of authorial responsibility and as the goal of the text's gradual atrophy towards nothing.

Gide's unremittingly ironic poetics of absence, identified in *Le Traité du Narcisse* with a Mallarméan "silence" set forth as the necessary

[16] André Gide, "Postface de la deuxième édition de *Paludes* et pour annoncer *Les Nourritures terrestres*," in *Romans, récits et sôties*, p. 1479.

precondition of the Symbol ("Et maintenant que manifester? — On apprend cela dans le silence"), and associated in *Le Voyage d'Urien* with the twin poles of desire and desire's unattainable or disappointing object, are risibly trivialized when extended in *Paludes* into a theory of contigency.[17] Originally subtitled "Traité de la Contigence," *Paludes*, in the words of Christian Angelet, "est fait d'événements négatifs."[18] Ancestors of the "acte gratuit," these "negative events" are the products of a backwards calculus stipulated by the protagonist in his agenda. Here, what was done is subtracted from what will be done and the "deficit" — what should be accomplished — completely forgotten. This poorly feigned attempt to convert procrastination into a deliberate course of action may be interpreted as part of *Paludes*'s overall endeavor to convert "nothing" into "something." Infinitely possible, eminently detachable, nowhere and everywhere, *Paludes* emerges as the essence of contigency, a remainder or "something else" to be carried over and interpreted differently by each individual reader. As the reader's role increases, the narrator's role accordingly diminishes, and like the Symbolist writer who serves as the principal object of the *sôtie*'s satirical bite, the narrator is left, contemplating an empty sign that reflects his own mirror image.

Narratus Interruptus

Paludes's Tityre — a fictional narrator created by a fictional narrator is represented, like Narcisse, through allusions to his conventional posture. The visual counterpart and complement to his confrère Narcisse, who as we may recall, is repeatedly described as "penché," Tityre is depicted as "recubans" — recumbent, bent backwards, supine. In Virgil's Eclogue I, he is introduced this way: "Tityre, tu patulae recubans sub tegmine fagi/silvestrum tenui musam meditaris avena" ("Tityrus, thou where thou liest under the covert of spreading beech, broodest on thy slim pipe over the Muse of the Woodland").[19] The narrator, an ardent admirer of the Latin poet, takes his cue for his characterization of Tityre from this evocation of contented repose, despite his distaste for the Virgilian shepherd's complacency.

[17] Gide, *Le Traité du Narcisse*, p. 9.
[18] Christian Angelet, *Symbolisme et invention formelle dans les premiers écrits d'André Gide*, Romanica Gandensia 19 (Ghent, 1982), p. 84.
[19] Paul Alpers, *The Singer of the Eclogues: A Study of Virgilian Pastoral, with a New Translation of the Eclogues* (Berkeley: University of California Press, 1979).

"Recubans," for him, connotes "l'homme couché:" "Dans Virgile il s'appelle Tityre — et il nous est dit expressément qu'il est *couché* — *Paludes*, c'est l'histoire de l'homme couché" (*P* 117).

Paludes, the story of a "man in bed," promises erotic fantasy, though the onanistic associations attached to the image of his classical namesake "playing on his thin reed," are transferred, as in Mallarmé's *L'Après-midi d'un faune*, to the dreamer's play with language. The links between song, poësis, and sexual reverie are furthered reinforced by the name Tityre, a Latin synonym of *satyros* meaning "billygoat" or "bellwether." Derived from "little bird," which qualifies, according to Weinberg, as a euphemism for phallus (with the root *tu*, "to swell"), the name itself elides the bird's song with a symbolic erection. Accordingly, as self-appointed bard of the marsh, Tityre salaciously sings its praises:

> ...J'habite les bas-fonds et ne songe pas trop à me hisser sur les collines...
>
> Parfois, à la surface des eaux croupies, s'étale une irisation merveilleuse et les papillons les plus beaux n'ont rien de pareil sur leurs ailes; la pellicule qui s'y diapre est formée de matières décomposées. Sur les étangs, la nuit éveille des phosphorescences, et les feux des marais s'élèvent semblent celles-là même sublimées,
>
> Marais! qui donc raconterait vos charmes? Tityre! (*P* 108; italicized in the text)

His hymn to the "bas-fonds" features Nature basking in her own delights and beauties through reflexive verbs such as "s'étaler" ("to spread, to parade, to display") and "se diaprer" ("to variegate, to adorn, to sprinkle"). This hymn could be dedicated to the God Priapus, who, like Tityrus (the "billy-goat") is a satyr, although he tends to be aroused in a sylvan glade rather than a putrid swamp. The imbrication of these onanistic innuendos can be discerned yet again in the bond between Tityrus and Orpheus, established in a phrase of Virgil's Eclogue VIII: "Sit Tityrus Orpheus" ("Let Orpheus be Tityrus") which Gide cited in his 1895 "Postface" to *Paludes*'s second edition. Often interpreted as an ancient phallic icon, the disembodied head of Orpheus, mouth gaping open and pouring out a song of frustrated love, was a favored Romantic and Symbolist allegory of the mysterious bond between Art and Eros and as such emerges as a target of parody in *Paludes*. But unlike Mallarmé's lusty antique faun, Nietzsche's modern satyr fired by the spirit of ancient Greece, George Meredith's savage egoist (whose "striking arms, running legs, glorious first flint and arrowhead" render him a symbol of Nature's "ripest issue") or Valéry's titanic athlete (also named Tityre), Gide's phlegmatic shepherd offers a paltry homage to the poetic Muse.[20] Far from being an active modern primitive, dreaming of the rape of nymphs, revelling in his god, removing obstacles to growth, displacing mountains and overturning monuments, he dreams of worms and waterfowl and passes his time "fishing for words": *"Des fenêtres de sa tour, Tityre peut pêcher à la ligne…* *—Attentes mornes du poisson; insuffisance des amorces, multiplication des lignes (symbole)—par nécessité il ne peut rien prendre"* (P 94; Gide's emphases). Tityre's fishing lines double as the lines of his journal with which he hopes to garner a meaning, or at the very least a small catch of symbolic value. Since the lines invariably bring in no reward, he must instead substitute the word "symbole" for the symbol itself. An author afflicted by sterility, his text is accordingly marked, like *Paludes*, with signposts of missing signs.

Despite the fact that he is plagued by setbacks and misfortunes, Tityre refuses to complain of his lot. In this respect, he resembles his Virgilian ancestor who had claimed to be satisfied with his unarable plot of land. Virgil wrote: "Et tibi magna satis quamvis lapis omnia nudus/Limosque palus obducat pascua junco," which the narrator of *Paludes* freely translates for his friend Hubert: "C'est un berger qui parle à un autre; il lui dit que son champ est plein de pierres et de marécages sans doute, mais assez bon pour lui; et qu'il est très heureux de s'en satisfaire" (P 91). Tityre is a litotic hero, for his motto, "too little is enough and more for me," valorizes insufficiency and lack. Though the narrator finds this contentment with "too little" a deplorable inducement to vice ("l'acceptation du mal l'aggrave, — cela devient du vice, Messieurs, puisque l'on finit par s'y plaire"), he is in fact no different from his literary alter-ego (P 123). Even as he militates vociferously in favor of ambitious adventures to exotic parts of the world, he allows his own departure to be thwarted by inclement weather. According to Jean Delay, the narrator is also Tityre, a Tityre reincarnated as a fin-de-siècle decadent—a Des Esseintes or Lord Chandos figure—introverted, enervated, and self-absorbed. Delay characterizes him as:

> …une petite nature, de constitution faible et de complexion délicate. On ne le voit pas, car Gide ne décrit guère la physique de ses personnages, mais on l'imagine menu, mièvre, maigrelet, pâlot, renchéri, maniéré, plein de l'afféterie et de mignardise, n'usant de ses chaussures

[20] George Meredith, *The Egoist* (New York: Random House 1951), p. 406.

que la pointe, buvant le thé le petit doigt levé, ou susurrant d'une voix de tête: "Dic cur his?" Il n'a pas de muscles et très peu d'os, mais ses nerfs sont en soie. Froissé, il crisse, et, contrarié, sanglote, se sent au bord de la crisette.[21]

The narrator, or Tityre II, qualifies, to borrow Nietzsche's words, as an example of the "contrived shepherd in his dress-ups" who, if confronted with an authentic modern primitive, would "shrivel into a mendacious caricature."[22] This element of caricature is accentuated by passive grammatical constructions further transforming Tityre's existential posture into a textual trope. Intellectually as well as physically supine, he prefers to "follow" rather than direct his train of thought: "suivait cette pensée (j'en écris à l'avance une pour chaque jour: elles décident de ma tristesse ou de ma joie)" he writes, or, in another context: "Je me souviens que cette idée m'est venue" (*P* 96-97). Completely reversing the Nietzschean will to power, Tityre postulates an ethics of under-achievement. Within this system, the aversion to committing evil deeds is twisted into an omnibus justification for total passivity:

> Souvent Richard m'affirme avec emotion que je suis incapable d'une action mauvaise, et cela me retient quand parfois je voudrais me décider à agir. Richard prise fort en moi cette passivité qui me maintient dans les sentiers de la vertu, où d'autres, pareils à lui m'ont poussé. (*P* 97).

Once passivity is identified with virtue, it follows that the most physically passive occupation — writing — is substituted for bourgeois enterprise. When Angèle inquires: "Pourquoi écrivez-vous?" Tityre replies: "Je ne sais pas — probablement que c'est pour agir" (*P* 93).

Writing, set up as the antithesis of "working," emerges as a supreme value in this negative economy of libidinal displacements. Fearful of the verb "faire," to which his rival Hubert does justice by managing four industrial companies, attending courses, delivering public lectures, and engaging in philanthropy and sport, Tityre resorts to the verb "écrire" (reiterated in the refrain "Moi, j'écris *Paludes*") as a buffer against the dreaded question "Qu'est-ce que vous faites?" Angèle's question is treated by the narrator like a sexual provocation prompting him to disclose what Barthes would call "le plaisir du text." An obvious channel or surrogate object of desire, the text of *Paludes* itself embodies erotic foreplay and postponed fulfillment. This reading is

[21] Jean Delay, *La Jeunesse d'André Gide*, *II* (Paris: Gallimard, 1957), 402.
[22] Friedrich Nietzsche, *The Birth of Tragedy* in *The Basic Writings of Friedrich Nietzsche*, tr. Walter Kaufman (New York: Random House, 1968), p. 61.

reinforced by Tityre's response to a question posed in the course of a heated discussion among literary men: "Qu'est-ce-que-vous voulez?" His excited, breathless answer: "Ce que je veux? Messieurs, ce que je veux, moi, personellement— c'est terminer *Paludes*," uses the "ending of *Paludes*" as the last card to be played against their relentless interrogation (*P* 123). But it is a card that he is clearly reluctant to deploy, for to finish *Paludes* is tantamount to arresting the titillating chain of metonymical substitutions that constitute the impetus to further pleasure. As Jean Delay so suggestively surmised: "Les possibilités de Tityre sont minimes, mais il se console en versifiant ses insuffisances. Du reste, il a du goût pour sa faiblesse et n'a que dégoût pour la force virile."[23]

As a "versifier of insufficiency," Tityre personifies the trope of extenuation ("rendre mince, amaigrir, déssecher, réduire à une grande faiblesse") which constitutes one of the family of figures clustering around litotes. Extenuation connotes the state of inertia normally associated with impotence, both in the sens of *impotens* (without power) and *impuissant* (sexually inadequate). His sexual inadequacy is explicitly revealed in the descriptions of his rapport with Angèle: "elle et moi nous ne sommes jamais aimés d'une façon bien décisive," he avows, and lest the reader suspect that their friendship has ever been more than platonic, he specifies: "après mon dîner, je m'en fus coucher chez Angèle. Je dis chez et non avec elle, n'ayant jamais fait avec elle que de petits simulacres anodins" (*P* 104). Like his text, which can also be seen as a series of erotic, mimetic plays or "simulacra" of the sexual act, Tityre's discourse with Angèle is constructed around the principles of displacement and transfer. At a particularly dangerous moment, the moment where Angèle, in a gesture of compassion offers herself to Tityre, he casts about for an excuse that will permit him to avoid the peril of a real encounter. He finds an ingenius ruse that consists in placing the onus of their "amour manqué" on Angèle, "Avouez d'aillers que vous n'avez pas grande envie," he insists maliciously, and then, advancing this flagrantly self-serving excuse yet another step, he proceeds to versify *her* insufficiencies:

> ...vous êtes, je vous assure, délicate, et c'est en pensant à vous que j'écrivais, vous en souvenez-vous, cette phrase: *'elle craignait la volupté comme une chose trop forte qui l'eût peut-être tuée.'* Vous m'affirmiez que c'était exagéré... Non, chère amie, — non — nous pourrions en être gênés; — j'ai même fait à ce sujet quelques vers:

[23] Delay, p. 404.

'Nous ne sommes pas
Chère, de ceux-là
Par qui naissent les fils des hommes.' (*P* 141; Gide's emphases)

Here Tityre deploys a litotic strategy of rationalization, evading his own disinterest by affirming the inhibitions of Angèle. This negative affirmation, enabling him to deny (to himself) the absence of his own sexual longing by denying (in another) the presence of desire, corresponds to a form of repression defined by Freud as *Verneinung* and translated by Lacan as "dénégation."[24] Like litotes, it is distinguished by a structure of doubled difference that ultimately confirms what it apparently seeks to negate. As in the analysand's "I saw someone in a dream. You are wondering who it could be. It was certainly not my mother," the figure of the mother is doubly refused; first, as an unconscious repression of Oedipal desire, and second, for the benefit of the analyst, as a consciously perceived dream image.[25] In *Paludes*, this definition of repression (for Freud interpreted his patients' two-tiered disavowals as positive proof of the existence of repression), forms part of a miniature melodrama occurring on one level between Tityre and Angèle, and on another between Tityre and the fraternity of letters. Though one must be wary of imposing a cumbersome psychoanalytical rubric on a text that so lightly satirizes erotic interplay, the explication of repression in *Paludes* nonetheless illuminates the complex relationship between sexuality and writing so profoundly informing the success of its grotesque humor.

The Drama of "Dénégation": Circuits of Exchange in the Literary Socius

Dans *le Banquet*, Eryximaque constate avec ironie qu'il a lu quelque part un panégyrique du sel, mais rien sur Éros; et c'est parce que Éros

[24] In his essay on Negation, Freud elaborated the notion of *Verneinung* as follows: "...Negation is a way of taking cognizance of what is repressed ...only one consequence of the process of negation is undone—the fact, namely, of the ideational content of what is repressed not reaching consciousness. The outcome of this is a kind of intellectual acceptance of the repressed, while at the same time what is essential to the repression persists... With the help of the symbol of negation, thinking frees itself from the restrictions of repression" (Sigmund Freud, "Negation," *Standard Edition of the Complete Psychological Works of Sigmund Freud*, 19: 235-36. Quoted in J. Laplanche and J.B. Pontalis, *The Language of Psychoanalysis*, tr. D. Nicholson-Smith (New York: Norton, 1973).

[25] See Jean Hyppolite, "Commentaire parlé sur la *Verneinung* de Freud," *La Psychanalyse* 1 (1956), 29-39.

est censuré comme sujet de conversation, que la petite société du *Banquet* décide d'en faire le propos de sa table ronde: on dirait des intellectuels d'aujourd'hui acceptant de discuter à contre-courant, précisément de l'Amour et non de politique, du Désir (amoureux) et non du Besoin (social). L'excentricité de la conversation vient de ce que cette conversation est systématique: ce que les convives essayent de produire, ce ne sont pas des propos prouvés, des récits d'expériences, c'est une doctrine: Éros est pour chacun d'eux un système.

(Roland Barthes, *Fragments d'un discours amoureux*)

Angèle, similar to most of Gide's female characters, acts as little more than a cipher. The hostess of a literary soirée, she circulates in the crowd like her ventilator: distributing refreshments, just as the machine disperses gusts of cool air, in an effort to soothe the hot temperaments of her male guests. A mechanical "bride stripped bare by her bachelors," she receives no signs of gratitude for her pains, which in any case are to no avail. The ventilator, described as "une grosse tache noire qui faisait du bruit," induces the guests to raise their voices, thereby abetting their predisposition to quarrel (*P* 118). Like Angèle, it becomes the object of verbal abuse: "Chère amie, c'est beaucoup trop petit," complains Tityre:

Je vous demande un peu ce que signifiait votre petit ventilateur! D'abord rien ne m'agace comme ce qui tourne sur place; vous devriez savoir cela, depuis le temps! — Eh puis en fait-il un vilain bruit quand il tourne! On entendait ça sous le rideau sitôt qu'on arrêtait de causer. Et tout le monde se demandait: "Qu'est ce que c'est?" — Vous pensez bien que je ne pouvais pas leur dire: "C'est le ventilateur d'Angèle!" Tenez, l'entendez-vous à présent, comme il grince. Oh! C'est insupportable, chère amie: arrêtez-le, je vous en prie. (*P* 124)

Tityre raises the question (absurd on a literal level) of what the ventilator "signifies." Clearly, as a utilitarian household object it signifies nothing. But we have learned in this text that "nothing" is capable of signifying a great deal. The machine's movements — an endless spinning on itself — has been recognized by many critics as a metaphor for the circular structure and cyclical motion of the text, reinforced, as Catherine Savage Brosman has argued in her article, "Le monde fermé de *Paludes*," by images of physical constriction and entrapment.[26] As a "large, black blotch concealed behind a curtain,"

[26] Catherine Savage Brosman, "Le Monde fermé de *Paludes*," *La Revue des Lettres Modernes*, André Gide 6 (March 1979).

the ventilator also invites association with Surrealist symbols of voyeurism, fetishism and the female sex (which, like Gide's, are drawn from a repertory of everyday objects). It is perhaps no wonder that Tityre treats this gaping vortex as a menacing presence and his obsessive dreams later that night reveal a classic case of castration anxiety. Chased down endless corridors by a "rigolateur" or "laughing-machine," pursued by a detached wooden leg (a spectre of the erect phallus that Tityre lacks?) which drags him into a bed of quicksand, and enveloped by a bed canopy that suffocates the sleeper with its entwining embrace, the narrator is perpetually terrorized by phantoms of female desire and it is no surprise that he repulses the advances of Angèle.

Tityre's pronounced aversion for the female sex, caricatured in stark relief in his dream of a castrating woman, and surfacing in his querulous conversations with Angèle, motivates a range of repressive rhetorical strategies and postures. In male company, the same posturing can be observed, but with quite different results. Where, with respect to the woman, negation carries a note of finality, operating as a kind of definitive rupture in communication, with men it is transposed into a dynamic circuit of exchanges that have the opposite effect of postponing closure. Though the narrator's disgruntled, vitriolic ripostes often resemble those which he directs at Angèle, in the context of the literary fraternity they are repaid in kind, so that the friction between him and his rivals appears as the inverted expression of male bonding. Rather than serve to alienate the speakers from each other (as with Angèle), "dénégation" — or the pitting of "not" against "not not" — is transformed through reciprocity into an open-ended series of mutually engendering denunciations that serve as the basis of an amusing game of rhetorical one-up-manship, or what René Girard has called "mimetic rivalry."[27] A fundamental relation of identity exists between members of the fraternity inducing the kind of competition on which the dynamic of mimetic rivalry depends. Here, the mutual efforts of the same sex to appear different (by repeating the words of the opponent differently or in reverse) on the one hand bolsters a sexual code of difference, that is, a homosexual counter-code, and on the other hand produces a paradoxical likeness-in-difference (each resembles the other in trying to appear different) which

[27] The expression "mimetic rivalry" is used by René Girard to denote the resemblance between the efforts of two rival parties to appear different. It is the counterpart of his concept of "mimetic desire," developed in *Deceit, Desire and the Novel*, tr. Yvonne Freccero (Baltimore: Johns Hopkins University Press, 1965).

consolidates the brotherhood. This tacit collusion, localized in intellectual "bavardage," emerges as the vehicle for communicating an unstated homoeroticism, or, if not outright homoeroticism, then at least an updated version of "Greek" love. The analogy to the Platonic colloquy of sophists and the ancient art of dispute is guaranteed, as we have already mentioned, by the device of a banquet scene. This analogy is further reinforced by the anachronistic antique names of the "littérateurs" (similar in effect to a costume conceit, as if Gide had cloaked his characters in togas).[28] As in Plato's *Symposium*, it is the seductive nature of dialogue, the "meeting of minds," the contest between equals, that cements the affectional ties between men.

The interchange between Tityre and his friends begins on the landing before they enter Angèle's apartment and implies an interesting gender code. Tityre passes a note to Martin with the elliptical message: "Etre aveugle pour se croire heureux," and Martin replies with "Etre heureux de sa cécité" (*P* 114). The two texts, suggesting a mirror reflection in which likeness is distorted by reversal, structurally resemble the paradigm of homosocial infatuation with a male other — the same gender but different. Similarly, in a subsequent missive commenting on the relationship between "odd" and "even," a subtle argument in favor of "difference" can be construed. The narrator writes:

> *Tu me rappelles ceux qui traduisent* "Numero Deus impare gaudet" *par:* "Le numéro Deux se réjouit d'être impair" *et qui trouvent qu'il a bien raison. — Or s'il était vrai que l'imparité porte en elle quelque promesse de bonheur — je dis de liberté, on devrait dire au nombre Deux:* "Mais, pauvre ami, vous ne l'êtes pas impair; pour vous satisfaire de l'être tâchez au moins de le devenir." (*P* 114)

This convoluted pronouncement urges the conversion of that which is even or identical (members of the same sex) into that which is odd (that is, deviating from the norm, homosexual). The interplay of likeness and difference, with the latter always maintaining a firm advantage, recurs in a series of discursive encounters among members of the literary socius starting with the discussion of the theater between two poets: "ils étaient en train d'affirmer qu'on pouvait plus

---

[28] Angelet, in his allusion to *Paludes*'s parody of the art of dispute cites Jean-Paul Dumont's discussion of Protagoras in *Les Sophistes: fragments et témoignages* (Paris, 1969), p. 36. Dumont provides a particularly apt description of the forensic quibbling in *Paludes*: "Les propositions qui se contredisent étant toutes vraies ensemble, il devient impossible de contredire." In *Paludes*, of course, noncontradictory statements are repeatedly contradicted as if they were incompatible. The noble art of heuristics is thus comically inverted.

faire de drames; chacun n'approuva pas les raisons que l'autre en don-
nait, mais ils s'accordèrent pour supprimer le théâtre" (*P* 109). Here,
specular disagreement generates a consensus itself grounded in a
negative act—the supression of the theater. This pattern recurs in
the narrator's confrontations with his detractors as when: "Evariste,
le fin critique argua: 'J'ai peur que ce ne soit un peu spécial comme
sujet'" in response to Tityre's mock-platonic description of *Paludes* as
a story about cave-dwelling animals who lose their sight as a result
of never using their eyes. To Evariste the narrator retorts: "Il n'y a
pas de sujet trop particulier," and when Evariste retaliates with "Vous
facilitez singulièrement votre tâche," he violently denegates his negation
with: "Et sinon je supprime la vôtre" (*P* 118). Here the collision between identical signs ("sujet" and "sujet," tâche" and "tâche"), yields
an absolute negative—that of "suppression"—which in turn prompts
a mimetic call for suppression. As soon as Tityre utters the word,
it is whispered excitedly by the auditors who finally cry out for the
"suppression" of Tityre.

One can see here how negation is inadvertently transformed into
a form of affirmation. Though it expresses in one sense the urge for
closure, in another, it perpetuates the discourse by provoking fresh
rounds of dissension. The negative disjunction operates as a positive
conjunction or elision, for its repetition thwarts the concerted effort
to have the "final say," to institute a reign of silence. Throughout these
innummerable altercations, objections are overruled: whether it is in
the context of curt imperatives such as "Chutt! Chutt! je vais parler,"
or in inverted exchanges such as "Ce que vous dites là est assez
curieux... — Mais non, Monsieur, ce n'est pas curieux de tout," and
"Alors de quoi plaignez-vous? — Mais précisément de ce que personne
ne se plaigne!" linguistic obstacles are set up repeatedly throughout
the discourse, but fail to adduce its conclusion (*P* 121-23). Quips are
followed by counter-quips as when the narrator says to Hubert:

> Un livre... mais un livre, Hubert, est clos, plein, lisse comme un oeuf.
> On n'y saurait faire entrer rien, pas une épingle, que par force, et sa
> forme en serait brisée.
> — Alors ton oeuf est plein? reprit Hubert.
> — Mais, cher ami, criai-je, les oeufs ne se remplissent pas: les oeufs
> naissent pleins... (*P* 112)

And puns are piled up on top of withering insinuations:

Alors, Monsieur, dit-il, vous écrivez *Paludes*?
— Comment savez-vous? m'écriai-je.
— Mais, reprit-il (exagérant) — il n'est plus question que de cela; — il paraît même que ça ne ressemblera pas à votre dernier ouvrage — que je n'ai pas eu le plaisir de lire, mais dont mon ami Hubert m'a beaucoup parlé. — Vous nous lirez des vers, n'est-ce pas?
— Pas des vers de vase, dit Isidore bêtement — il paraît que c'en est plein dans *Paludes*, — à ce que raconte Hubert. (*P* 116)

As both of these examples illustrate, each party tries to expropriate the major metaphor — the book as egg in the former case, the verse as slimy worm in the latter. In both instances, the metaphor's repetition spurs an aggressive reaction that forges a new link in the chain of negative sign production. However, it is precisely these provocatively negative signs which reinvigorate the discourse, investing the competition for literary power with new energy, and ultimately transforming the quarrel into a ritual of courtship.

The carefree verbal license animating these whimsical rounds of repartee parallels the spirit of hermeneutical liberty which endows *Paludes* with its textual eroticism. This can be most clearly discerned in the arguments over "what Paludes is about." The narrator launches the offensive by cryptically characterizing his text as the story of the "third man" (a play on the "third sex?"), a kind of Everyman's daemon, who, he claims, derives from Virgil's recumbent Tityrus. Patras begs to differ with the author, offering an alternative version of *Paludes* based on hearsay: "Tiens,... je croyais que c'était l'histoire d'un marais." "Monsieur," replies Tityre, "les avis diffèrent, le fond permane. — Mais comprenez, je vous prie, que la seule façon de raconter la même chose à chacun, — la même chose, entendez-moi bien, c'est l'histoire du salon d'Angèle" (*P* 117). Tityre's rejoinder, in addition to providing an ironic moment in the text insofar as it calls the bluff of *Paludes*'s presence as absence, contains a hermeneutical formulation of likeness-in-difference. "Opinions," he says "differ," but the essence of the text remains the "same" because its essence *is difference*; it changes according to each reader so that each will receive the same message, but in the terms which he alone can understand. This protean notion of the literary work is further elaborated with the help of yet another metaphor — the image of the "keyhole," which, if approached, yields a picture of the world general enough to accommodate everyone's vision:

— L'art est de peindre un sujet particulier avec assez de puissance pour que la généralité dont il dépendait s'y comprenne. En termes abstraits cela se dit très mal parce que c'est déjà une pensée abstraite; — mais vous me comprendrez assurément en songeant à tout l'énorme paysage qui passe à travers le trou d'une serrure dès que l'oeil se rapproche suffisamment de la porte. Tel, qui ne voit ici qu'une serrure, verrait le monde entier au travers s'il savait seulement se pencher. Il suffit qu'il y ait possibilité de généralisation; la généralisation, c'est au lecteur, au critique de la faire. (*P* 118)

Vinio Rossi, commenting on this passage, interprets the keyhole metaphor as an aesthetic "parable" about mythology and the emblematic theory of symbols which Gide termed the "mise en abyme." Like the myth or symbol, what is perceived through the keyhole is truth elevated from the particular to the general. As Rossi argues, it "represents itself as object and also what it contains upon closer scrutiny, what lies beyond it."[29] For this reason, Rossi likens the keyhole metaphor to Gide's aesthetic of litotes which condenses (in less) the universal (more). But Rossi could equally well have interpreted the keyhole as a metaphor for the act of interpretation itself. The gap or hole, through which the observer voyeuristically peers, is comparable to the textual gap or missing referent which generates a fiction — namely, the "key" to "what *Paludes* is about." As each member of the literary group tries his hand at the interpretation of *Paludes*, he engages in the collective enterprise of fiction-making. What is *Paludes* if not the sum of its interpretations? if not the narrative which describes the giving and taking of "tall tales" each inflating the paltry visions of the individual viewer to the grandiose proportions of high art?

With "tall tales," Tityre "versifies his insufficiencies": those of his text (which, as we have seen, is no better than an empty, floating signifier attaching itself to any available reader) and those of his sexual exploits. In his story of the duck hunt, which, Holdheim claims, "he relates in order to compete with Hubert's panther-hunting story," the text is inadvertently telling when it comes to deciphering the hieroglyphics of impotence. The fatal clue is lodged in his description of the weapon — an antiquated air rifle ("un fusil à air comprimé"):

... — Un petit réservoir à air faisait manoeuvrer la détente, — au moyen d'un tube élastique que l'on se passait sous l'aisselle; on tenait dans sa

[29] Vinio Rossi, *André Gide: The Evolution of an Aesthetic* (New Brunswick: Rutgers University Press, 1967), p. 137.

main une poire un peu fatiguée, — car c'était un vieux appareil; — à la moindre pression, la poire en caoutchouc faisait partir la balle... Votre ignorance de la technique m'empêche de vous expliquer mieux.

— Vous auriez dû me montrer cela, dit Angèle.

— Chère amie, ces instruments ne peuvent être touchés qu'avec une toute particulière adresse, — puis, je vous l'ai dit, je ne le gardai point. D'ailleurs cette seule nuit de chasse suffit, tant elle fut fructifère, à user définitivement la poire, — comme je vais vous raconter: (*P* 133)

The sexual subtext could scarcely be more thinly veiled. It is replete with a "tired bulb" held in the hand, an "elastic tube," firmly grasped, and specification of the "instrument's sensitivity to the slightest pressure." As Holdheim has noted: "instead of the concentrated violence of a single detonation, there is a cumulative series of discreetly inaudible shots (a muffler is being used) which continue with delicate monotony until they peter out at dawn."[30]

Though Holdheim offers this observation to exemplify Gide's use of enumeration as a technique of humor rather than to illustrate the distance between Tityre's imaginary potency and real inadequacy, the two readings may in fact be easily reconciled. The story's embellishment with superfluous details and meticulous precisions attests to a textual impotence (its failure to weave a good yarn) that mirrors the narrator's ill-concealed revelation of his sexual impotence. Like the duck-hunting story, *Paludes* records the sexual and textual "misfiring" of signs. Scattered in random, indiscriminate patterns like so many seeds or splotches of ink, the signs of the text resemble a negative, automatic writing, the scribble of an uncontrollable impulse, the "brownian motion" of dispersed erotic energy. Unable or unwilling to explain this cryptic sign language, the narrator devises instead ingenious mathematical systems that tabulate or quantify the empty signifiers of his text. "His day is fruitful," Holdheim observes, "because he writes *twenty* definitions and finds as many as *eight* new epithets for "blastoderm."[31] In addition to this labor of numerical notation, Tityre supplements his codification of "non-sense" by inventing a negative theory of value in which deficits are treated as credits. This theory is contained *in nuce* in his "agendas," which themselves embody the dismal fate to which literature is destined — the surrender of the letter to pure number.

[30] Holdheim, p. 176.
[31] Holdheim, p. 176.

The Negative Economy of Textual Production

> "Penser à Hubert", écrit comiquement sur son agenda le narrateur de
> *Paludes*, qui est le livre du Rien.
>
> (Barthes, *Fragments d'un discours amoureux*)

Gide, as is well known, was a compulsive list maker and collector
of self-addressed messages. As Cocteau once teasingly remarked: "il
chérissait notes et notules."[32] In addition to littering his private, confessional writing with schemes and outlines for future literary projects, he invented systems of distributive justice which meted out
rewards and punishments to the writer. These systems often found
their way into his literary works, most notably in *Les Caves du Vatican*
where, in a "carnet" locked inside a secret "tiroir," Lafcadio keeps a
ledger of all his pecadillos each paid for according to its gravity with
"puntas" — self-inflicted pricks with a knife (a kind of negative writing
of the body). Whereas in *Les Caves*, this normative code is designed
primarily to undermine the values of bourgeois society, in *Paludes*,
it aims to justify a private neurosis — the narrator's endemic inadequacy. The agenda endeavors to convert this neurosis into an asset
by placing value on nothing, or what is referred to as a "déficit":

> Dans mon agenda il y a deux parties: sur une feuille j'écris ce que
> je ferai, et sur la feuille d'en face, chaque soir, j'écris ce que je n'ai pas
> fait. Ensuite je compare; je soustrais, et ce que je n'ai pas fait, le déficit,
> devient ce que j'aurais dû faire. Je le récris pour le mois de décembre
> et cela me donne des idées morales. (*P* 96)

Tityre's system of deficits implies a thoroughly negative economy
because it trades an empty past against a tentative, uninsured future.
Though it appears to subtract what has been accomplished from what
will be done, it in fact takes away what has *not* been realized (in the
past) from what has *not* been realized (in the future). The product
of this "zero sum game" is yet another deficit — a moral imperative
prescribing what *should* have been done, but what is particularly
singular about this deficit is that for Tityre, it *possesses* a positive value:

> — L'agenda a du bon, pensai-je, car si je n'eusse pas marqué pour ce
> matin ce que j'eusse dû faire, j'aurais pu l'oublier, et je n'aurais pu me
> réjouir de ne l'avoir point fait. C'est toujours là le charme qu'a pour

[32] Jean Cocteau, *Journal d'un inconnu* (Paris: Grasset, 1953), p. 111.

moi ce que j'appelai si joliment 'l'imprévu négatif'; je l'aime assez car
il nécessite peu d'apport, de sorte qu'il me sert pour les jours ordinaires.
(*P* 130)

"L'imprévu négatif,"considered by Alain Goulet to be the forerunner
of the "acte gratuit" in *Les Caves du Vatican*, ostensibly denotes an un-
motivated deed; an eruption of the unpredictable into the seamless
fabric of bourgeois order.[33] The interpretation is misleading, however,
because it renders "the negative unforeseen" virtually synonymous with
simple unpredictability or surprise, both of which are "negative" only insofar as they represent an anarchic disturbance in society. Tityre's
further adumbration of the term emphasizes a different definition.
He implies that the unforeseen is negative precisely because it constitutes the negation of surprise. Though it may suddenly impose itself
between an intention and an act, thwarting the latter, its appearance
is not an accident. Rather, it has been painstakingly planned, carefully
determined, nurtured by its author's awareness that negativity is essential to his way of life:

> ...Dans mon agenda je puise le sentiment du devoir; j'écris huit jours
> à l'avance, pour avoir le temps d'oublier et pour *me créer des surprises*,
> indispensables dans ma manière de vivre; chaque soir ainsi je m'en-
> dors devant un lendemain inconnu et *pourtant déjà décidé par moi-même*.
> (*P* 96; my emphases)

Tityre's "imprévu négatif " is an ironic denominator of temporali-
ty and action because it demonstrates the properties of a negation
that affirms "something," which itself is a minus sign. It also furnishes
a versatile justification for all that is "difference"—whether a deduc-
tion from the future or a deviation from conventional mores. Though
Tityre himself is clearly enchanted with his theory as a means of spicing
his existence with unknowns and endowing his text with a raison-
d'être, his friends' reception of the theory is extremely cool. Barnabé,
"the moralist," detects a threat to individual freedom in this theology
of over-determined surprises. In his eyes, it is no better than a smoke
screen for a highly repressive machine; an untrustworthy "divine plan"
behind which lurks the author as dictator:

> Divers de vos amis m'ont parlé de *Paludes* suffisament pour que je
> voie assez clairement ce que vous voulez faire; je viens vous avertir
> que cela me paraît inutile et fâcheux.—Vous voulez forcer les gens à

[33] Alain Goulet, *'Les Caves du Vatican' d'André Gide: étude méthodologique* (Paris: Larousse, 1972). See also Fillaudeau, pp. 253-64.

agir parce que vous avez horreur du stagnant—les forcer à agir sans considérer que plus vous intervenez, avant leurs actes, moins ces actes dépendent d'eux. Votre responsabilité s'en augmente; la leur en est d'autant diminuée. Or la responsabilité seule des actes fait pour chacun leur importance—et leur apparence n'est rien. Vous n'apprendrez pas à vouloir: *velle non discitur*; simplement vous influencez; la belle avance alors si vous pouvez à la fin procréer quelques actions sans valeur! (*P* 119)

Barnabé divines two seminal features of Tityre's negative economy: first, by attempting to determine freedom it negates individual liberty, and second, it is committed to "actions without value"; it purchases a meaningless future whose sole value is the negation of value or social deviancy. Though Tityre angrily contests this accusation, his refutation is belied by the enthusiasm which he manifests for Valentin Knox's equally negative calculus. Knox concurs with Tityre in condemning the qualities associated with the "normal man," and like Tityre he defends his condemnation with the aid of a logic that assigns positive value to negation. Thus "health," seen by Knox as a form of mediocrity, is defined as the absence of deviation from the norm ("l'absence d'hypertrophies") just as a one-legged man is defined as "un homme plus la bosse" (*P* 120). According to this rule of reversal, lameness, like illness, is perceived as a positive condition because it "adds" absence rather than "subtracts" presence. This positive absence (positive because it exalts the superior value of difference) is the principle enabling Knox to eliminate the normal man, who, he reasons mathematically, is nothing better than a "common denominator" that cancels itself out:

L'*homme normal* nous importe peu; j'aimerais dire qu'il est supprimable—car on le retrouve partout. C'est le plus grand commun diviseur de l'humanité, et qu'en mathématiques, étant donné des nombres on peut enlever à chaque chiffre sans lui faire perdre sa *vertu personnelle*. L'*homme normal* (ce mot m'exaspère), c'est ce résidu, cette matière première, qu'après la fonte ou les particularités se subtilisent, on retrouve au fond des cornues. C'est le pigeon primitif qu'on réobtient par le croisement des variétés rares—un pigeon gris—les plumes de couleur sont tombées; il n'a plus rien qui le distingue. (*P* 120; Gide's emphases)

For Knox, it is the negative value of abnormality that constitutes "personal virtue." "Vertu," derived from the latin *virtus* or "mérite de l'homme" implies above all, "force," in the sense of virility, sexual potency. The word, moreover, contains the root *vir*, or "man" which, when resituated in Knox's theory, insinuates that the superiority of the abnormal man derives from the fact that in contra-distinction to the normal man, he cultivates his "vertu" in his desire for *vir*; his homosexual desire. According to this rationale, Tityre's aborted overtures to Angèle are recast as the felicitous signs of his attraction to the "abnormal man" — the exotic pigeon of the variegated plumes. By analogy, the same argument implies that *Paludes*'s merit rests on its failure to satisfy the requisites of a conventional, "normal" genre of prose fiction, such as the novel. Its textual idiosyncrasies, the mirror reflections of its author's heterosexual impotence are thus defined through a negative economy, as its greatest "virtue."

With its satire of parlor politics and literary billingsgate, *Paludes* appears today to be a proleptic parody of the world which Proust would later depict with secret awe and admiration — a world comprised of high-bourgeois esthetes, flamboyant "arrivistes," and querulous "invertis." Certainly this interpretation has helped to explain Gide's initial refusal of the manuscript of *A la recherche du temps perdu*. But if *Paludes* anticipates the swerve away from Symbolism and the glamour of the Belle Epoque, it also qualifies as a forerunner of the "nouveau roman." Its exposure of fictive illusions; its ambiguous first person pronoun (confusing narrator, author, character and reader); its multiple framing of events and non-events; its mechanical repetitions of phrases and narrative fragments; its dialogue punctuated by *non-sequiturs* and its typographical and stylistic likeness to a sketch or tentative plan of a narrative (close to what Marguerite Duras, in reference to her own work, dubbed "blueprints of novels"), all these features, as many critics have noted, announce "l'ère de soupçon" — the era in which the presumed innocence of fiction is severely and irrevocably called into question. Similar in its narrative experimentation to the works of Robbe-Grillet, Sarraute, Butor, Simon and Duras among others, *Paludes* offers an early paradigm of the twentieth-century "oeuvre-critique," or genre of theoretical fiction.

Conflating the two coordinates of "irony" and "critique" which Gide ascribed to his modern rendition of the medieval *sôtie*, the oeuvre-critique as defined in *Paludes* retains its ludic spirit and psychological interest through the invention of a narrator who, in Barthes's formulation, acts the part of village gossip, or petty Informer: "L'Informateur, ingénu ou pervers, a un rôle négatif. Si anodin que soit le message qu'il me passe (comme une maladie), il réduit mon autre à n'être qu'un autre. Je suis bien obligé de l'écouter (je ne puis *mondainement* laisser voir mon agacement)…"[34] (Barthes's emphasis). Clearly tending more towards the perverse than the ingenuous in his dealings with that "réseau farce" or "immense micmac" in which, according to Barthes, all encounters whether dialogical or social, Gidean or Proustian, are ultimately revealed as grotesquely coincidental, *Paludes*'s narrator personifies the textual trope of the eternal "réplique," of literary "dénégation."

[34] Roland Barthes, *Fragments d'un discours amoureux*, p. 166.

IV

HOMOTEXTUAL COUNTER-CODES*

THE HYPERBOLIC DISCOURSE OF
LES NOURRITURES TERRESTRES

Les Nourritures terrestres, first published in its entirety in 1897, is probably at first reading the least classical of all Gide's works. Its style is epiphanic, apostrophic, hortatory and above all hyperbolic. The lyrical voice, formerly checked by deflation, understatement, autocritique and irony, is suddenly unfettered and accorded full range.

Where *Le Traité du Narcisse* called for "manifestation" but cautiously removed its polemic to the extraneous pasture of the Footnote, *Les Nourritures* openly and defiantly "manifests" itself in the style and structure of its narrative. Where *Paludes* couched its criticism of Symbolism in passive constructions, derision and the humor of parody, *Les Nourritures* actively and seriously promulgates its credo, arguing for immediacy, sensual apperception and free love over and against critical distance, intellectual mediation and Calvinist repression. Here, as nowhere else in Gide's oeuvre, the classical norm of "le frein" or "restraint" appears to be discarded: "pudeur" is abandoned for the sake of an emphatic release of emotion, and the conventions of unity characteristic of prose fiction are undercut by the random motions of a mock travelogue of the soul, tergiversating between genres if it deigns to respect their integrity at all. Decentered and desultory, this reckless narrative qualifies as yet another form of "negative writing," an anti-*Bildungsroman*, charting the "disinstruction" of a young man in the mores and morals of bourgeois education, and his initiation to the joys of homoeroticism. In this respect, it bears a thematic affinity to other works, most of which treat homosexuality at the very least

* Portions of this chapter have been published previously in *Michigan Romance Studies* 6 (1986) and are reprinted here by permission of the editors.

indirectly. Stylistically, however, it appears to stand apart, as a brief history of the work's reception will indicate.

Les Nourritures has been grossly neglected by literary critics as Gide himself irately pointed out in his preface to the 1927 edition of the work: "A quel point ce livre heurtait le goût du jour, c'est ce que laissa voir son insuccès total. Aucun critique n'en parla. En dix ans, il s'en vendit tout juste cinq cents exemplaires." Upon initial publication it was thought to be morally suspect (particularly the "Récit de Ménalque" published separately in 1896 in *L'Ermitage* prior to the completion of *Les Nourritures*), unnecessarily harsh towards Symbolism, and of dubious originality. The editors of *Le Centaure*, to which Gide originally submitted and then withdrew the manuscript, found it derivative, Gide's friend Marcel Schwob considered it a blatant imitation of his *Livre de Monelle*, and other readers thought it pandered to the rather modish "Naturist" school whose figurehead was Gide's close friend Francis Jammes. Jammes himself was firmly convinced that the work, even prior to its publication, was to be interpreted as the sign of Gide's willingness to join the Naturist fold. In a letter to Gide, Jammes wrote:

> On dirait que tu as eu, dans ton évolution, et avec *Paludes*, un moment d'arrêt. Comprends bien ce mot. Tout maintenant... va se porter contre les Mallarméens et les Regniéristes, contre le faux mysticisme, etc.
>
> On a tort d'attaquer Mallarmé et Regnier, qui sont deux grand poètes...
>
> Toi, non seulement tu es en dehors, mais toute cette nouvelle littérature, naturiste ou non, est formée et sera formée d'un triangle dont les angles sont toi, Bouhélier et moi.
>
> ...La clique dans laquelle je vis te place en dehors de la poésie marmoréene, figée, mythologique et symbolique. Il me semble que tu es appellé à vivre avec nous et, pour un petit moment, "d'attendre... d'attendre..., d'attendre..."
>
> ...Le précipité s'est cristallisé au fond du verre pour ceux avec qui tu vivais. Tu es resté en suspens. Je sens bien que la *nouvelle* école doute si tu veux fuir ou demeurer. *Les Nourritures terrestres*, rien que par ce titre, indiquent que tu es, comme nous, de Jean-Jacques et de Bernardin. Pourrai-je l'affirmer au besoin? Tu es appellé à beaucoup. Il me semble que, ton influence se mêlant à la nôtre, tu ne peux échapper. Réfléchis à tout cela et brûle cette lettre. Elle pourrait dénoncer un esprit de parti pris qui n'est pas en moi.[1]

[1] Letter, Jammes to Gide, October 1896. Cited by Yvonne Davet, *Autour des 'Nourritures terrestres': histoire d'un livre* (Paris: Gallimard, 1948), pp. 30-31.

Gide, deeply disconcerted by Jammes's eagerness to assimilate the work as a contribution to his "school" and concerned that he maintain his distance, wrote back:

> Je ne t'écrivais pas parce que je travaillais. Mes *Nourritures* avancent; j'ai absolument besoin que ça paraisse très vite pour empêcher les fausses idées de s'enraciner sur mon compte (tu remarqueras cette métaphore). ..."Je suis ton *voisin* de triangle."[2] (Gide's emphasis)

Distinguishing himself as a "neighbor" rather than a member did little to hinder the complaint against Naturism registered by many of his early readers. Nor did it serve to prejudice favorably the work's reception in general. Though its libertine advocacy of liberation appealed to postwar youth, it continued to sell poorly until, in the twenties, it suddenly began to enjoy a remarkable vogue. Out of print in the early twenties, copies when discovered, were eagerly seized and consumed. Martin du Gard memorialized its impact on a generation in the 1923 installment of *Les Thibaut*:

> Le livre se déplaça. Daniel eut encore le temps de déchiffrer le titre qui courait au haut des pages: *Les Nourritures terrestres*.
> Intrigué, il entra, le jour même, chez plusieurs libraires. L'ouvrage y était ignoré. L'homme du wagon garderait-il son secret? "Une existence pathétique," se répétait Daniel, "plutôt que la tranquillité..." Le lendemain matin, il courut dépouiller des catalogues sous les galeries de l'Odéon: et, quelques heures plus tard, le volume en poche, il venait s'enfermer chez lui.
> Il le lut d'un trait. L'après-midi y passa. Vers le soir, il sortit. Jamais encore il n'avait connu pareille fièvre, exaltation aussi glorieuse: il allait devant lui, à grand pas, comme un conquérant. La nuit vint. Il avait suivi les quais, il était fort loin de chez lui. Il dîna d'un croissant, et rentra. Le livre attendait, sur la table. Daniel tournait autour, sans plus oser l'ouvrir. Il se coucha, mais ne put trouver le sommeil. Alors il capitula, s'enveloppa d'un manteau, et reprit sa lecture, lentement, depuis le début. Il sentait bien que l'heure était solonnelle, qu'un travail, une germination mystérieuse, s'élaborait au plus intime de sa conscience. Lorsqu'à l'aube il eut, une fois encore, achevé la dernière page, il s'aperçut qu'il posait sur la vie un regard neuf.[3]

Here, the reading of Gide, fraught with temptation and resulting in a complete transformation of world-view, mimics the conventions of a "first night," a symbolic rite of passage from adolescence to

---

[2] Letter, Gide to Jammes, October 1896. Cited by Davet, p. 32.
[3] Roger Martin du Gard, *Les Thibauts*, troisième partie, *La Belle Saison* (Paris: Gallimard, 1923), pp. 39-40.

manhood. Ironically, the book rather than the lover effects this dramatic change in the account of Martin du Gard, who was perhaps also inadvertently recording the opinion of a prior generation, which felt that *Les Nourritures*'s inspiration derived more from "bookish" sources than from actual romantic initiation.

The heterogeneity of literary sources posed problems for readers of all generations. Valéry, though he adopted a more indulgent position than most, identified this difficulty in a letter to Gide in 1897: "Ce qui fait l'amusement de ton petit Baedaker, c'est qu'il y a un peu de tout. Il y a d'Annunzio, des soukhs, des Donatelli, et les fruits qui sont à la mode (Cur?)."[4] Other sources that he neglected to mention but which others noticed were Rimbaud's *Illuminations*, Whitman's *Leaves of Grass*, Goethe's *Römische Elegien* and *Faust II*, Nietzsche's *Zarathustra* (which, as is well known, Gide obstinately refused to acknowledge having read despite the fact that letters to friends dated prior to the publication of *Les Nourritures* contain explicit references to Nietzsche) and Virgil's *Eclogues*. The imprint of these influences complicated the reader's acceptance of *Les Nourritures*'s diatribe against the book, so strongly pronounced in incendiary injunctions that framed the *récit*: in the preface, "Et quand tu m'auras lu, jette ce livre, — et sors," and in the envoi; "jette mon livre. Emancipe-t-en..." "Jette mon livre; ne t'y satisfais point..." "Jette mon livre; dis-toi bien que ce n'est là *qu'une* des mille postures possibles en face de la vie." For many, this dictum was imbued with hypocrisy given the intensely literary nature of the writing. If the dictum were to be taken seriously, if literature were to be deplored on account of its derogatory effect on the pure, unmediated experience of life, then why write a "book" so riddled with literary formulas and models, so encrusted with quotations from great literary works of the past? Even the gentle Valéry was irked by these contradictions, as evinced by his confession to Gide that he found the work over-written: "L'ensemble est peut-être trop écrit; et les impressions pas assez inédites... on sent très souvent le morceau qui commence. Aussi souvent tu l'arrêtes, et il n'en reste qu'une phrase, mais la sensation demeure. Tu réponds illico: ce n'est pas un bouquin, et puis zut..."[5] Valéry implies that the "puis zut" attitude is a poor excuse for affected, uneven form.

In a similar way to *Paludes*, *Les Nourritures* starts with a series of aborted efforts at a beginning. Like a manuscript, left at intermittent intervals on a table, picked up and reworked from its original

[4] Letter, Valéry to Gide, September 1897. Cited by Davet, p. 118.
[5] Letter, Valéry to Gide, September 1897. Cited by Davet, p. 118.

point of departure, *Les Nourritures* follows an aleatory, retrogressive, narrative movement. This becomes particularly evident when, in Book V, the paragraphs circle round and back to the evocation of a misty, troubled, "scene of writing," composed under the epigram "Pluvieuse terre de Normandie; campagne domestiquée..."[6] We imagine the writer, having made his autumnal retreat to a Normandy estate not unlike Cuverville, fretting late at night in demi-consciousness over a false start: "Il y a des jours et d'autres jours encore. Il y a des matins et des soirs. Il y a des matins où l'on se lève avant l'aube, plein de torpeur" (*NT* 205).

As a foil against the terrifying prospect of closure and completion, the voyage *cum* literary work is repeatedly postponed before being taken up anew: "Partons! et ne nous arrêtons que n'importe où..." (*NT* 205). However, the resolve to progress is stymied when the traveller finds himself retracing the steps of a familiar route leading back to the old sites of feeling, back to the texts of his early education:

> Je suis la même route et je reconnais tout. Je remets mes pas sur mes pas et mes émotions... Il y avait un banc de pierre où je m'assis. — Voici. — J'y lisais. Quel livre? — Ah!: Virgile. (*NT* 206-07)

and back to the books which he himself has written in the past, in this case to the dialogue with Angèle in *Paludes*. This "mise en abyme" of the act of writing together with the reversals, stops, broken trajectories and multiple unfinished phrases so typical of narrative paralysis in *Paludes*, implies that the consummately ironic earlier text is in some sense still vestigially present, despite *Les Nourritures*'s apparent lack of irony. Moreover, as in the early *sôtie*, a plethora of quotations (some readily identifiable such as the *Koran*, Virgil's *Eclogues*, and "The Exile's Song" translated from the Anglo-Saxon by Taine and included in his *Littérature anglaise*), is elided with the pastiche of numerous genres encompassing the journal (Gide's own in particular), the aphorism, the rondeau, the blason, the ballad, and the pastoral epic.[7]

This compendium of poetic and prose forms provoked and continues to provoke consternation among critics. The overall effect of such quotation, though in some respect "postmodern" in the most contemporary sense, lends the text an academic quality that clashes with its didactic insistence on liberation from tradition. What on the one

---

[6] André Gide, *Les Nourritures terrestres*, in *Romans, récits et sôties* p. 204. All further references to this work will appear in the text abbreviated *NT*.

[7] For a more complete discussion of the literary sources of *Les Nourritures*, see Davet, *Autour des 'Nourritures terrestres'* and Angelet, *Symbolisme et invention formelle dans les premiers écrits d'André Gide*.

hand appears to be a sophisticated formal experiment with the mixture of discourses, on the other may be seen as a monotonous repetition of mood pieces divorced from suspenseful story line and rendered even more inaccessible by the absence of an ironic narrator (such as one finds in *Paludes*).[8] Though a single first-person narrative voice seems to prevail, its inflections are alternately saccharine and insistent, bathetic and manipulative. This psychologically untrustworthy tone, akin in many respects to the spurious "sincerity" of Michel in *L'Immoraliste*, is exacerbated by the fact that the omnibus addressee — Nathanaël — is never given the opportunity to challenge his mentor's opinions, point of view or implicit authority.

Perhaps the greatest source of difficulty, however, lies in the style of *Les Nourritures*. Aside from Léon Blum in *La Revue Blanche*, Paul Dermée in *L'Esprit Nouveau*, and Jacques Rivière in his *Etudes*, there are virtually no stylistic analyses of *Les Nourritures* by Gide's contemporaries. Though later scholars of Gide such as Jean Hytier, Jean Delay and Ralph Freedman concede its importance in the evolution of Gide's style and examine the more salient attributes of its lyricism, there exist no endeavors to interpret this style within the history of modernism. Possibly for today's readers, its lyrical excess, the impassioned tenor of its axioms and the overly insistent didacticism of its narrator, seem hopelessly superannuated. Such exaggerated enthusiasm, such hyperbolic flights, are irksome to the reader of Gide accustomed to savoring the pleasures of reserved, litotic prose.

How do we account for such hyperbole? Is it simply an aberration within Gide's oeuvre? Or is it the partner of themes and polemics that comprise a particular oeuvre within the oeuvre? Is it simply the object of litotic repression, bursting forth suddenly and then subsequently censored; a confirmation of the Sartrean theory that there are "two Gides" constantly at war with one another? Or is this hyperbole simply

---

[8] In Book IV, commonly referred to as the "Récit de Ménalque" (since Gide published it separately under this title), there are specific indications of intervening narrators. Ménalque, who would subsequently reappear in *L'Immoraliste*, expounds his philosophy of free love at the beginning, his speeches demarcated by quotation marks. Later, re-employing the conversational technique of *Paludes*, the floor is relinquished to other characters: Josèphe is reproved for self-pity; Hylas, Moelibée, Mopsus and Cléodalise each take their turn to sing; and Lothaire and Ulrich argue about snow. Aside from Ménalque, however (whose strong character as mentor to the rest is well defined), there is little if anything to distinguish the voices of these minor characters. It is thus fair to allege that *Les Nourritures* is dominated by a single, first-person narrator, interrupted only briefly by Ménalque who himself shares the opinions of the principal speaker.

another version of litotes, another dimension of rhetorical negativity?[9]
In a commemorative essay, published in 1951 in *Les Temps Modernes*
shortly after Gide's death, Sartre articulated this rhetorical dialectic
in terms of binary oppositions that fuse together in uneasy, but
dynamic "compromise":

> Courage et prudence: ce mélange bien dosé explique la tension in-
> térieure de son oeuvre. L'art de Gide veut établir un compromis entre
> le risque et la règle; en lui s'équilibrent la loi protestante et le non-
> conformisme de l'homosexuel, l'individualisme orgueilleux du grand
> bourgeois et le goût puritain de la contrainte sociale; une certaine
> sécheresse, une difficulté à communiquer et un humanisme d'origine
> chrétienne, une sensualité vive et qui se voudrait innocente; l'obser-
> vance de la règle s'y unit à la quête de la spontanéité.[10]

Aside from delineating important links between the dominant chords
of Gide's personal character and the thematic and stylistic dimensions
of art, Sartre uncovers the way in which thesis and antithesis in-
terpenetrate each other, give rise to each other mutually in a single
upsurge. Thus the "search for spontaneity" gives birth immediately
to the "observance of regulation" and vice versa. This elusive division-
in-fusion helps to explain characterizations of Gide that emphasize
his reputation as a "Protée insaisissable." Consider, for example, the
opening of Maurice Blanchot's 1949 essay entitled "Gide et la littérature
d'expérience":

> Pour qui s'efforce de regarder avec un esprit juste l'oeuvre et la per-
> sonne d'André Gide, le premier trait qui frappe est celui-ci: on ne peut
> guère parler de cette oeuvre que d'une manière injuste. Si l'on voit d'elle
> fortement un seul aspect, on néglige ce que cet aspect a d'important,
> qui est de n'être pas seul et d'admettre aussi la vérité de l'aspect op-
> posé. Souligne-t-on, en elle, cette *affirmation des contraires, on oublie la ten-*
> *dance à l'equilibre, à l'harmonie et à l'ordre qui n'a cessé de l'animer. Oeuvre d'ex-*
> *cès, oeuvre d'extrême mesure...*
> ...enfin oeuvre immense, d'une extraordinaire variété, mais aussi épar-
> pillé et étroite et monotone, ouverte à la culture la plus riche, tournée
> vers la spontanéité la moins livresque, naïve par goût de l'effort, libre
> par souci de la contrainte, discrète dans la franchise, sincère jusqu'à
> l'affectation et comme poussée par l'inquiétude vers le repos et la sérénité
> d'une forme à laquelle rien ne saurait être changé.[11] (my emphases)

[9] Pierre Fontanier, *Les Figures du discours*, p. 123.
[10] Jean-Paul Sartre, "Gide vivant," *Les Temps Modernes*, no. 65 (March 1951), p.
89. This text was later included in *Situations IV*.
[11] Maurice Blanchot, "Gide et la littérature d'experience" *L'Arche*, no. 23 (1946), p. 87.

Blanchot, like Sartre, exhibits a tendency towards rhetorical contradiction in speaking of the same effect in Gide's style. His characterization of all readings of Gide as necessarily "unjust" implies an interesting appreciation of the Gidean bias: a slant or inclination that tilts backwards at the slightest pressure in a single direction (making hyperbole a postponed swerve towards litotes and vice versa), or, in the moral sense, a neglect or disdain for the "just" measure, the "mean" which is stable and secure. Blanchot also demonstrates a willingness to extend the rhetorical posturing of Gide's writing to his mode of being in the world, treating the life as a set of tropes in much the same way as Jacques Rivière many years earlier and Sartre several years later. In 1911, Rivière had equated the indefinability of Gide's ontology with that of his books:

> Mais Gide, il nous est impossible de le définir; non pas qu'il se cache, mais c'est qu'il se dit tout entier. Il refuse de s'en tenir à ce qu'il a déjà posé de lui-même. Le voici devant nous plein de sourire et de nouveauté. Tant il change, et sous nos yeux, ne se moquerait-il pas de nous?...
>
> ...Vraiment il serait temps qu'il se rangeât; il faudrait qu'on fût enfin sûr de pouvoir le retrouver désormais toujours pareil à l'idée qu'une bonne fois on se serait formée de lui. Alors il serait permis de lui décerner des éloges... tout au moins de choisir, pour qualifier ses livres, des épithètes irrévocables. — Mais non. Il augmente de choses épris, à plus d'idées, à plus d'êtres attaché, moins définitif que jamais. Il n'a même pas la pudeur de dépouiller franchement son passé à mesure qu'il use. Si du moins il déclarait ce qu'il repousse! Mais il se complique toujours davantage et l'on ne sait même pas bien ce qu'il n'est plus.[12]

In Gide's chronic "dédoublement" Rivière recognizes a single style rather than an array of permanently distinguishable, mutually exclusive styles. The problem, he suggests, is that the Gidean phrase is avowedly complicated; rather than relinquish the dissenting voice and alleviate internal dissonance in its multiple variations, his phrase juxtaposes contraries in a state of suspended, protracted, and potentially ironic uncertainty.

Perhaps the text that comes closest in its irony of rhetorical attitude to *Les Nourritures* is Barthes's *Fragments d'un discours amoureux*. Superficially the similarities are striking: both capitalize on a modern reinterpretation of the Romantic fragment, evoking with their respective epigrams, maxims and apostrophes a memorial destined to console

---

[12] Jacques Rivière, *Etudes* (Paris: Gallimard, 1924), p. 176. All further references to this work will appear in the text abbreviated *E*.

the posterity of unrequited or unsatisfied lovers. Both in their common concern with the dilemma of how to "write love" oscillate furiously between daring, full-fledged affirmations of homosexual desire (a mode most typified by *Corydon* with its rather hackneyed use of Platonic dialogue) and a furtive, tentative, "secret language," best described in the famous opening of *Si le grain ne meurt*. Here Gide's origins as a writer were traced to a scene of masturbation under the dining room table of his childhood home — literally a figure of "writing under the table." Both texts are structured around a discernible protocol decreeing how lovers should behave; the maxims, entreaties and, in Barthes's case, lexical definitions of erotic poses can be read as so many rules governing the treatment of the object of desire. These rules yield an ideal of aestheticized, distantiated veneration eventually culminating in the virtual suppression of the fetishized homosexual body; indeed it is this very suppression which, interpreted figuratively, can be seen as the motivating force behind the repertory of stylistic and rhetorical postures that comprise the lover's discourse. Specific parallels between the favored erotic tropes of Gide and Barthes are easily drawn: what we have referred to as Gidean hyperbole corresponds to the Barthesian concept of "affirmation" in itself "dédoublé" and derived, like Gide's, from Nietzsche:

> Il y a deux affirmations de l'amour. Tout d'abord, lorsque l'amoureux rencontre l'autre, il y a affirmation immédiate (psychologiquement: éblouissement, enthousiasme, exaltation, projection folle d'un avenir comblé: je suis dévoré par le désir, l'impulsion d'être heureux): je dis *oui* à tout (en m'aveuglant). Suit un long tunnel: mon premier *oui* est rongé de doutes, la *valeur* amoureuse est sans cesse menacée de dépréciation: c'est le moment de la passion triste, la montée du ressentiment et de l'oblation. De ce tunnel, cependant, je puis sortir; je puis "surmonter", sans liquider; ce que j'ai affirmé une première fois, je puis de nouveau l'affirmer, sans le répéter, car alors, ce que j'affirme, c'est l'affirmation, non sa contingence: j'affirme la première rencontre dans sa différence, je veux son retour, non sa répétition. Je dis à l'autre (ancien ou nouveau): *Recommençons.*[13]

[13] Roland Barthes, *Fragments d'un discours amoureux*, p. 31. One could easily, following Barthes's invention of a dictionary of lover's tropes, plot the rhetorical moves and strategies of Gide's *Nourritures* accordingly. Figures such as "Absence," "Altération," "Attente," "Dédicace," "Dépense," "Errance," "Etreinte," "Ravissement," and "Rencontre," among others, have appropriate corollaries in *Les Nourritures*. Barthes, moreover, cites Gide in the margins of this text, thereby designating him as one

And just as Gide's hyperbole, also a kind of "oui-non," is inextricably entwined with litotes, so Barthes's affirmation is interlocked with a comparable figure — askesis:

> ASCESE. Soit qu'il se sente coupable à l'égard de l'être aimé, soit qu'il veuille l'impressioner en lui représentant son malheur, le sujet amoureux esquisse une conduite ascétique d'autopunition (régime de vie, vête-ment, etc.).
>
> 1. Puisque je suis coupable de ceci, de cela (j'ai, je me donne mille raisons de l'être), je vais me punir, je vais abîmer mon corps: me faire tailler les cheveux très court, cacher mon regard derrière des lunettes noires (façon d'entrer au couvent), m'adonner à l'étude d'une science sérieuse et abstraite. Je vais me lever tôt pour travailler pendant qu'il fait encore nuit, tel un moine. Je vais être très patient, un peu triste, en un mot, *digne*, comme il sied à l'homme du ressentiment.[14] (Barthes's emphasis)

One is struck by the obvious congruence between the bent towards self-inflicted punishment and self-imposed deprivation inherent in Barthes's concept of askesis and the "return to the monk's cell" witnessed in Gide's early *Journal*. In *Les Nourritures*, a comparable regimen can be detected in rituals of divestiture and dispossession: "A cinquante ans, l'heure étant venue, je vendis tout... Je vendis absolument tout, ne voulant rien garder de *personnel* sur cette terre (*NT* 189; Gide's emphasis). In this evacuation of the personal, and by extension, of the "persona," one retraces the now familiar signifying chain of autonegation: from Narcisse's murky looking glass, to Tityre's clouded fishbowl, through to their modern day equivalent, the "lunettes noires" of Roland Barthes. The spurning of worldly comforts and goods, like the willful shielding of the eye, qualify as modulations of a negative trope, itself ramified to apply both to the lover's discourse and the lover's text.

Hyperbolic Postures

One of the first, most astute and generous reviews of *Les Nourritures* — Léon Blum's 1897 essay in *La Revue Blanche* — offers a sophisticated definition of hyperbole, again in the context of a dialectical, comparative approach:

of his elected, textual "lovers." Finally, Gide and Barthes seem to converge yet again in their common dependence on Goethe's *Werther* as a supreme model for the lover's discourse.

[14] Barthes, *Fragments d'un discours amoureux*, p. 41.

Il y a toujours eu, en M. Gide, un grand écrivain. Pourtant chacun de ses livres vient révéler à son tour une perfection plus secrète et plus sûre de la forme. Je n'imaginais rien qui fût mieux écrit que *Paludes*, et je ne puis ne pas préférer *Les Nourritures*. Les qualités du style assurément n'ont pas changées. On retrouvera la même exactitude, la même force serrée et approchée, jointe à une fluidité limpide et insensible de l'usage, ce mélange de dons presque opposés qui semblent faire de chaque phrase de M. Gide un mélange d'éléments contraires, et laissent l'expression la plus précise et la plus solide de la pensée comme baignée d'un air vaporeux et matinal. Mais la beauté de la forme me paraît ici plus intime que jamais, plus cachée, obtenue par des moyens moins sensibles. Elle semble l'effet d'une déviation presque insensible de la phrase, du choix ténu d'une épithète, du changement insensible et nécessaire d'un mot.[15]

Blum's commentary is particularly pertinent because it assures the possiblity of establishing some measure of continuity between the style of *Les Nourritures* and that of previous prose pieces, thus countering the temptation to treat it as an anomaly within Gide's corpus. At the same time, Blum articulates many of the qualities of stylistic aberration that one would associate with litotic hyperbole: the "limpid fluidity" of its "exactitude" and "rigor," the "vaporous air" of its "precision" and "intellectual solidity" and most importantly, the "effect of its almost imperceptible deviation" from the norms of grammatical usage. Blum's stress on "imperceptible" deviation is particularly significant, for it is not the wild, far-reaching curve, but rather, the gentle "écart," a restrained penchant towards unconventional syntax, that conditions *Les Nourritures*'s formal technique. For Gérard Genette, the "écart" constitutes the defining feature of hyperbole:

...on appellerait "hyperboles" les effets par lesquels le langage, au contraire, rapproche comme par effraction des réalités naturellement éloignées dans le contraste et la discontinuité. Cette opposition sommaire n'a évidemment qu'une valeur indicative et transitoire. Elle nous permet cependant, peut-être, de mieux sentir une des affinités qui unissent la poétique du baroque et celle de la poésie moderne: toutes deux sont fondées sur ce que les marinistes nommaient la *surprise*, et qu'on définirait plus volontiers aujourd'hui par la distance ou l'*écart* que le langage fait franchir à la pensée. L'image surréaliste, qui vaut explicitement, par l'ampleur de l'écart et l'*improbabilité* du rapprochement, c'est-à-dire sa teneur en information, est le type même de la figure hyperbolique.[16]

[15] Léon Blum, "André Gide: *Les Nourritures terrestres,*" *La Revue Blanche* (1897), p. 77.
[16] Gérard Genette, *Figures I* (Paris: Seuil, 1966), p. 252.

Unlike the baroque or surrealist image, the referential margin of which is often radically removed from the original point of comparison, the Gidean "écart" ranges over a limited circumference, tolerating a comparatively minimal degree of irrational analogy, contrived disjunction, or oxymoron. The hyperbolic effect is generally a product of minor deviation from the syntax of logical sequence and the elision of explanation. However, despite the restraint of Gide's hyperbole, *Les Nourritures* has been judged "coquettish" and "mannerist." On what foundation do these judgements rest?

In her exhaustive and technical analysis of Gide's phrase, Marie-Thérèse Veyrenc refers to Gide's predilection for *archaism* in this regard. Archaism emerges primarily in the superimposition of Latinate constructions on French word order, as in "Les plus grandes joies de mes sens / C'ont été des soifs étanchées" where, according to Veyrenc, the replacement of "étanchements de soifs" with "soifs étanchées" goes against the grain of modern French.[17] She also considers the frequent detachment of negative markers such as "ne pas" or "ne plus" from their conventional positions as part of the same phenomenon, citing a particularly jarring example of this dislocution: "De là me vint d'ailleurs un peu de cette aversion pour n'importe quelle *possession* sur la terre; la peur de n'aussitôt plus posséder que cela" in which "n'aussitôt plus posséder" supplants the expected "ne plus posséder aussitôt."[18] The effect, according to Veyrenc, is to approach and unite two separate phrases by doubling the function of "ne plus." Thus, instead of "ne plus posséder aussitôt" followed by "ne plus que cela" which would yield "la peur de ne plus posséder aussitôt ne plus que cela," the two meanings are governed by a single "ne plus." Their combination within a single phrase produces a rather foreign sounding syntax.

In Veyrenc's opinion, though such archaisms abound, their overall "ungrammaticality" is neutralized by their fusion with Gide's personal style causing the reader to accept them as rhetorical innovations or classical refinements.[19] Jean Hytier reaches a similar conclusion

[17] Marie-Thérèse Veyrenc, *Genèse d'un style: la phrase d'André Gide dans 'Les Nourritures terrestres'* (Paris: Nizet, 1976), pp. 22-23.

[18] Veyrenc, p. 196.

[19] Michael Riffaterre uses the term "ungrammaticality" as something of a synonym for what the rhetoricians commonly refer to as "catachresis," that is, the verbal abuse of literal meaning inherent in most tropes and metaphors. What interests Riffaterre is the reader's ability to assimilate such "incompatibilities between words," by making the necessary "semantic transfer" from the literal to the figurative level of meaning. This "competence" on the part of the reader is qualified by Riffaterre as "linguistic"

("Comme tout grand écrivain, et d'une manière toute classique, qui rappelle Racine, il rapprochera des mots pour établir entre eux un rapport à la fois saisissant et naturel"), after a long and dense enumeration of stylistic divarications ranging from the neologism to the displacement of adjectives:

> Gide gardera longtemps une prédilection pour le mot rare, ou plutôt pour l'emploi rare du mot, de même que pour le néologisme, ou plutôt pour la recréation d'un terme: il parlera de "vision miragineuse," de "monomorphie des palmes," de "ternissares de chaleur," d'"immédiatité des souvenirs"; il emploiera un infinitif comme "emboire," un adjectif comme "prévespéral." D'autre part, il hasardera l'adverbe "clémentement," il forgera un adjectif verbal comme "surodorant," il créera toute une série de verbes privatifs: "déponderer," "déséprendre," "désennoblir." Il affectionnera de même des tours anciennement usités, comme l'imparfait du subjonctif pour marquer le souhait: — "Ah! que m'emportât une lame assez forte." Il transformera un pronom en substantif: "le quelconque de sa banalisation," des participes présents en adjectifs verbaux, et il abusera de ce maniérisme: "les attendantes réponses."[20]

Hytier's favorable appraisal of such deviations stems from his appreciation of Gide's debt to classical precedent, a debt serving to moderate and therefore justify his inventive abuse of grammar in Hytier's eyes. Like Veyrenc, he conflates the classical and hyperbolic in his discussion of the latter within Gide's style, and like Veyrenc, he designates the Latinate quality of the syntax as an area where tradition and modernity merge.

Perhaps the most sensitive account of litotic hyperbole (or controlled deviation) in the early Gide can be found in Jacques Rivière's *Etude*. In addition to exploring the subtle varieties of this rhetorical figure, Rivière provides the invaluable service of linking it directly to the explication of Gide's ambivalent lyricism. Rivière's own writing is itself

when "the physical fact that a phrase has been generated by a word that should have excluded it" is overcome. Alternatively "literary competence" consists of "the reader's familiarity with the descriptive systems, with themes, with his society's mythologies and above all with other texts. Wherever there are gaps or compressions in the text— such as incomplete descriptions, or allusions, or quotations— it is this literary competence that will enable the reader to respond properly" (*Semiotics of Poetry* [Bloomington: Indiana University Press, 1978], p. 5).

Gide's "quotation" of the archaism fits most appropriately into the category of "literary competence" its "ungrammaticality" resolved by the reader's familiarity with classical texts or modern works contriving to be classical in their use of stylistic allusion.

[20] Jean Hytier, *André Gide* (Alger: Fréminville, 1938).

so lyrically expressive and so deeply in harmony with the passages
he cites, that it merits extensive transcription. He begins by identifying the "écart" with the sense of movement inherent in both the individual phrase and its ensemble:

> Le délice du premier style est surtout dans le mouvement des phrases.
> Elles bougent; elles se déroulent, elles ont mille inclinations diverses
> au gré desquelles elles se laissent porter. Elles sont pleines de direc-
> tions comme l'eau. On les lit en se penchant; tout le corps s'intéresse
> à leurs modifications; on les accompagne tour à tour avec une ployante
> et voluptueuse attention. (*E* 181)

The motion embodied in the hyperbolic swing recalls the "leaning"
and "bending" so prevalent a *topos* in Gide's previous work. Like Narcisse bent over his reflection and Tityre *recubans*, Rivière's reader of
Gide leans towards the book and moves in concert with the sensual
penchants of the prose. The rhetoric of the text animates the physical
person of the reader, who then communicates his fervor by personi-
fying the critical language used to describe this effect. Here adjective, noun and pronoun acquire an animus:

> Les adjectifs viennent doucement précéder les noms (cf. "une vie au
> monotone cours"...), les pronoms prennent une place exquise et écartée;
> ils semblent vouloir effacer dans l'ombre des mots plus graves. De
> souples échanges, de petites inversions. Tout plie sous un long souffle
> modéré. (*E* 181-82)

They motivate the text, and by extension the reader, with an apparent
will of their own, engaging in transactions and assuming positions
that suggest their independence from an omniscient authorial presence.

Rivière builds up a lexicon of descriptive and passional terms that
contain or replicate hyperbole: "déroulent — inclinations — se laissent
porter — directions — se penchant — tour à tour — écartée — plié — élans —
errer — courants — tendances divergentes — détours délectables —
amours qui s'élancent — bougements — versent," thereby implying
that the hyperbolic code provides a key to deciphering desire's hieroglyphics:

> Voici d'abord les phrases qu'animent les élancements du désir. Elles
> ont toutes une sorte d'extase désemparée; elles s'attardent de partout,
> elles s'alentissent passionément; et, en même temps. Je ne sais quelle
> fièvre les inquiète et les empêche de se reposer dans la défaite. Les unes
> fuient longtemps comme le désir qui a échappé vainement du coeur;

elles rebondissent en s'affaiblissant toujours, elles se perdent plutôt qu'elles ne s'achèvent. Elles sont pareilles à des promontoires: au moment où leur ligne bleue va finir dans la mer, un bleu plus pâle les reprend et les prolonge encore en les atténuant davantage. (*E* 183)

To this vivid evocation of Gide's phrase one might impute a theory of textual Eros, best exemplified by a passage from Book IV in which the gradual accretion of images describing the crescendo of the sunset simulates the act of love. It begins with a tiny wisp of smoke, then becomes a cloud of gilded dust suddenly bursting into flame upon contact with a mysterious rocket, "une fusée lancée on ne sait d'où." Throughout the description, hyperbole structures the erotic subtext:

De la ville montait ce qui semblait une fumée; c'était de la poussière illuminée qui flottait, s'élevait à peine au-dessus des places où plus de lumière brillait. Et parfois jaillissait comme spontanément, dans l'extase de cette nuit trop chaude, une fusée, lancée on ne sait d'où, qui filait, suivait comme un cri dans l'espace, vibrait, tournait, et retombait défaite, au bruit de sa mystérieuse éclosion. J'aimais celles surtout dont les étincelles d'or pâle tombent si lentement et si négligemment s'éparpillent, qu'on croit, après, tant les étoiles sont merveilleuses, qu'elles aussi sont nées de cette subite féerie, et que, de les voir, après les étincelles, demeurantes, l'on s'étonne... puis, lentement, on reconnaît chacune à sa constellation attachée, — et l'extase en est prolongée. (*NT* 192)

Here, the spatial sense of the "écart," projected by words such as "montait," "s'élevait," "au dessus lancée," "filait" is reinforced by hyperboles resulting from excessive repetition, as in the sequence: "filait, suivait, vibrait, tournait et retombait." In this case, the sonoric aspect of the signifier greatly enhances the erotic implications of affirmation (the sound "ait, ait" connoting a cry of pleasure that complements the "cri dans l'espace") as do the semantically charged words "extase" and "merveilleuses."

In the curve of a sentence that forms an arch leading back to its point of origin, Rivière seems to identify a form of textual onanism. The phrase, "Petite chambre au-dessus de la mer; m'a réveillé la trop grande clarté de la lune, de la lune au-dessus de la mer," prompts him to remark: "...la phrase est de son commencement tout entière occupée, elle s'est tournée vers lui, elle ne le quitte pas en s'éloignant de lui, elle en garde doucement mémoire" (*E* 185). Here he implies that the phrase courts its own beginning as if it were an infatuating Other, and later in his commentary, he personifies Gide's style through an array of dramatic poses—torment, shame, pleasure and the thrill of touch—which further imply auto-eroticism. Indeed, for Rivière, the particular delight of Gide's style resides in its communication of desire and sensual pleasure "through the fingers": "Parfois elle est faite de propositions parallèles qui tâtonnent ensemble; elle est pareille aux sensations qui viennent par les doigts et que l'on se donne plusieurs fois pour être bien sûr de leur délice…" (*E* 185). Gide's propensity for parallel structure characterized by Rivière as "propositions, groping towards each other, is at one moment skillfully instrumentalized to accentuate the sensation of progressive inebriation, with "à mon troisième verre de kirsch" gradually truncated to become "au cinquième" (*NT* 208). Elsewhere anaphora, and asyndeton—the latter apparent in passages where a private shorthand predominates as in: "*Cinq heures*—Réveils en sueur; coeur battant; frissons; tête légère; disponibilité de la chair; chair poreuse et que semble envahir trop délicieusement chaque chose" (*NT* 221), also in some sense exemplify the "rubbing together" of digressions and autonomous fragments. But Rivière's rather abstract notion of rhetorical touch acquires a more literal dimension in the context of a description of hygienic ritual. In a scene that would later become famous when reworked in *L'Immoraliste*, the narrator of *Les Nourritures* portrays the act of being shaved as a kind of masturbatory pleasure:

> …On s'abandonne. Est-ce que cela va durer longtemps? Quiétude. Gouttes de sueur aux tempes. Frisson de la mousse de savon sur les joues. Et lui qui raffine après qu'il a rasé, rase encore avec un rasoir plus habile et s'aidant à présent d'une petite éponge imbibée d'eau tiède, qui amollit la peau, relève la lèvre. Puis, avec une douce eau parfumée, il lave la brûlure laissée! puis, avec un onguent, calme encore. (*NT* 175)

The repetition of "rasé, rase encore avec un rasoir" underscores the passive state of the subject who submits to each stroke of the barber's hand with increasing satisfaction.

Perhaps the most extended figure of textual onanism is the "seed,"—the "grains" that would appear later in the title of Gide's confessional account of the discovery of his sexual preferences (*Si le grain ne meurt*). The parable of the sower, of Lot, the Sodomite forefather of Gide whose seed fertilized the sterile plain just as the narrator's fecondates the sterile text, surfaces obliquely in the prevalent motifs of the desert's cultivation, the pollination of nature, and the apostrophe to seed in Book V: "Grains, je garde de vous une poignée; je la sème en mon champ fertile…" (*NT* 211-12).

If in parts of the text the onanistic hyperbole seems to prevail, in other sections the hyperbolic caress is directed, with fear and the excitement of transgression, towards the novice: "O! petite figure que j'ai caressée sous les feuilles... Et les corps délicats épousés sous les branches. J'ai touché d'un doigt délicat sa peau nacrée" (*NT* 176). Here the sexual gesture is considerably more measured and restrained than in the passages on autoeroticism; its "écart" curtailed by the dictates of "pudeur" governing the overtures of man to boy. Gide's description follows the code of "homogenic" (*homos* 'same' and *genos* 'sex') "comrade-love" set forth by the English socialist and homosexual theoretician Edward Carpenter, who, in drafting his own case history for Havelock Ellis, wrote: "I have never had to do with actual pederasty, so called. My chief desire in love is bodily nearness or contact, as to sleep naked with a naked friend."[21]

The counterpoint between askesis and affirmation, evident in the rhetoric of the homoerotic encounter, also informs the use of the polyvalent expression "Ah," defined as "une interjection expressive, marquant un sentiment vif (plaisir, douleur, admiration, impatience...)" and, "une interjection d'insistance, de renforcement" (*Petit Robert*). An onomonopoeic word, situated at the bridge between non-linguistic and linguistic utterance, "Ah" conveys complex emotions with complete economy. Condensed and emphatic, it perfectly exemplifies litotic hyperbole. Mme de Rysselberge referred to Gide's use of the high Romantic "Ah" in his earliest works as "la respiration même de son lyrisme," and Jean Delay, affiliated it with the "transports" and "ravissements" of Gide's erotic experiences, ranging from extreme euphoria to extreme melancholia.[22] Though Delay concedes that these primordial cries are "tempérés et maîtrisés par l'art," in Gide's writing, he nonetheless construes them as indexical signs of unmediated feeling, often appositely positioned to maximize contrast. In "Ah! croisées! que de fois mon front s'est venu rafraîchir à vos vitres, et que de fois mes désirs, lorsque je courais de mon lit trop brûlant vers le balcon, à voir l'immense ciel tranquille, se sont évaporés comme des brumes," desire is unleashed and dissipated (*NT* 159). Conversely, pain and depression are registered through the same sign: "Ah! que vienne enfin, suppliais-je, la crise aiguë, la maladie, la douleur vive!" (*NT* 159).

[21] Edward Carpenter, *Sex*, vol. I of *Selected Writings* (London: GMP Publishers 1984), p. 290.
[22] M. Saint-Clair, Galérie privée, pp. 153, 154 as cited by Jean Delay, *André Gide avant André Walter* vol. I of *La Jeunesse d'André Gide* (1869-1890) (Paris: Gallimard, 1956), p. 550.

In the narrator's autobiographical account of his "palingenesis" (his transformation from pious believer to joyful sybarite) the changing resonances of the utterance calibrate the stages of the narrator's existential metamorphosis. Subsequent to his change, it denotes the exclamation of ecstasy and the prosopoeic address of an absent Other, sometimes a lover, sometimes a pantheistic, munificent god of Nature. As a celebration of Nature, it resembles the antique "a!" of Virgil's pastoral poetry, breaking into the strophe and sounding the depths of lyricism: "Quem fugis, a! demens?" ("From whom fliest thou, ah infatuate" [II, 60]); "Alpinas a! dura, nives et frigora Rheni me sine sola vides. A! te ne frigora laedant! a! tibi ne teneras glacies secet aspera plantas!" ("ah cruel, lookest on Alpine snows and the frosts of the Rhine. Ah may the frost not hurt thee! Ah may the rough ice not cut thy delicate feet!" [X, 47-49]).[23] These lines from the *Eclogues* are selected by Justin O'Brien as proof of the influence of Virgil on *Les Nourritures*, where he locates no fewer than nineteen instances in which the "Ah!" erupts inside the sentence.[24] Interspersed in the middle of a phrase as in "Devant moi, ah! que toute chose s'irise" or "Nous chercherions, ah! Sulamite! si la voulpté de nos corps, sur les pommes mouillées, est moins prompte à tarir...," it directly evokes Virgilian syntax as it was Virgil who was the first and only Latin author to place it in this position.[25] Gide's use of interjection might also be read as a quotation of Goethe's quotation of the same device in his *Römische Elegien*, a short collection of erotic, lyrical poems perused by Gide shortly before commencing *Les Nourritures*. Defined then as a metaleptic conceit inscribed within two classical traditions, the Latin and the German, "Ah!" qualifies as a two-fold deviation from the conventions of modern prose.

Curiously, however, not all of Gide's readers interpreted this classical affectation as a derivative anachronism. In an article on Gide published in 1925 in *L'Esprit Nouveau*, a journal under the direction of Ozenfant and Le Corbusier dedicated to the quest for a modernist classicism, Paul Dermée treated what he called "une aspiration dans le silence" as the hallmark of a classicism bearing no resemblance to the French classicism of "le grand siècle":

> Mais comment André Gide ne voit-il pas que cette syntaxe n'a rien de commun avec celle du grand siècle? Là tout est architecture logique

[23] *Virgil's Works*, tr. J.W. MacKail (New York: Random House, 1950).

[24] Justin O'Brien, *'Les Nourritures terrestres' d'André Gide et 'Les Bucoliques' de Virgile* (Boulogne-sur-Seine: Prétexte, 1953), p. 40.

[25] Gide, *Les Nourritures terrestres* as cited by O'Brien, pp. 38-39.

aux gros blocs chevronnés par les fortes conjonctions. Ici, c'est une par-
tition d'orchestre où les instruments jouent tour à tour ou simultané-
ment, à deux, trois, quatre, puis tous ensemble — ou se taisent soudain
pour laisser s'élever une aspiration dans le silence devenu le plus vide.

Untroubled, as were later critics (Hytier, Veyrenc, O'Brien) by the
atavistic resonance of Gide's lyrical "élans" and syntactic irregularities,
Dermée preferred to treat them as signs of naturalism, faithful to the
mannerisms and idiosyncrasies of authentic speech. He hailed the
famous "tremblement" of Gide's style as a progressive invention — "la
phrase moderne":

> Cette phrase moderne, qui reste identiquement semblable à elle-
> même lorsqu'on la morcelle en ses éléments et qu'on supprime les tran-
> sitions, n'a rien de commun avec la rhétorique d'un Guez de Balzac,
> l'augmentation d'un Descartes ou la démonstration éloquente d'un
> Bossuet.
> L'inquiétude encore, et au moment le plus pathétique, le "tremble-
> ment," voilà ce qui signera les oeuvres de notre temps. Que M. André
> Gide se méfie des habilités syntaxiques du grand siècle.[26]

Dermée isolates two fundamental forms of modernism within Gide's
phrase; the first, corresponding to the notion of "morcellement," refers
to a hyperbolic vivisection of orthodox sentence structure, to the process of fracturing, proliferation, digression, or what we saw already
developing in *Paludes*, the "hétéroclite." The second, correlating to
Dermée's concept of "suppressed transitions," embodies the litotic emphasis on contraction and refers to the poetics of the discrete,
detachable unit, to the sentence which, in the words of Veyrenc, constitutes a "phrastic universe" unto itself.[27]

The Litotic Discourse of the Maxim

If the emphatic "Ah!" falls into the litotic category of the "phrase
moderne," distinguished as its purest, most reduced variant, then the
maxim or adage can be situated at the next order of verbal complexity. Recognizable in a range of absolute pronouncements, the maxim
pervades *Les Nourritures*, carrying with it the aura of a *doxa* comprised
of a priori principles:

Chaque créature indique Dieu, aucune ne le révèle. (154)

Que ton désir soit de l'amour, et que ta possession soit amoureuse. (162)

[26] Paul Dermée, "André Gide," *L'Esprit Nouveau* 25 (1925), n. pag.
[27] Veyrenc. See her excellent chapter on the maxim, pp. 39-45.

Voilà pourquoi, Nathanaël, j'ai nommé Dieu tout ce que j'aime, et pourquoi j'ai voulu tout aimer. (170)

Tout être est capable de nudité; toute émotion de plénitude... (157)

Où tu ne peux pas dire: tant mieux, dis: tant pis. Et où je dis: tant mieux, tu n'as pas à dire: tant pis. (168)

Chacun naît de son besoin, et n'est pour ainsi dire qu'un besoin extériorisé (170).

Whether they parrot the rhetorical conventions of the religious injunction or the pithy, gnomic verities of philosophy, these abbreviated utterances share the structure of the "phrase bouclée" — the phrase which turns back on itself or inverts itself through chiasmus. As a genre they confer aesthetic value on economy, closure, the essential Idea, careful grammatical composition, and the logical operation (over and against the appeal of exotic or abstruse vocabulary.) Gide owed his facility with this difficult form to his familiarity and taste for the classical moralists: in French, La Rochefoucauld; in Latin, Seneca, Tacitus and Virgil; and in German, Goethe, Schopenhauer and Nietzsche.

The aphoristic qualities of the maxim, Boethius' "proposito maxima," appealed to Gide on a number of levels: as pretending to universal truth, it provided a form for the statement that was, by definition, the most sincere; as economic and pithy, devoid of proviso, qualifications and explanations, it conveyed its content stripped of superfluity; as a statement enclosed on itself, it was in a sense a fragment, capable of being inserted, substituted and juxtaposed in relation to other fragments of the same kind. Here, the example of the classical maxim was for Gide, supplemented and extended by the Romantic theory of the fragment, defined paradigmatically by Friedrich Schlegel as "like a miniature work of art fully isolated from the surrounding world and turned in on itself like a hedgehog."[28] Independent of context and internally coherent, this kind of statement was for the Romantics also unfinished, emblematic of a project to be completed, of the "inachevée." As analyzed by Philippe Lacoue-Labarthe and Jean-Luc Nancy:

> ...le fragment se délimite par une double différence: si d'une part il n'est pas pur morceau, de l'autre il n'est pas non plus aucun de ces

---

[28] Friedrich Schlegel, *Athenäumsfragmente*, ed. Behler (1963). Cited and tr. Siegbert Prawer, *The Romantic Period in Germany* (New York: Schocken, 1970), p. 207.

termes-genres dont se sont servi les moralistes: pensée, maxime, sentence, opinion, anecdote, remarque. Ceux-ci ont plus ou moins en commun de prétendre à un achèvement dans la frappe même du "morceau." Le fragment au contraire comprend un essentiel inachèvement. C'est pourquoi il est, selon *Ath. 22*, identique au *projet*, "fragment d'avenir," en tant que l'inachèvement constitutif du projet fait précisément tout le prix de celui-ci par "la faculté de tout ensemble idéaliser et réaliser immédiatement." En ce sens tout fragment est projet: le fragment-projet ne vaut pas comme programme ou prospective, mais comme projection *immédiate* de ce que pourtant il inachève.[29] (their emphases)

Lacoue-Labarthe and Nancy identify the paradoxical quality of the fragment as that which is both a completed container of discourse and a carrier of the understated, partially suppressed unfinished message. It is of course precisely this paradox which renders this quintessentially Romantic form so "modern." In it, the aesthetics of completion give way to the aesthetics of incompletion or anticlosure, and the Romantic fragment emerges as the precursor of the modern technique of fragmentation in which parts are metonymically substituted for greater wholes or juxtaposed to each other in collage or montage. For Gide, this aspect of the "partially finished" allowed the fragment to signify both plenitude and its opposite; the organicism implicit in the concept of the self-sufficient part is undermind by the fact that the part refers to a depleted, absent, lost or not yet found totality.

In one sense, *Les Nourritures* can be seen as an assemblage or pastiche of such "romantic-modern" fragments, with the transformed classical maxim set in the text as simply one of its multiple metonymic variations. But the maxim, as utilized by Gide, holds also the dimensions of a litotic stylistic device, one that is precisely distinguished by its lack of metaphor. In fact, it approximates a litotic ideal of "naked" writing which Gide articulated in his own reading of *Les Nourritures*. In his *Journal* of 1921-1922, he wrote: "H.C. m'accusa de coquetterie dans l'arrangement de mes phrases; rien n'est plus faux. Je n'aime que le strict et le nu. Quand je commençai d'écrire mes Nourritures, je compris que le sujet de mon livre était d'en bannir toute métaphore."[30] Gide later developed this concept in the Preface to the 1927 edition of *Les Nourritures* in terms of an aesthetics of "dénuement":

[29] Philippe Lacoue-Labarthe and Jean-Luc Nancy, *L'Absolu littéraire* (Paris: Seuil, 1978), pp. 62-63.

Un mot encore: Certains ne savent voir dans ce livre, ou ne consentent à y voir, qu'une glorification du désir et des instincts. Il me semble que c'est une vue un peu courte. Pour moi, lorsque je le rouvre, c'est plus encore une apologie du dénuement que j'y vois.

"Dénuement," implying a state of metaphysical nakedness resulting from the sincere, unobstructed expression of truth is a term used both figuratively and literally, particularly when initially introduced in the 1927 preface:

J'écrivais ce livre à un moment où la littérature sentait furieusement le factice et le renfermé; où il me paraissait urgent de la faire à nouveau toucher terre et poser simplement sur le sol un pied nu. [31]

Here the "naked foot" functions not only as a metaphor for the urge to strip away literary artifice and reduce literature to the scale of the maxim, but also as a direct allusion to one of the text's most prevalent rhetorical principles. Like the maxim as a stylistic device in relation to its containing text, so the "pied nu" stands in relation to the naked body, metonymically.

The Body and the Text

Gide's poetics of nudity was based on classical standards of beauty, in particular the hellenistic beauty of the male nude as canonized by Renaissance sculpture and the aesthetics of Winckelmann, a tradition that joins the idealization of the young male form to its eroticized homosexual implications. He first began to develop the figuration of nudity in *Feuilles de route* (composed during his travels through Italy and published in the *Journal* of 1895). In his description of Donatello's *David*, the statue's anatomy is broken down into an assortment of eroticized component parts:

Après le déjeuner nous retournons au Bargello. Merveilleux *David* de Donatello! Petit corps de bronze! nudité ornée; grâce orientale; ombre du chapeau sur les yeux, où la naissance du regard se perd et s'immatérialise. Sourire des lèvres; douceur des joues.

Son petit corps délicat, de grâce un peu frêle et guindée; — dureté du bronze; — cuirasses ouvragées des jambes, qui n'emprisonnent que le mollet et d'où la cuisse après semble sortir attendrie.

[30] Gide, *Journal* (1889-1939), pp. 717-18.
[31] Gide, preface to the 1927 edition of *Les Nourritures terrestres* in *Romans, récits et sôties*, pp. 250 and 249.

> Etrangeté même de cet accoutrement impudique, et la nervosité ten-
> due des petits bras qui tiennent ou la pierre ou le sabre. J'aimerais à
> mon gré l'évoquer devant moi. Longtemps j'ai regardé — tâchant d'ap-
> prendre, de retenir en moi ces lignes délicieuses, ce pli du ventre im-
> médiatement sous les côtes et que creuse la respiration, et jusqu'à cette
> sécheresse du muscle qui joint le haut du sein à l'épaule droite — et ce
> pli un peu cassé du haut de la cuisse — et cette extraordinaire planitude
> des reins sitôt au-dessus du sacrum...[32]

Here, the observer animates the statue, infusing his body with life
through a prurient gaze, itself the vehicle of homosexual signals. The
degree of its fixity determines whether or not the erotic "rencontre"
will take place. David's return gaze is coy, as if veiled in the shadow
of a hat, at once inviting and evasive. It beckons the viewer to follow
each alluring detail of the body with his eyes: from lips and cheeks
to the smallest muscle and subtlest fold or joint. Each part is reduced
to an ornament of nudity ("nudité ornée") and then subdivided into
qualities or properties ascribed to the part: "sourire des lèvres,"
"douceur des joues," "pli du ventre," "planitude des reins." The result
is an interconnecting chain of charged synechdoches articulating the
unspoken text of desire. Later, in *Les Nourritures terrestres*, mouth, eyes
and hands provide the *locus amoenus* of magnetic attraction:

> Et comme, pour le ressusciter, Elisée, sur le fils de la Sunamite — "la
> bouche sur sa bouche, et les yeux sur ses yeux, et les mains sur ses
> mains, s'étendit" — mon grand coeur rayonnant contre ton âme encore
> ténébreuse, m'étendre sur toi tout entier, ma bouche sur ta bouche,
> et mon front sur ton front, tes mains froides dans mes mains brûlantes,
> et mon coeur palpitant... ("Et la chair de l'enfant se réchauffa," est-il
> écrit...) afin que dans la volupté tu t'éveilles — *puis me laisses* — pour une
> vie palpitante et déréglée. (*NT* 171; Gide's emphasis)

In this passage, the cool, sublimated contemplation of the novice yields
to a more volatile register. Each part of the body is electrically united
with its mirror likeness in a male Other, thus breaching the distance
required by aestheticized love. The words "palpitante" and "déréglée"
underscore the sense of trangression which has already been established
by the travesty of an Old Testament miracle (Elijah's resuscitation
of the widow woman's son [1, Kings 17:1]).

While the sense of transgression is never dispelled, nor the technique of metonymy abandoned, they are nonetheless diffused throughout

---

[32] Gide, *Journal* (1889-1939), p. 63.

the text by means of poetic associations that spatialize and enlarge the figuration of what might now be called the "homotextual body." This effect is achieved in part through extended metaphors that double as erotic euphemisms. Pores and orifices are penetrated like the eight doors in Book V (which parallel the eight books of *Les Nourritures*) and the doorway in the grain cellar reveals the place where symbolic seed is stored: "Grains, je garde de vous une poignée; je la sème en mon champ fertile…" (*NT* 211-12). The dairy harbors the acrid odor and taste of sweat, the damp and pliant texture associated with cheese, but also with flesh. In the fruit room, the raisins and apples arranged in coquettish piles recall the rounded contours of shoulders, thighs and buttocks, and the distillery, described as a "foyer ardent" containing "machines ténébreuses" induces a state of inner intoxication (*NT* 213). Here, the body is transformed into a sacred barn — a folk version of Solomon's temple (whose pillars were crowned with pomegranates). Indeed, the pomegranate, which like the fig enjoys a privileged status as an emblem of sexuality and fertility, emerges as one of the primary figures of *Les Nourritures*; it is the only fruit to which an entire poem is dedicated ("Ronde de la Grenade").

A complex system of metonymical displacements provides the mediation between sense and sexuality and between internal and external nature. The body is broken up into synecdoches of food and drink, "literalized" through the evocation of hunger and thirst, and then "remetaphorized" as spiritual states or euphemisms for sexual appetite. These images are further developed into a network of signs organized around the crossing of corporal topography with humanized landscape. The body is featured as a world map comprised of sensitive sites of feeling just as place-names and geological formations constitute the landmarks of emotional peregrinations. In the "travelogue" sections, predominant in Books III and VII, erotic localities such as "Alger," "Biskra," "Blidah," "Chetma" and "Touggourt" are comparable to the peripheral regions of the body where pleasure is concentrated. The head, normally considered the seat of reason and self-control, is subordinated to the body's tactile surface and outermost extremities. Desert sands are apprehended through naked feet, and refreshing oases experienced through cupped hands.

The dispersal and relocation of sensation to marginal zones embodies a discursive, rambling narrative movement which, in addition to eroding the traditional hierarchy of the anatomy, also undermines traditional narrative organization. In this sense, Gide's deployment of homosexual signs combines a poetics of marginality with an antiestablishment narrative strategy based on the diffusion and dissipation of textual energy.

The Homotextual Counter-Code

Though the "homosexual sign" is hardly susceptible to systematic definition, a suggestive attempt at one has been offered by Harold Beaver, itself derivative of Proust's four-page sentence describing the behavioral rituals of homosexuals in *Contre Sainte-Beuve*. Proust dilates on every aspect of homoerotic sighting. Where Beaver summarizes the homosexual's "urge to interpret whatever transpires, or fails to transpire, between himself and every chance acquaintance" with a list of signs equally applicable to heterosexual communication ("the momentary glimpse," "the sporadic gesture," "the sudden slippage," "the lowered guard"), Proust sets this semiotics in motion with a social vignette that records the exchange of signals between the narrator and a certain "comte de Quercy":

> Non seulement il n'avait vu, mais me voyait, car dès que je me tournai vers lui pour le saluer, tâchant d'attirer l'attention de son visage souriant d'un autre côté du salon et de ses yeux épiant "la rousse," il me tendit la main et n'eut qu'à utiliser pour moi sans bouger son sourire disponible et son regard vacant que je pouvais prendre pour une amabilité pour moi puisqu'il me disait bonjour de sa main libre, que j'aurais pu prendre pour une ironie contre moi si je ne lui avais pas dit bonjour,...

Each discernible nuance of coded expression is enumerated by Proust, from the ambiguously "vacant stare," to the displaceable vector of eye contact, to the cover or alibi lest the signs be betrayed. The locking of little fingers between the narrator and the Count ("J'avais serré le quatrième doigt qui semblait regretter dans une inflexion mélancholique l'anneau d'archevêque; j'étais pour ainsi dire entré par effraction dans son bonjour incessant..."), and Proust's subsequent comparison of homosexual solidarity to "une sorte de franc-maçonnerie qui est plus vaste que celle des Juifs" also seems to inform Beaver's assertion that[33]:

> Homosexuals, like Masons, live not in an alternative culture but in a duplicate culture of constantly interrupted and overlapping roles...

[33] Marcel Proust, *Contre Sainte-Beuve* (Paris: Gallimard, 1954), pp. 300, 304.

Every sign becomes duplicitous, slipping back and forth across a wavering line, once the heterosexual antithesis between love and friendship has been breached.[34]

Proust's projections of "la race maudite" together with Beaver's interpolations allow us to interpret numerous thematic structures within *Les Nourritures* in terms of a generalized play of "homosexual signs." The notion of the chance encounter is exemplified by the "Ballade de toutes les rencontres" in Book VI, by Gide's use of "Rencontres" as a subheading throughout the *Nouvelles nourritures* (1935), and by Ménalque's doctrine of "disponibilité":

...je disais que chaque nouveauté doit nous trouver tout entiers disponibles. (184)

Je vivais dans la perpétuelle attente, délicieuse, de n'importe quel avenir... (185)

...Mon âme était l'auberge ouverte au carrefour; ce qui voulait entrer, entrait. Je me suis fait ductile, à l'amiable, disponible par tous mes sens, attentif, écouteur jusqu'à n'avoir plus *une* pensée personnelle, capteur de toute émotion en passage, et réaction si minime que je ne tenais plus rien pour mal plutôt que de protester devant rien. (185-86)

Mon coeur naturellement aimant et comme liquide se répandait de toutes parts; aucune joie ne me semblait appartenir à moi-même; j'y invitais chacun de rencontre, et lorsque j'étais seul à jouir, ce n'était qu'à force d'orgueil. (188).

Ménalque defines what might be called the "promiscuous sign": a free-floating signifier that attaches itself to any "available" referent. The "inn at the crossroads" with its doors flung open suggests a haven where marginal, exiled signs can freely associate. Such signs point allusively to stages of sexual emancipation: the excitement of erotic anticipation ("la perpétuelle attente, délicieuse"), the joy in removing barriers to access to the body ("ce qui voulait entrer, entrait"), the rejection of intellectual discrimination (jusqu'à n'avoir plus une pensée personnelle"), the sensations of elasticity, penetration ("...je ne cherchais plus rien qu'une pénétration toujours plus simple de la nature" [*NT* 185]) and pure "jouissance." The body, as a text, becomes a fluid, fluctuating scene of encounter that temporarily unites difference— heterogeneous sense impressions, banished emotions, alienated

[34] Harold Beaver, "Homosexual Signs," *Critical Inquiry* 8, no. 2 (Autumn 1981), 104-05.

strangers. Homosexual difference, analogous in Proust's less optimistic account to the fatal "tare" or stigma of Judaism, is now glorified as the agent of a revolutionary potentiality that refutes the realm of sterile expectations and substitutes in its place a principle of fantasy and surprise. "Le rêve de demain est une joie, mais la joie de demain en est une autre," says the narrator of *Les Nourritures* to the young novice Nathanaël, and with such alluring promises of a future filled with real and imaginary conquests — each accruing the supreme value of *differing* from the foreseeable options available to conventional men — he encourages his charge to embrace the cause of difference (*NT* 168). He will achieve this end both by *dis*-possessing himself of worldly ambitions, prudish mores and material goods, and by submitting himself to the rituals of *di*-vestiture, that is, stripping down and rendering naked mind and flesh alike.

Here we might begin to establish specific thematic affinities between the poetics of "dénuement" and an antibourgeois moral code that would ultimately induce Gide to become a fellow traveller in the 1930s. When in 1932 he published an excerpt of his "Pages de Journal" in the *Nouvelle Revue Française* claiming, "De coeur, de tempérament, de pensée, j'ai toujours été communiste," he was presumably referring to the diatribes against capitalist accumulation propounded as early as 1897 in *Les Nourritures*.[35] If one traces allusions to nakedness, in addition to finding

[35] André Gide, "Pages de *Journal*, " *La Nouvelle Revue Française* 29 (October 1932), 481-506. "Dénuement," grafted onto Marxism after first taking root in Gide's early reading of the Gospels (particularly Pauline abnegation), was transformed from an abstract principle and purely literary construct *into an act*, when Gide in preparation for his trip to the Congo sold off a major portion of his personal library. The gesture caused consternation among close friends and colleagues for the collection included numerous original editions of Symbolist works, often signed or personally dedicated. Gide undoubtedly only added flame to the fire with his "preface" to the catalogue of the auction, a statement promulgating intellectual and material divestiture with the same high moral tone of *Les Nourritures*:

Le goût de la propriété n'a, chez moi, jamais été bien vif. Il me paraît que la plupart de nos possessions sur cette terre sont moins faites pour augmenter notre joie, que nos regrets de devoir un jour les quitter. Au surplus, peu soigneux, j'ai sans cesse la crainte que les objets que je détiens ainsi ne s'abîment; qu'ils ne s'abîment davantage encore si, partant en voyage, je les abandonne longtemps. Projetant une longue absence, j'ai donc pris le parti de me séparer de livres acquis en un temps où j'étais moins sage, que je ne conservais que par faste; d'autres enfin qui me sont demeurés chers entre tous aussi longtemps qu'ils n'éveillaient en moi que des souvenirs d'amitié. J'y ajoute les exemplaires que je m'étais réservés de mes premiers livres, dont les éditions

it associated with the traditional prelapserian ideals of spiritual purity, moral sincerity and the innocent primitive, one also discovers it
is closely tied to the act of casting off clothes, money, worldly possessions and domestic obligations. Books, the clothing of the mind, are
undressed, shed like the bark of a tree, rejected like the tenets of
middle-class morality:

> Du plus haut de leurs hautes branches, les eucalyptus délivrés laissaient
> tomber leur vieille écorce; elle pendait, protection usée, *comme un habit
> que le soleil rend inutile, comme ma vieille morale qui ne valait que pour l'hiver.*
> (*NT* 180; my emphasis)

Interpreting the capitalist notion of "property" in its fullest sense —
namely, as containing an ideology of sexual possession and
exclusivity — the narrator poses against it yet again the notion of
"dénuement," similarly extended, to include a counter-ideology of anti-
marriage and sexual availability. His lament, "Ames jamais suffisament dénuées pour être enfin suffisament emplies d'amour — d'amour,
d'attentes et d'espérance, qui sont nos seules vraies possessions" (*NT*
205), serves as a pendant to a didactically explicated principle of
"nomadism" presented in Book IV:

> Certains m'accusèrent d'égoïsme; je les accusai de sottise. J'avais la
> prétention de n'aimer point quelqu'un, homme ou femme, mais bien
> l'amitié, l'affection ou l'amour. En le donnant à l'un je n'eusse pas voulu
> l'enlever à quelque autre, et ne faisais que me prêter. Pas plus je ne
> voulais accaparer le corps ou le coeur d'aucun autre; nomade ici com-
> me envers la nature, je ne m'arrêtais nulle part. Toute préférence me
> semblait injustice; voulant rester à tous, je ne me donnais pas à quel-
> qu'un. (*NT* 188).

Sexual nomadism is predicated on an economy of pleasure that undermines the capitalist conventions of exchange: partners are no longer
to be bought and sold, their fidelity guaranteed with either sentimental
or material bonds; rather, pleasure will circulate freely, with the body
of the beloved "lent," borrowed at no cost, or offered as a gift. "Rien,"
Gide would argue later in *Les Nouvelles Nourritures* (a sequel written
in 1935 at the height of his enthusiasm for Marxist precepts), "ne

---

originales sont devenues rares. A quoi bon les garder dans une armoire d'où
jamais je ne les sortais? Ils pourront amuser quelques bibliophiles, mieux
capables que moi de les apprécier. (*Catalogue de Livres et Manuscripts provenant
de la Bibliothèque de M. André Gide* [Paris: Librairie Ancienne Honoré Cham-
pion, 1925]).

s'épanouit que par offrande... Tout mûrit pour le don et se parachève en offrande"[36] (italicized in text).

This emancipatory principle of gifts — of unrecompensed exchange and unmonitored circulation — emerges as one of the absolute laws of the homotextual counter-code in both the early and later versions of *Les Nourritures*. Where in the earlier text this law is conjoined with a polemic against marriage (informed in part by the intertext of Gide's own troubled conjugal life), it is further ramified in *Les Nouvelles Nourritures* to encompass the repudiation of motherhood. The denatured infant who refuses his mother's breast, preferring to her milk a hardy "nourriture" or his own sap, is heralded as the agent of a new society. Later the myth of Achilles' heel is re-read as a caveat against a castrating maternal presence: "Sache comprendre la fable grecque: Elle nous enseigne qu'Achille était invulnérable, sauf en cet endroit de son corps qu'attendrissait le souvenir du contact des doigts maternels" (*NN* 298). Finally, the entire nuclear family is rejected in favor of a society no longer governed by outmoded structures of kinship, legitimacy and conventional sex roles. This incendiary message is transmitted most emphatically when Lot's story is retold as a parable of the forthcoming sexual revolution: "L'on raconte que la femme de Loth, pour avoir voulu regarder en arrière, fut changée en statue de sel, c'est-à-dire: de larmes figées. Tourné vers l'avenir, Loth couche alors avec ses filles. Ainsi soit-il" (*NN* 299).

Gide's subversive transformation of Greek myths and biblical parables, particularly those that underscore the violation of taboos or the testing of blood ties, implies a radically new society grounded on open sexuality, a kind of homosexual utopia, ideologically compatible with Marxist ideals of individual self-realization. On a less political level, however, these revisionist foundation myths also suggest a hearkening back on Gide's part to what Barthes refers to as the "archaic forms" of love — forms distinguished by that quality of having already been rehearsed elsewhere, yet retaining the aura of a sacred drama.[37] "L'énamoration," Barthes put forth, "est un *drame*, si l'on veut bien rendre à ce mot le sens archaïque que Nietzsche lui donne: 'Le drame antique avait en vue de grandes scènes

---

[36] Gide, *Les Nouvelles Nourritures*, in *Romans, récits et sôties*, p. 261. All further references to this work will appear in the text abbreviated *NN*.

[37] The mythical "types" of love are commemorated most explicitly in the "Ballade des plus célèbres amants" where, among others, Soleiman and Balkis, Bathsheba and David, Ariadne and Theseus and Eurydice and Orpheus each make a ghostly appearance.

déclamatoires, ce qui excluait l'action (celles-ci avait lieu *avant* ou *der-rière* la scène).'" As Barthes dilates on Nietzsche's derivation of Greek "offstage love," one is tempted to insert into the sequence the ensem-ble of romantic postures, postulates and expostulations furnished by Gide's *Nourritures*, for they too convey the sense of being surrogate expressions of rigorously excluded actions. In the beseeching gaze and speechless awe of Nathanaël's tutor, in the cold, yet gracious ac-quiescence of the neophyte, in the quavering voice and oblique glance, one detects the age-old performance of rapture, a performance which, at least for Barthes and Gide, will eventually evolve into private ritual, secretly enacted between the lover and himself: "C'est ma propre légende locale," Barthes confesses, "ma petite historie sainte que je me déclame à moi-même, et cette déclamation d'un fait accompli (figé, embaumé, retiré de tout faire) est le discours amoureux."[38] Gide's nar-rator also engages in private declarations of love, revivals of dead memories, interiorized pantomines of an act occurring elsewhere, parodic, histrionic ceremonies attesting to the displacement of the homosexual body to the homotextual sphere of discourse. This discourse, like the lover it replaces, situates itself just beyond the margins of bourgeois society, complementing on a narrative level the dislocation or "off-staging" of the reader's perspective.

In *Si le grain ne meurt*, a work that treats homosexuality far less poetically, the same discourse can be found, though cloaked in the more traditional narrative conventions of autobiography. Here an elite caste of exiles from heterosexual society (Gide, Oscar Wilde, Lord Alfred Douglas) embark on a pilgrimage through North Africa (the symbolic periphery of European values) in quest of society's marginals: the *ragazzi* of the casbah, the shepherd boys who languish in remote Kabylian villages, the "enfants prodigues" who obligingly wait for hours in public parks and gardens. Without a doubt, Gide was drawn to this nomadic, *déclassé* population just as he was drawn to textual equivalents for marginality, difference and dispossession.[39] The seduc-tion of the margin is what ultimately draws out the "écart" of Gide's hyperbole, luring it from its dignified retreat into classical askesis.

---

[38] Barthes, *Fragments d'un discours amoureux*, p. 110.

[39] The homosexual novel that Barthes never wrote (or displaced into the superficially more theoretical genre of *Fragments*), a novel of homoerotic encounters, brushes with the slightly dangerous underworld of Turkish baths and sleazy bars, and aimless voyages coupled with accounts of the dispossessed life of the social marginal, was iden-tified by Barthes in the oeuvre of Renaud Camus. The fictive counterpart of Bar-thes's theory, heavily inflected with Barthesian stylistic conceits, Camus's writings

Though the gestures of hyperbole remain tempered, governed by the laws of abstinence and restraint which Foucault would trace in the Greek ethics of sexuality ("diététique," "économique," "érotique"), they nonetheless communicate to the Other a counter-code of homotextual signs, calibrating the nuances of erotic experience and simulating the hypostatized forms of "deviation."[40]

include: *Passage* (1975), *Travers* (1978), *Tricks* (1979) for which Barthes wrote the preface, *Buena Vista Park* (1980), and *Journal d'un voyage en France* (1981).

In the preface to *Tricks*, Barthes praises "ce *passage* du sexe au discours," holding up Camus's thirty-three miniature *récits* as examples of a kind of homotextual "writing degree zero": "Notre époque interprète beaucoup, mais les récits de Renaud Camus sont neutres, ils n'entrent pas dans le jeu de l'Interprétation. Ce sont des sortes d'à-plats, sans ombre et comme *sans arrière-pensées*. Et encore une fois, seule l'écriture permet cette pureté, ce matin de l'énonciation, inconnu de la parole, qui est toujours un enchevêtrement retors d'intentions cachées. N'étaient leur taille et leur sujet, ces *Tricks* devraient faire penser à des Haïkus; car le Haïku unit un ascétisme de la forme (qui coupe net l'envie d'interpréter) et un hédonisme si tranquille, qu'on peut dire seulement du plaisir qu'*il est là* (ce qui est aussi le contraire de l'Interprétation)" (Paris: Mazarine, 1979, p. 15; Barthes's emphasis). This pure, unmediated enunciation of the sexual act — beyond Interpretation — finds its corollary in Gide's *Carnets d'Egypte* and *Ainsi soit-il* in which Gide, self-portrayed as a homosexual Robinson, openly recounts the vagaries of his sexual exploits behind the great pyramids. The fact that Barthes also lauded Gide for the "récit neutre" implies that Gide and Camus were Barthes's two principal models of an ideal homosexual writing.

[40] Michel Foucault, *L'Usage des plaisirs*, vol. II of *Histoire de la sexualité* (Paris: Gallimard, 1984), especially ch. 2-4.

V

THE ETIOLOGY OF THE UNSPOKEN

NEGATION AND GENDER IN THE *RÉCITS**

> Le récit, construction médiate, retardée:
> Freud ne fait pas autre chose en écrivant ses
> "cas."
>
> Roland Barthes, *L'Obvie et l'obtus*

In 1901, just one year prior to the redaction of Gide's first *récit*, *L'Immoraliste*, Freud published his *Psychopathology of Everyday Life*. In this work, Freud introduced the concept of *Fehlleistung*, translated with the English neologism "Parapraxis" (for there as yet existed no precise English equivalent), in turn devised as a synonym for the literal sense of "faulty function." What is now loosely alluded to with a host of interrelated designations ranging from "the Freudian slip" or "lapsus" to the "misreading," possessed in Freud's native tongue a more unified frame of reference. "The German language," as Laplanche and Pontalis point out, "brings out the common denominator of all these mistakes by giving the prefix 'ver-' to many of the words which describe them: *das Vergessen* (forgetting), *das Versprechen* (slip of the tongue), *das Verlesen* (misreading), *das Verschreiben* (slip of the pen), *das Vergreifen* (bungled action), *das Verlieren* (mislaying)."[1]

---

* The section of this chapter on "Female Impersonations in *L'Ecole des femmes*, *Robert* and *Geneviève*" has appeared as an article in *Romanic Review* 78, no. 3 (May 1986) 264-78. Reprinted here by permission.

[1] J. Laplanche and J.B. Pontalis, *The Language of Psychoanalysis*, tr. Donald Nicholson-Smith (New York: Norton, 1973), p. 300.

105

Although other linguists and psychoanalysts (Meringer and Meyer, Ruths, Ernest Jones) had already identified significant theoretical aspects of the slip, it was Freud who interpreted them inventively as psychical phenomena, explicable as indications of suppressed motives, intuitions or neuroses. Commenting on the corrections of detail made by friends and former patients to his own reports of their analyses (errors that he may have made subconsciously to enhance the ingenuity or credibility of his case studies), Freud unabashedly noted: *"Here once again we find an unobserved error taking the place of an intentional concealment or repression"* (Freud's emphases). [2]

In an analysis of Gide's *récits* — the most unequivocally classical and rhetorically understated of his writings — Freud's concept of the slip or "unobserved error" is particularly useful, especially in interpreting the psychosexual implications of yet another form of negative writing — *the unspoken*. Though the theory of the slip applies ostensibly to what is said rather than to what is not stated, Freud leaves open the specification of the possible forms such "verbal disturbances" can take. One can thus assume that inadvertent omissions or ellipses qualify as legitimate slips of the tongue just as easily as figures of spoken language, such as accidental obscenities, unintentional puns, or mispronounced names. Using this category of the inadvertent omission, we might even add to Freud's list of errors governed by the prefix 'ver-' a new term: *das Verschmieren* ("to smear, daub, to waste paper in writing"), a term that could be stretched to mean "a slip of the text." Unlike Freud's "slip of the pen," which focuses on the writer's personal motives for committing an error, the "slip of the text" would refer to a purely *textual* stratum of unintentionality, the *un*written implications of what is pointedly implied by the *un*spoken. We will be looking then not only at what Gide's narrators seem to be withholding from their confessions, but also at specific moments in the *récit* where what is said by these fictional narrators is belied by what the text, as a narrative system, "accidentally" suggests (and we put accidental in quotations because these unwritten implications may in fact be fully intended by the author).

The *récit* lends itself particularly well to the double-pronged, metanarrative problematic of the unspoken and the unwritten because it constitutes the quintessential genre of *spoken* confession and auto-analysis. From *La Princesse de Clèves* and *Adolphe* to Gide's *L'Immoraliste*

[2] Sigmund Freud, *The Psychopathology of Everyday Life*, tr. Alan Tyson (same as Vol. VI of Standard Edition) (New York: Norton, 1965), p. 220.

(1902), *La Porte étroite* (1909), *La Symphonie pastorale* (1919) and the trilogy of *L'Ecole des femmes* (1929-1936), professions of truth, sincerity and contrition, typical of the *récit's* first-person narrators, automatically alert the reader to traces of duplicity, unreliability or outright mendacity. Indeed, one could argue, and many critics have, that for the *récit* what is dissimulated or not articulated plays a more significant role in the text's interpretation than what is actually reported.

The figures of the unspoken have received considerable attention in recent poststructuralist theory, but it is Barthes who perhaps goes the farthest in extending the definitions of such figures into the critical discourse of textuality. Most of Barthes's major books are structured as tropologies (*SZ*, *Le Plaisir du texte*, *Fragments d'un discours amoureux*) or assemblages of expressive fragments ("tableautins") indexed according to "idées reçues," coded citations, or seemingly detached perceptions falling roughly in a field of philosophical inquiry. Barthes even acknowledged Gide as the instigator of this practice. "Son premier texte," Barthes writes of himself, "...est fait de fragments; ce choix est alors justifié à la manière gidienne parce que l'incohérence est préférable à l'ordre qui déforme. Depuis, en fait, il n'a cessé de pratiquer l'écriture courte."[3] Guided by Gide, Barthes devoted himself to inventing a nomenclature for verbal and textual lacunae, the pauses and gaps enabling discourse to collapse into fragments or condense into allusive axioms. Among his most suggestive labels for these deletions were: "l'in-dicible" (corresponding approximately to unspeakable "jouissance"); "l'inter-dite" (that which is read "between the lines," or which outlaws "jouissance" to the speaking subject); and "l'inter-texte" (roughly, referentiality "en abyme"). Introduced in *Le Plaisir du texte*, the first two terms, "l'in-dicible" and "l'inter-dite," directly call up Barthes's master-trope of textual pleasure ("plaisir/jouissance") itself dependent on a Lacanian "inter-texte." "Qu'est-ce que c'est que la jouissance?" Lacan had queried rhetorically in *Encore* in order to obtain a rejoinder with obvious significance for the problem of negative

[3] Roland Barthes, *Roland Barthes* (Paris: Seuil, 1975), p. 97. This section, subtitled "Le cercle des fragments," contains a chain of associations in which the links are, ironically, missing. Barthes offers the chain to illustrate that fragments are also fragmented unto themselves: "Soit les mots: *fragment, cercle, Gide, catch, asyndète, peinture, dissertation, Zen, intermezzo*; imaginez un discours qui puisse les lier. Eh bien, ce sera tout simplement ce fragment-ci." Resituating each of these elements in "ce fragment-ci," we discover that the fragment entitled "Gide" breaks down into smaller "fragments-Barthes."

writing: "Elle se réduit ici à n'être qu'une instance négative. La jouissance, c'est ce qui ne sert à rien."[4] With the addition of Lacan's concept of "jouissance" as "that which amounts to nothing," that is, gratuitous and thoroughly disinterested, we return full circle to Gide's positive valuation of nothing, of "*rien*" via Barthes's expansion on the same term in his essay on Pierre Loti:

> Donc, il se passe: *rien*. Ce *rien*, cependant, il faut le dire. Comment dire: *rien*? On se trouve ici devant un grand paradoxe d'écriture: *rien* ne peut se dire que *rien*; *rien* est peut-être le seul mot de la langue qui n'admet aucune périphrase, aucune métaphore, aucun synonyme, aucun substitut; car dire *rien* autrement que par son pur dénotant (le mot "rien"), c'est aussitôt remplir le rien, le démentir: tel Orphée qui perd Eurydice en se retournant vers elle, *rien* perd un peu de son sens, chaque fois qu'on l'énonce (qu'on le dé-nonce). Il faut donc tricher. Le *rien* ne peut être pris par le discours que de biais, en écharpe, par une sorte d'allusion déceptive.[5]

One might begin here to construct a three-way "imaginary interview" (Gide's favorite form of intimate exchange) between Gide, Barthes and Lacan, revolving around the volatile topic of sexuality and the unspeakable. Lacanian "jouissance," predicated on an erotico-textual ideal of "nothing," seems to prompt Barthes's theory of "nothing" as the sign which refers to insatisfaction and structurally resembles the paradoxical myth of Orphic love (its expression "speaks" the impossibility of its expression). The only means of outsmarting this paradox, Barthes insinuates, is "to cheat," and with this curious recommendation he brings to mind Gide's most sophicaticated narrative formulas for representing the unspeakable on the sly. Plunging his readers into a matrix of unreliable narrators characteristically divided between their wish on the one hand to "de-negate" the repressive silence surrounding their homosexual penchants and, on the other hand, to maintain the appearances of a heterosexual conscience, Gide approaches the unspeakable theme of his own complicated sexual identity "on the bias," from the oblique angle, as a "tricheur." Even in

[4] Jacques Lacan, *Le Séminaire, Livre XX (Encore)*, ed. Jacques-Alain Miller (Paris: Seuil, 1975), p. 10. The extent to which this seminar on "jouissance" dated 1972 directly informs Barthes's writing on the same subject in *Le Plaisir du texte* is confirmed by Barthes's allusions to Lacan as well as to the proximity in dates (*Le Plaisir* was published in 1973).

[5] Roland Barthes, *Nouveaux Essais critiques* in *Le Degré zéro de l'écriture* (Paris: Seuil, 1972), p. 173.

one of his last works to be published — *Et nunc manet in te* (1947) — Gide's frank and highly personal account of the impact of his preference for the male sex on his marriage, is introduced indirectly in the guise of a regretful homage to the memory of his dead wife. Is it a "slip of the text" that his alleged "ignorance" of Madeleine's desire strikes a false note, revealing itself upon close inspection as a subterfuge for his unwillingness to acknowledge at the time what failed to take place in their conjugal life? Despite his avowal of the unutterable "whiteness" of the marriage, and by implication his covert denial of feminine "jouissance," one senses an overly convenient expiation of guilt that shelters his homosexual "parti pris" from the barbs of an unspoken feminine accusation:

> Je m'étonne aujourd'hui de cette aberration qui m'amenait à croire que, plus mon amour était éthéré, et plus il était digne d'elle — gardant cette naïveté de ne me demander jamais si la contenterait un amour tout désincarné. Que mes désirs charnels s'adressassent à d'autres objets, je ne m'en inquiétais donc guère. Et même j'en arrivais à me persuader confortablement, que mieux valait ainsi. Les désirs, pensais-je, sont le propre de l'homme; il m'était rassurant de ne pas admettre que la femme en pût éprouver de semblables; ou seulement les femmes de "mauvaise vie." *Telle était mon inconscience, il faut bien que j'avoue cette énormité, et qui ne peut trouver d'explication ou d'excuse que dans l'ignorance où m'avait entretenu la vie,* ne m'ayant présenté d'exemples que de ces admirables figures de femmes, penchées au-dessus de mon enfance: de ma mère d'abord... (my emphases)[6]

But to be fair, Gide, in this passage, can hardly be accused of advancing his own pedophilic interests at the expense of his late wife's memory, for he appears genuinely anxious to somehow posthumously vitiate the reproach of her lost voice. Taking up her abandoned role, speaking her part like a prompter or ventriloquist, pleading her case by describing the void that he himself, as her husband, helped to create, Gide effects a transition from "ignorant" spouse to angry feminist.

The strange invention of this "feminist Gide" implies a novel development in the evolving gender of the Gidean narrative voice. It emerges as a fundamentally bisexual voice, a male voice born of the feminine unspoken, a homosexual voice identifying with the historical oppression of women and apologizing for its own failure

---

[6] André Gide, *Et nunc manet in te* (Neuchâtel: Ides et Calendes, 1947), pp. 22-23.

to remedy the negation of "Her" desire. Like the voice perfected by Marguerite Yourcenar in *Les Mémoires d'Hadrian*, in which one finds a "homotextual" inflection grafted onto a "gynotextual" sensibility, Gide's entails an equally complex "voice-over" of gender. When he speaks the part of Eveline in *L'Ecole des femmes* (whose journal plots the nascence of a kind of pre- or proto-feminist consciousness) and later that of her daughter Geneviève (whose antisexism is a given), the contemporary reader becomes acutely aware of the potentially counterfeit nature of a masculine author who sets himself up as the master of a stridently feminine "écriture." Can the suppressed voice of a woman be authentically and adequately represented by a man? Is the homosexual, because of the marginality of his status in society (which he shares with women), thus a better spokesman for feminism than the heterosexual male? Or, is the woman's voice, as spoken by Gide, ultimately returned to another order of the unspoken, slipping through the net of the narrator's sexual indeterminacy — the neither/nor of masculine/feminine — into an even denser realm of negation? These questions are difficult to answer without raising the controversial issue of Gide's misogyny or confronting the charged opinions surrounding sexual politics in today's academic institutions, but it is precisely these concerns that render the thematic intersection of writing, sexuality, gender and negation in Gide's stylistically classical works of particular interest to contemporary theory and criticism.

Slips of the Text (L'Immoraliste)

An incompletely formulated yet nonetheless coherent definition of the slip or lapsus can be discovered *in nuce* within Gide's oeuvre, not in relation to his *récits* (where we intend to resituate it), but in the context of his critical remarks on the nature of myth and his efforts to transpose classical myths into the idiom of modern theater. As Walter Benjamin noted in his review of Gide's *Oedipe* (staged in 1930), this was a theater of language — of excessive "bavardage" in which archetypal heroes (Oedipus, Saul, Theseus) were allowed to define themselves as *myths* in an outburst of anger, a flash of tenderness, or a slip of the tongue. Benjamin emphasized in his essay entitled "Oedipe ou le mythe raisonnable," that unlike the Sophoclean Oedipus who remains a mute pawn of Fate, Gide's Oedipe dares to speak out, to interpret his destiny subjectively. During the second act of the play, he angrily refuses Tiresias' orthodox recourse to the Gods' will as a

means of explaining the origin of his personal and political tribulations: "Que chercher près d'un Dieu? Des réponses. Je me sentais moi-
même une réponse à je ne savais encore quelle question."[7] The fact
that Gide's Oedipe is allowed to "answer back" to the supercilious pro-
phet is, according to Benjamin, a long overdue settling of accounts:

> Le drame de Sophocle a cinq actes; c'est à la fin du second que le
> voyant Tirésias quitte la scène. Oedipe aura dû attendre deux
> millénaires pour engager avec lui, chez Gide, le grand débat au cours
> duquel il exprime ce que, chez Sophocle, il n'eût pas même osé penser.[8]

As willful author of both question and answer, this Oedipus reserves
the right to define his own fate even when this necessitates the recognition of his own inner "monstrosity": "Engourdi dans la récompense,
je dors depuis vingt ans. Mais à présent, enfin j'écoute en moi le
monstre nouveau qui s'étire. Un grand destin m'attend, tapi dans les
ombres du soir. Oedipe, le temps de la quiétude est passé. Réveille-
toi de ton bonheur."[9] Oedipe's premonition of his future monstrosity
(as a myth) gives him the right to both define the crime and determine the nature of his punishment. No longer is his guilt the result
of parricide and incest; it resides instead in the realization that his
twenty years of "bonheur" were purchased through ignorance of the
power-hungry motives of his family. He chooses to blind himself not
because he aims to do penance for crimes that were accidents of fate,
but because he can no longer endure contemplating the ignominious
scheming of Etéocle, Polynice, Créon, Ismène and Antigone.

In his reading of Oedipus, Gide seems intent on traveling beyond
Freud. Where Freud stops at a psychological allegory of mother-loving
and father-killing (the inherent drama of which is heightened by
theatrical representation), Gide gravitates towards the more prosaic
moment of the subject's verbal cure—often brought on by a slip of
the tongue. In *Thésée*, Gide's final *récit* (1946), it is the "bêtise" lodged
in pure "bavardage" that dismantles the protective facade of repression. Here, in the course of his uncontrollable chatter to himself,
Theseus stumbles unwittingly on the explanation for his "forgetting"
of the black sails (thereby provoking his father's suicide):

[7] André Gide, *Oedipe* in *Théâtre* (Paris: Gallimard, 1942), p. 288.
[8] Walter Benjamin, "Oedipe et le mythe raisonnable," *Walter Benjamin: Oeuvres*, II,
tr. Maurice de Gandillac (Paris: Denoël, 1971), 47.
[9] Gide, *Oedipe*, p. 289.

...J'ai regret d'avoir causé sa mort par un fatal oubli: celui de remplacer par des voiles blanches les voiles noires du bateau qui me ramenait de Crète, ainsi qu'il était convenu si je revenais victorieux de mon entreprise hasardeuse. On ne saurait penser à tout. Mais à vrai dire et si je m'interroge, ce que je ne fais jamais volontiers, je ne puis jurer que ce fût vraiment un oubli. Egée m'empêchait, vous dis-je, et surtout lorsque, par les philtres de la magicienne, de Médée, qui le trouvait, ainsi qu'il se trouvait lui-même, un peu vieux en tant que mari, il s'avisa, fâcheuse idée, de repiquer une seconde jeunesse, obstruant ainsi ma carrière, alors que c'est à chacun son tour. Toujours est-il qu'à la vue des voiles noires... j'appris en rentrant dans Athènes, qu'il s'était jeté dans la mer.[10]

In the colloquial expressions and commonplaces littered throughout Theseus' monologue, phrases such as "On ne saurait penser à tout," "il se trouvait lui-même, un peu vieux en tant que mari," "repiquer une seconde jeunesse" or "c'est à chacun son tour" one can locate instances of verbal lapsus. To carefully attuned post-Freudian ears, it is painfully obvious that "à chacun son tour" is a euphemism for patriarchal displacement—an act the violence of which is elided yet conveyed by the gap in the last sentence. In addition to euphemisms that have the effect of blocking out unpleasant truths, Theseus exhibits (and even admits to) the same tendency towards resisting self-questioning as do typical patients in analysis ("si je m'interroge, ce que je ne fais jamais volontiers..."). But as resistance erodes and the unconscious ploy of the "oubli" is abandoned, Theseus approaches the verge of speaking the unspeakable—acknowledging his parricide outright. By catching him at this pivotal moment in his "talking cure" Gide rewrites the legend of Theseus as Freud might have rewritten it—as a symbolic rendering of "dénégation," or the function of resistance in the affirmation of repression. Indeed, it is this rationality of repression (explicated so brilliantly by Freud in psychoanalytical terms) that constitutes what Benjamin identified as the "reasonableness" of the Gidean myth, noting how his characters "speak" the logic of their unconscious desires and fears. Gide himself, long before writing *Thésée*, had given theoretical expression to this notion in a brief essay on Greek mythology (1919):

Et l'on a rien compris au caractère de Thésée, par exemple, si l'on admet que l'audacieux héros

---

[10] Gide, *Thésée* in *Romans, récits et sôties*, pp. 1416-17.

> *Qui va du dieu des morts déshonorer la couche,*
>
> a laissé par simple inadvertance la voile noire au vaisseau qui le ramène en Grèce, cette "fatale" voile noire qui, trompant son père affligé, l'invite à se précipiter dans la mer, grâce à quoi Thésée entre en possession de son royaume. Un oubli? Allons donc! Il oublie de changer la voile comme il oublie Ariane à Naxos. Et je comprends que les pères n'enseignent pas cela aux enfants; mais pour cesser de réduire l'histoire de Thésée à l'insignifiance d'un conte de nourrice, il n'est qu'à restituer au héros sa conscience et sa résolution.[11]

Insisting on the implausibility of Theseus' plea of "not guilty" on the grounds of faulty recollection, Gide insinuates that the metonymy of the fatal black sails is itself the equivalent of a textual lapsus in the Greek version of the myth, thinly concealing yet exposing Theseus' underlying wish-fulfillment. In his modern adaptation of the myth, Gide, following the implied prescription of his argument, devised linguistic corollaries for the black veil — the insipid blunders, horrendous clichés and maladroit euphemisms that festoon Theseus' speech.

One of the major differences between the use of the lapsus in *Thésée* (Gide's final *récit*) and its uses in the early *L'Immoraliste*, lies in the fact that Theseus is a far less intelligent, hence less manipulative, narrator than Michel. The latter reveals himself as constantly on guard against the reader's powers of supposition, which means that Michel's slips of the tongue, like the author's slips of the text, are more difficult to localize. Frequently, evidence of Michel's narratorial circumspection is registered through anacoluthon, technically defined as "the failure, accidental or deliberate, to complete a sentence according to the structural plan on which it was started" and used more loosely by Barthes to signify "a break in sense or construction."[12] The first instance of this rupture occurs when Michel, having summoned his friends to North Africa to listen to his story, finds himself unable to articulate precisely why he needs them or what he wishes to say: "Car je suis à tel point de ma vie que je ne peux plus dépasser. Pourtant ce n'est pas lassitude. Mais je ne comprends plus. J'ai besoin... J'ai besoin de parler, vous dis-je."[13] Here, the verb "parler" is ironically

[11] André Gide, "Considérations sur la mythologie grecque," *Incidences* (Paris: Gallimard, 1924), p. 129.

[12] Barthes, "Pierre Loti," *Nouveaux Essais*, p. 173 (my paraphrase).

[13] André Gide, *L'Immoraliste*, ed. Elaine Marks and Richard Tedeschi (Toronto: Macmillan, 1963), p. 29. All further references to this work will appear in the text abbreviated *I*. I have used this edition because of its useful notes.

substituted for the "faille" or temporary failure of speech on Michel's part. As in the discourse of Theseus, it is the impromptu utterance or uncontrolled pause that signals the speaker's fear of disclosure.

What is it that Michel fears to disclose? Initially it appears to be the ambivalence of his sentiments towards his new bride Marceline: "j'étais habitué à sa grâce... Pour la première fois je m'étonnai, tant cette grâce me parût grande" (I, 33). Here, the gap records the shock as he recognizes his former indifference to Marceline. Suddenly, he senses her presence and though he claims at this moment to welcome it, assuring the reader of his pleasure, the ellipsis foreshadows the awkward moments of silence that will occur when communication between them deteriorates, and Marceline's presence resented as an imposition. This begins to happen soon enough during what turns out to be a grotesque travesty of a conventional wedding night. The blood which is shed comes not from Marceline's deflowering, but from Michel's diseased lungs, and, as if to add to the horror, it is staunched by a scarf that Marceline wears aroung her waist (a symbolic chastity belt), stealthily procured by Michel while she sleeps. Throughout this scene, Michel engages in a debate with himself marked by hesitations and ellipses, which themselves signal the textual spaces of transgression:

> Pourtant je me sentais très faible et fis monter du thé pour nous deux. Et tandis qu'elle l'apprêtait, très calme, un peu pâle elle-même, souriante, une sorte d'irritaion me vint de ce qu'elle n'eût rien su voir. Je me sentais injuste, il est vrai, me disais: si elle n'a rien vu, c'est que je cachais bien; n'importe; rien n'y fit; cela grandit en moi comme un instinct, m'envahit... à la fin cela fut trop fort; je n'y tins plus: comme distraitement, je lui dis:
> —J'ai craché le sang, cette nuit. (I, 37)

Michel's "irritation" at Marceline escalates rapidly into rage as he struggles inwardly against uttering the unspeakable revelation of his illness. Here the rupture in his narration, directly following the allusion to an "invading instinct," provides a clue, perhaps, to what he fears to divulge for it is this very instinct, so strong as to defy constraint, that will ultimately impel him away form his wife and towards members of his own sex.

If Michel's latent homosexuality is *pre*-figured in the "creux" or hollows of a spoken sentence, it also emerges after his return to health, as a *sub*-text in the analogy drawn between himself and a palimpsest:

> Et je me comparais aux palimpsestes; je goûtais la joie du savant, qui, sous les écritures plus récentes, découvre sur un même papier un

texte très ancien infiniment plus précieux. Quel était-il, ce texte oc-
culte? Pour le lire, ne fallait-il pas tout d'abord effacer les textes récents?
(I, 60)

The palimpsest is used as a metaphor of the quest for lost origins,
both in the historical sense (Adamic man, the Greek pagans) and in
the personal sense (childhood, freedom from social inhibitions, the
novelty of sensual experience). All this seems laudable in the context
of Michel's renewed resolve to live and fortify himself until one recalls
that the "textes récents" of the life that he would so eagerly "efface"
include his marriage to Marceline. Moreover, as we gradually learn,
references to "origins" are encoded as the original nature of the "vieil
homme," which, like the palimpsest, has been submerged in artificial
layers of civilization. It is for this reason that the new Michel no longer
devotes his intellectual energies to abstract, philological research, but
rather to studying the periods in history where political authority is
undermined (as when Altharic, a young Italian king, rebels against
his mother and aligns himself with the wicked Goths) or when high
culture begins to degenerate. In the course that he offers at the Col-
lège de France, he delights in focusing on the most decadent phase
of the late Roman empire for it permits him to fashion a thesis with
Nietzschean and Spenglerian overtones in its prophecy of decline and
fall in the West.

In Michel's description of the public's reaction to his lectures, Gide
may be seen not only to be alluding to the unstated subtext of
homoeroticism, but also to be committing a slip of the text in relation to his own narrative control over the reader. Implying that only
the inferior scholar is capable of enthusiasm ("Les historiens blâmèrent
une tendance, dirent-ils, aux généralisations trop rapides. D'autres
blâmèrent ma méthode; *et ceux qui me complimentèrent furent ceux qui
m'avaient le moins compris*" [I, 93; my emphasis]), Michel places the
scholar-reader in a double bind. If, like the historians in relation to
Michel's interpretation of history, we discern in *L'Immoraliste* a certain "tendency," then we reveal ourselves as morally prudish and
narrow-minded. If, on the other hand, we admit to being moved by
the text, then we betray our ignorance of its subversive content. The
work apparently falls at this point into its own trap: Michel's scorn
of the sympathetic reader parallels Gide's, who, by implication, ex-
horts the reader to relinquish his naïveté and adopt an attitude of suspicion towards the ruses of writing. But by rendering the reader less
susceptible, *L'Immoraliste* undoes a measure of its reader-manipulation.

Is this accident or plan? Certainly it can be interpreted as a version of the Freudian "unobserved error."

A comparable example of textual lapsus occurs in the treatment of a hallowed (even hackneyed) Gidean theme: the relationahip between truth and sincerity. After an extenuating soirée during which he has been compelled to "feign his feint," that is, disguise the fact that he is pretending to share the views of his colleagues, Michel concludes: "On ne peut à la fois être sincère et le paraître" (I, 90). Whether this is interpreted as a statement of fact or a moral admonition, the axiom unwittingly drives a wedge between the reader and the text, for *L'Immoraliste* is replete with instruments of literary artifice specifically chosen for their effectiveness in making the text *appear* sincere. From the frame conceit of multiple prefaces (with each narrator echoing the sincerity claims of the other), to the use of the gaze as a mirror of the lie (a kind of "regard regardé," as when Moktir watches Michel watch him steal Marceline's scissors), to an inverted rhetoric of self-exposure that grotesquely ranks dissimulation as the highest expression of truth, these techniques are in evidence. The last is particularly well exemplified in one of Michel's reports on the evolving patterns of his married life:

> Mes rapports avec Marceline demeurèrent donc, en attendant, les mêmes—quoique plus exaltés de jour en jour, par un toujours plus grand amour. Ma dissimulation même (si l'on peut appeler ainsi le besoin de préserver de son jugement ma pensée), ma dissimulation l'augmentait. Je veux dire que ce jeu m'occupait de Marceline sans cesse. Peut-être cette contrainte au mensonge me coûta-t-elle un peu d'abord: mais j'arrivai vite à comprendre que les choses réputées les pires (le mensonge, pour ne citer que celle-là) ne sont difficiles à faire que tant qu'on ne les a jamais faites; mais qu'elles deviennent chacune, et très vite, aisées, plaisantes, douces à refaire, et bientôt comme naturelles. Ainsi donc, comme à chaque chose pour laquelle un premier dégoût est vaincu, je finis par trouver plaisir à cette dissimulation même, à m'y attarder comme au jeu de mes facultés inconnues. (I, 66)

According to this convoluted logic, dissimulation "protects" from the truth, and the artifice of dissimulation—the tricks that forge the appearance of sincerity—are perversely valorized as a labor of love. Even the lie is naturalized ("comme naturelle"), presented as a vice which, like tobacco or alcohol, becomes through force of habit a sophisticated, acquired taste. If one re-juxtaposes this passage to the previously cited axiom—"one cannot be sincere and appear to be so at the same time" — it would seem that the narrator is deceiving us with the appearance of appearances, craftily substituting an ethic of falsehood for what seems to be a version of the noble lie. The axiom, however, belies the lie — like a slip or mistake, it signals the aesthetics of mimetic truth that undermine Michel's courageous avowals of duplicity and render his entire discourse of sincerity a kind of preamble or founding text for the postmodernist practice of dissemblance. As Alice Jardine, expanding on Deleuze's post-Nietzschean reflections on the modern status of falsehood has surmised:

> In effect, for many contemporary theorists and writers, to be radical in our culture may require new kinds of mental acrobatics: for example, to be radical may no longer be to work for the side that is "right," speaks the "truth," is most "just." It may in fact be to work rather for the *Pseudos*, for "the highest power of falsehood"; it may be to opt for overwhelming falsehood, thereby confusing and finally destroying the oppressive system of representation which would have us believe not only in its sub-systems of models (the real, the first) versus simulacra (the unreal, inauthentic), good versus bad, true versus false; but would also have us believe in a world ultimately obsessed with self-destruction.[14]

Examined thus from the hindsight of our own critical climate, Michel emerges as the prototypically Nietzschean king of the "Pseudos," even more than Ménalque, Michel's sinister mentor, whose characterization parodies and oversimplifies the stereotypical essentials of Nietzsche's thought. Privileging the simulacrum or semblance of truth over truth itself by means of such techniques as the partial avowal, the withheld inference, or the deceptive sign, Michel makes of the error a textual precondition.

In the cat and mouse encounters between Michel and Ménalque, the latter stalks the former and eventually traps him through the rhetorical manipulation of silence. As if to emphasize this point, Ménalque's persona is introduced under the sign of the unspoken; in his first words to Michel, he indicates his fundamental antipathy to idle chatter: "Je ne cause pas volontiers, mais voudrais causer avec vous" (I, 94). By breaking his habitual "code of silence," Ménalque begins his initiation of Michel into a secret society whose members recognize each other by their reserve in conversation. For this reason, Ménalque's discourse, with its pregnant pauses and pointed omissions, serves a didactic function as a model of the coded language that Michel

[14] Alice Jardine, *Gynesis* (Ithaca: Cornell University Press, 1985), p. 146.

has yet to master. The first lesson posits the necessity of indiscretion (foreshadowing the voyeurism in which Michel will later indulge after learning of the bestial sexual practices of some of his laborers). In the ellipsis into which Ménalque's speech trails, Michel receives his first prodding to respond in code:

> Je n'ai coutume d'être discret que pour ce qu'on me confie; pour ce que j'apprends par moi-même, ma curiosité, je l'avoue, est sans bornes. J'ai donc cherché, fouillé, questionné partout où j'ai pu. Mon indiscrétion m'a servi, puisqu'elle m'a donné désir de vous revoir; puisqu'au lieu du savant routinier que je voyais en vous naguère, je sais que je dois voir à présent... c'est à vous de m'expliquer quoi.
>
> Je sentis que je rougissais. (I, 95)

Michel's blush — the biblical sign of shame — shows that he is beginning to divine the missing texts of his interlocutor. When he reddens for a second time, it is because the unspoken comes dangerously close to enunciation; but ironically, what is revealed is yet another silence — Michel's silence as, on that fatal day, he watched Moktir furtively pocket Marceline's scissors:

> Vous aviez vu le vol et vous n'avez rien dit! Moktir s'est montré fort surpris de ce silence... moi aussi.
>
> — Je ne le suis pas moins de ce que vous me dites: comment! il savait donc que je l'avais surpris!
>
> Là n'est pas l'important; vous jouiez au plus fin; à ce jeu, ces enfants nous rouleront toujours. Vous pensiez le tenir et c'était lui qui vous tenait... Là n'est pas l'important. Expliquez-moi votre silence.
>
> — Je voudrais qu'on me l'expliquât.
>
> Nous restâmes pendant quelque temps sans parler. (I, 96)

Here it becomes evident that in remaining silent in the face of Moktir's theft, Michel was giving the sign of his assent to the tacit contract that will in future hold between them. The contract is grounded in a masochistic paradigm described by Fredric Jameson as "stealing from oneself."[15] Jameson identifies the pattern in relation to a later episode in which Michel is portrayed poaching on his own land, an accomplice to his most brutish farmhands. For Jameson, the travesty of the trope lies in its perversion of capitalism, and indeed, this is the explicit

---

[15] Fredric Jameson, *The Prison-House of Language* (Princeton: Princeton University Press, 1972), p. 178. Jameson writes: "Vice, said Sartre once is a taste for failure; and it is in Gide (think of the situation in which Michel ends up helping the poachers steal from himself) the penalty for an allegiance to the myth of some absolute and original presence."

reproof communicated by the young manager of Michel's estate, Charles Bocage: "Il faut prendre ces devoirs au sérieux et renoncer à jouer avec... ou alors c'est qu'on ne méritait pas de posséder" (I, 125). Taken as a figure, however, this "stealing from oneself" may be interpreted in its wider ramifications as a synonym of the self-undermining text; the text that robs itself, depleting its stock of moral integrity just as Michel depletes his own territories of valuable game, because he simply is unable to resist the temptation to "jouer avec..."

What is it about these games that excites Michel so profoundly? More than just the risk of being caught, his reputation tarnished by scandal, his name (and that of his wife) the object of public ridicule, it is the delight in being duped that spurs Michel towards danger. Having learned that Alcide, the wildest of the poachers, has tricked old Bocage into paying him to destroy illegal traps which he himself has laid, Michel confesses:

> Et ce qui me dépite en cette affaire, ce n'est pas le triple commerce d'Alcide, c'est de le voir ainsi me tromper. Et puis que font-ils de l'argent, Bute et lui? Je ne sais rien; je saurai jamais rien de tels êtres. Ils mentiront toujours, me tromperont pour me tromper. (I, 122)

Like both Swann and Marcel in *A la Recherche du temps perdu*, Michel reveals his vulnerability to the seductive powers of what Deleuze has called the "deceptive sign," a sign which, by "concealing what it expresses" alludes to those mysterious "possible worlds" of concupiscence and coquetry from which the jealous lover is excluded by the beloved.

Alcide, through his transparent lies, draws Michel deeper into the underworld of deception, a world governed, as Deleuze has advanced, by its own inverted "system," of rules and "laws":

> Si le mensonge obéit à des lois, c'est parce qu'il implique une certaine tension dans le menteur lui-même, comme un système de rapports physiques entre la vérité et les dénégations ou inventions sous lesquelles on prétend la cacher: il y a donc des lois de contact, d'attraction et de répulsion, qui forment un véritable "physique" du mensonge. En effet, la vérité est là, présente dans l'aimé qui ment; il en a une connaissance permanente, il ne l'oublie pas, tandis qu'il oublie vite un mensonge improvisé. La chose cachée agit en lui de telle manière qu'il extrait de son contexte un petit fait vrai destiné à garantir l'ensemble du mensonge. Mais c'est précisément ce petit fait qui le trahit, parce que ses angles s'adaptent mal avec le reste, révélant une autre origine, un appartenance à un autre système. Ou bien la chose cachée agit à distance, attire le menteur qui ne cesse de s'en rapprocher.[16]

[16] Gilles Deleuze, *Proust et les signes* (Paris: PUF, 1964), pp. 93-94.

When Michel covers for Alcide, fabricating excuses that will in turn signal his complicity to the young criminal even at the expense of putting his own credibility into question, he discovers the magic point of contact that connects him to that "autre système," that society of marginals tainted by poverty, incest and rape ("la famille Heurtevent"). But as Alcide is to Michel, so Michel is to Marceline: her point of intersection with the shady, mediated world of middle-class deception: her prevaricating beloved. Often, as Deleuze points out in relation to Proust's Marcel, Michel's "mensonge improvisé" is forgotten, as when he pretends to Marceline during the period of his malady that she should continue to engage young Arab companions, only in order to keep the enviable example of their health (rather than their animal sensuality) before him. Alternatively, in some of the subtle, almost imperceptible shifts in his interior monologues, one can discern the "petit fait vrai" which according to Deleuze gives away the lie. At one point, after exclaiming selfishly over the cost of a proper apartment for his ailing wife, he cunningly reverses his position: "D'ailleurs, qu'ai-je besoin d'argent? Qu'ai-je besoin de tout cela? Je suis devenu fort, à présent... Marceline, elle, a besoin de luxe; elle est faible" (I, 131). The sudden change in attitude from respect to scorn for private property acts as a disguise for Michel's shift in allegiance from the weak to the strong, the strong being the unbridled clan instructed by Ménalque, deserting responsibility, sleeping in barns, and heaping contempt on bourgeois moral protocol.

In his gradual withdrawal from Marceline, Michel saturates his own discourse with deceptive signs, as he progressively bankrupts the discourse of Marceline, and it is in this rhetorical negation of the female signifier, that one can begin to observe the broader relationship between negation and gender. Although he would never be so brutal as to voice openly the complaint that Marceline's conversation amounts to little more than a tissue of moral platitudes, the complaint is nonetheless communicated through textual juxtaposition, the requotation of her phrases in a hostile context. Shortly after one of their habitual evening "causeries," Michel remarks angrily on the conformity of opinion that appears to prevail among their friends, to which his wife replies: "Mais, mon ami,... vous ne pouvez demander à chacun de différer de tous les autres." "Plus ils se ressemblent entre eux," he retorts, "et plus ils diffèrent de moi" (I, 91). The manifest vehemence of this rebuke renders what happens later in the course of his discussion with Ménalque all the more astonishing:

> Je laissais Ménalque parler; ce qu'il disait, c'était précisément ce que, le mois d'avant, je disais à Marceline; et j'aurais donc dû l'approuver. Pourquoi, par quelle lâcheté l'interrompis-je, et lui dis-je, imitant Marceline, la phrase mot pour mot par laquelle elle m'avait alors interrompu:
> — Vous ne pouvez pourtant, cher Ménalque, demander à chacun de différer de tous les autres. (I, 101)

Repetition of the trivial phrase brings on swift and exigent punishment. Ménalque turns his back abruptly on Michel and only subsequently relents on the condition that Michel disown his words. Michel capitulates, condemning the phrase as a worthless commonplace, then furthering condemning its speakers ("Je hais tous les gens à principes"), thereby implicitly repudiating his wife. This seems to be what is understood by Ménalque who concurs, with satisfaction, that "Les gens à principes" qualify as "ce qu'il y a de plus détestable au monde" (I, 102). Marceline's words, read metonymically for her entire person, are thus radically negated, but with impunity, for Michel has not actually uttered a single word against her directly. Indeed, he even allows himself the luxury of "forgetting" the slip, as he masquerades as the most devoted of husbands after she has lost her child. The only overt signs of his betrayal can be found in the silent recrimination of the dead infant (a ghoulish metaphor of absence) and in the prohibition of all speech pertaining to the miscarriage: "Pas un mot ne fut échangé, au sujet du triste accident qui meurtrissait nos espérances" (I, 108). Here, Barthes's concept of the "Inter-dite," as that which is linguistically forbidden or taboo, as well as "read between the lines," appropriately describes the new mode of censorship to which all future exchange between them will be subjected.

If on one level, Marceline's discourse is rhetorically negated (judged to be conformist, "detestable," and finally unspeakable by Michel), on another and even more sinister level, the representation of her diseased and decomposing body merges horrifically with the textual figuration of the "abîme" or abyss. The association between the feminine body and the "abîme" as hole or gap acquires further semiotic dimensions with the help of its secondary meaning, the verb "abîmer" denoting the process of rotting, spoiling, or deterioration. It is in this sense that Michel initially uses the word in conjunction with Marceline's metonymical scissors after their theft by Moktir: "Et pourquoi les avait-il volés," he wonders, "si c'était aussitôt pour les *abîmer*, les détruire?" (I, 100; my emphasis). Michel's perplexity in regard

to the motives of a thief who defaces the booty which he has run such
risks to procure is left unresolved, but perhaps, as is intimated, Moktir's
perversely destructive gesture was guided by the unconscious wish-
fulfillments of Michel. Is it simply a slip of the text that as Marceline's
condition worsens, her body becoming the mirror of her husband's
growing immoralism, it is as "une chose abîmée" that she appears to
Michel? "La maladie était entrée en Marceline, l'habitait désormais,
la marquait, la tachait. C'était une chose abîmée," he observes with
chilling detachment (I, 109). The semantic links implicit in the verb
"abîmer" between organic decay (the body as transitively decomposed,
reduced to the holes of the death's head), are luridly personified in
the description of Marceline's face as it reflects the advanced stages
of the disease: "Comme elle paraît faible et changée; dans l'ombre,
ainsi, je la reconnaîtrais à peine. Que ses traits sont tirés! Est-ce que
l'on voyait ainsi les deux *trous noirs* de ses narines?" (I, 131; my
emphasis).

Michel's projected vision of the "black holes" in Marceline's head
is prefigured several times in *Les Cahiers d'André Walter*, conforming
with the alarming exactitude of a classic case history, to the Freudian
description of fetishism. The curious gaze that travels from below to
above, pruriently investigating beneath a woman's skirt, is duly recorded by the tormented narrator of *André Walter*: "Oh! me blottir auprès
de toi, m'asseoir à tes pieds, dans ta chaleur enveloppante, ma tête
sur tes genoux, dans le pli profond de ta robe," And if here the "pli
profond" evokes the dark space of the absent female phallus, so terrifying to the fetishist, it later develops into the even more redoubtable
apparition of a "nothingness," featured as "noir comme un trou":

> Cauchemar:
> Elle m'est apparue, très belle, vêtue d'une robe d'orfroi qui jusqu'à
> ses pieds tombait sans plis comme une étole;...
> Sous la robe, il n'y avait rien; c'était noir, noir comme un trou; je
> sanglotais de désespoir. Alors, de ses deux mains, elle a saisi le bas
> de sa robe et puis l'a rejetée jusque par-dessus sa figure. Elle s'est
> retournée comme un sac. Et je n'ai plus rien vu; la nuit s'est refermée
> sur elle...[17]

André Walter's nightmare of the womb shockingly emptied like a bag
(another figure of female castration) foreshadows the placement in

[17] André Gide, *Les Cahiers d'André Walter*, in *Oeuvres complètes*, ed. L. Martin Chauffier,
I (Paris: Editions de la Nouvelle Revue Française, 1932-1938), 144, 169-70.

later works of the female signifier "en abyme." The text of Marceline's body becomes the site of gaps, disfigurations, and defamiliarizing anatomical displacements. Most sinister is the grotesque displacement of the eyes, and by implication the spiritual value of her gaze, to the nostrils, which encircle the black hollow of physical dematerialization:

> O goût de cendres! O lassitude! Tristesse du surhumain effort! J'ose à peine la regarder; je sais trop que mes yeux au lieu de chercher son regard, iront *affreusement* se fixer sur les *trous noirs* de ses narines; l'expression de son visage souffrant est atroce. Elle non plus ne me regarde pas. (I, 146; my emphases)

In addition to the "trous noirs," the adverbial qualifier "affreusement" (denoting "horror" from the root *affre*, but also, significantly enough, that which is "détestable") serves to underscore the fine line between Michel's sympathy and contempt for his wife. The repressed significa- tion of "détestable" (the very word used by Ménalque in reference to people like Marceline) resurfaces in the ambivalent word "affreux." The adverb is even carried over as an adjective in the description of Marceline's death-throes, in which the awful silence between husband and wife is transferred back from the gaze to the lips, just as the abyssal signs of lifelessness are redisplaced back to the eyes from the nose:

> Marceline est assise à moitié sur son lit; un de ses maigres bras se cramponne aux barreaux du lit, la tient dressée; ses draps, ses mains, sa chemise, sont inondés d'un flot de sang; son visage en est tout sali; *ses yeux sont hideusement agrandis*; et n'importe quel cri d'agonie m'épouvanterait moins que *son silence*. Je cherche sur son visage transpirant une petite place pour poser un *affreux baiser*; le goût de sa sueur me reste aux lèvres. (I, 147; my emphases)

The transfixed expression of Marceline's cavernous eyes is harrowingly transcribed yet again a moment before her death ("mais ses yeux restent grands ouverts" [I, 148]), as if to punctuate the end-point in the abyssal chain stretching from the dark patches of discoloration on her body, to the blank spaces in dialogue, to the black orifices of nose and eyes.

Without imputing a vulgar misogyny to Michel, or for that matter to Gide, we are nonetheless left with the dilemma of how to interpret this censorship of the feminine—of the woman's body and the woman's "parole." Has Marceline simply been sublated, interred and inscribed in the homotextual "inquiétude" that reverberates in each of the *récit's* elisions? Or can her negation, her disappearance into the "abîme," be read as a protofeminist fable in which masculine and feminine "jouissance" are presented as mutually exclusive? Perhaps it is only in the slips of the text, in those flashes of simultaneous concealment and disclosure that the full complexity of these unspoken issues can be glimpsed.

Dead Letters (La Porte étroite)

At the mid-point in Gide's second *récit*, *La Porte étroite*, Alissa, the over-weeningly spiritual heroine whose letters become a paradigm of "textual penitence," offers up a disapproving review of a recent best-seller (written by her suitor's closest friend) that bears an unmistakable resemblance to *L'Immoraliste*. The work has been praised by respected critics for its stylistic felicities but Alissa confesses to Jérôme that she is grateful that the author has refrained from sending it to her. She was unable to peruse it, she confessed, without experiencing "shame," and even its purchase was difficult, for the very title of the book was too "ridiculous," too compromising *to utter* before the bookseller.[18]

Skirting, for the moment, the obvious biographical explanation of this conceit, namely, that Gide was recording Madeleine's reaction to his first *récit*, we might, on an intertextual level, interpret the framing of *L'Immoraliste* (a paean to hedonism) by *La Porte étroite* (with its Gospel quotations and its set-piece journal of an ascetic virgin) as a technique of ironic contrast, intended to highlight the textual enigma of how two works with such apparently opposite moral tendencies could be composed by the same author within a short period of time. But are these works really as dissimilar as they initially appear? To be sure, *L'Immoraliste* ends on a note of complicity with the self-indulgent Michel, who, after burying his wife, makes his home in Algeria attended by a compliant boy, whereas the finale of *La Porte étroite* presents an outer limit of self-abnegation in the unattended funeral of its heroine; but in the "excess" of difference between the two books we can begin to discern the logic behind Gide's own commentary: "c'est dans l'excès de l'un que j'ai trouvé pour l'excès de l'autre une sorte de permission." This chiasmatic formulation implies that it is their common exaggeration, on the one side, hyperbolic immoralism, on the other, hyperbolic virtue, which allows these works to be seen as a complementary pair, indeed, as Gide's own metaphor of childbirth intimates, as virtual "twins":

[18] Gide, *La Porte étroite*, in *Romans, récits et sôties*, p. 551. All further references to this work will appear in the text abbreviated *PE*.

Ceux qui s'étaient pris de mon *Immoraliste* ne me peuvent pardonner la *Porte étroite*. Je ne puis pourtant séparer dans mon esprit ces deux livres; *c'est ensemble que je les ai portés;* ils se font pendant, se maintiennent; c'est dans l'excès de l'un que j'ai trouvé pour l'excès de l'autre une sorte de permission. Si l'auteur avait pu *les produire similtanément, comme ils avaient été conçus,* sans doute eût-il échappé à un malentendu assez grave...[19] (my emphases)

If one begins to look for "common markings" confirming the consanguinial status of the two works, one stumbles on striking parallels between the principal narrators. The serious, Huguenot principles bequeathed to Michel on his mother's side ("Cette sorte *d'austérité* dont ma mère m'avait laissé le goût en m'en inculquant les principes") closely match Jérôme's "enseignement *austère*." The quality of a case history is, moreover, imparted to each *récit* by the respective narrators: the first preface to *L'Immoraliste* speaks of those who will read Michel's confession as a "cas bizarre" revolving around a "malade," and Jérôme, who will piece together ("repiécer") the fragments ("lambeaux") of Alissa's tragic neurosis as recorded in her letters and diary, undertakes the task much like a psychoanalyst, with an eye to its "instructive" value: "Je copie, des lettres qui suivirent, tout ce qui peut instruire ce *récit*" (*PE* 548). Indeed, it is in their mutual capacity as arbiters and editors of reported speech or written testimony that Michel and Jérôme resemble each other most significantly, thereby encouraging the comparison between their *récits* and the genre of the classic psychoanalytical case history. Though Michel plays the role of analysand, coyly withholding or providing information to his auditors, whereas Jérôme plays the role of analyst, sifting and cutting through the debris of memory and memorabilia to reconstruct the essentials of the case, both narrators justify the histrionic, at times even shocking excesses of their stories in terms of their purported didactic value, and both exhibit the propensity for strategic excision as editors of what is ultimately recorded.

The case history analogy gains legitimacy if, for a moment, one shifts from a comparison between Gidean *récits*, to a summation of parallels between *La Porte étroite* and Freud's celebrated *Dora*, published a mere four years earlier in 1905. In addition to its current privileged position as a "text à clef" for feminist theorists and critics of what is alleged to be the phallocentrism of Freudian theory (viz, Cixous' *Portrait de Dora* or the even more recent volume of essays: *In Dora's*

---

[19] Gide, *Feuillets*, in *Oeuvres complètes* as cited by Jean-Jacques Thierry, in Pléiade notes, p. 1549.

Case: Freud-Hysteria-Feminism), *Dora* fascinates through its imbrication of the analyst's anxieties, professional concerns and literary decisions within the sequence of narrated "facts."[20] It is for this reason that the similarities between Freud as case writer and Jérôme as psychoanalytical narrator may come as no surprise. Jérôme, as was pointed out, fabricates his narrative out of scraps, "pieces" and fragments, and Freud, in addition to noting that in his practice of analysis, "Everything that has to do with the clearing up of a particular symptom emerges piecemeal," entitled Dora's history, *Fragment of an Analysis of a Case of Hysteria*. Here the emphasis may be placed on its conditional autonomy as fragment, its dependency on the quirks of circumstance (for Dora "broke off" her analysis, leaving Freud unsatisfied, just as Alissa's destruction by her own volition of portions of her journal together with her untimely death, take Jérôme entirely off-guard in the course of his collation and interpretation of her writings).[21]

Additional correlatives begin to emerge as we observe that Freud, in answer to the willful withdrawal of Dora, endeavors to fill in the missing parts of her case through "archeological" excavation into the sites of comparable cases:

> In the face of the incompleteness of my analytic results, I had no choice but to follow the example of those discoverers whose good fortune it is to bring to the light of day after their long burial the priceless though mutilated relics of antiquity. I have restored what is missing, taking the best models known to me from other analyses; but like a conscientious archeologist I have not omitted to mention in each case where the authentic parts end and my constructions begin. (*D* 27)

The association between Freud the medical man and Freud the archeologist is uncannily reproduced in the character of Jérôme, who, the son of a doctor, is later accepted as a member of the *Ecole d'Athènes*

---

[20] See Hélène Cixous, *Portrait de Dora* (Paris: Edition des Femmes, 1976) as well as her *Le Jeune née* co-authored with Catherine Clément (Paris: Editions 10/18, 1975). The book referred to here, *In Dora's Case: Freud-Hysteria-Feminism*, ed. Charles Bernheimer and Claire Kahane (New York: Columbia University Press, 1985) contains essays of particular pertinence to the literary reading of Dora's case by Stephen Marcus, "Freud and Dora: Story, History, Case History," and Neil Hertz, "Dora's Secrets, Freud's Techniques."

[21] Sigmund Freud, *Dora: An Analysis of a Case of Hysteria*, ed Philip Rieff (New York: Macmillan, 1971), p. 27. All further references to this work will be to this edition and will appear in the text abbreviated *D*.

(*PE* 574). The symmetries between their "archeological" methods of investigation may be further extended to their tampering instincts (despite disclaimers) as transcribers of the material set before the reader. Freud avows that:

> the record is not absolutely—phonographically—exact, but it can claim to possess a high degree of trustworthiness. Nothing of any importance has been altered in it except in several places the order in which the explanations are given; and this has been done for the sake of presenting the case in a more connected form. (*D* 24)

His concern with "connected form" betrays the traditional preoccupation of the writer of literature with the creation of seamless narrative, thereby attracting more attention to suppressions and omissions than might otherwise have occurred. Jérôme, the perfect mirror image, presents the reader with Alissa's journal "sans commentaires," that is, exactly as he found it, with the *exception* (and here the paradigm fits) of some of its pages: "J'en transcris ici nombre de pages" (*PE* 580). As Albert Sonnenfeld has perspicaciously queried with respect to this admission: "What proportion of the page in the diary does Jérôme transcribe? What did the suppressed pages contain? What were the reflections those pages inspired in Jérôme as a reader? Is not the choice of pages to transcribe itself the 'commentaires' Jérôme denies making?"[22]

The same questions, particularly the last, can be directed on a microcosmic scale to Alissa's letters where it is not so much a matter of pages removed as sentences or even single words. Here the difficulty of intuiting the referent of these elisions is compounded by the occasional ambiguity of diacritical notation. For example, when Alissa writes: "Te l'avouerais-je? je saurais que tu viens ce soir... te fuirais. Oh! ne me demande pas de t'expliquer ce... sentiment, je t'en prie" (*PE* 549-50), one assumes that it is the editor who has introduced the ellipses, though it could be the writer herself in an attempt to convey the natural rhythms of her quavering deliberations. But this conclusion hardly simplifies the vexed question of what Jérôme has suppressed and why. In the first sentence, one would be inclined to fill in the blank as follows: "je saurais que tu viens ce soir (mais si tu viens, je) te fuirais" simply because these words are congruous with Alissa's perverse impulse to retreat (demonstrated throughout) whenever her

[22] Albert Sonnenfeld, "On Readers and Reading in *La Porte étroite* and *L'Immoraliste*," *Romanic Review* 67 (1976), 174.

lover approaches in the flesh. However, this still fails to dispel the mystery of why Jérôme has deemed worthy of "constructive" cutting the words that we have parenthically supplied. The same issue emerges in the second phrase where it appears that an adjective has been left out, though what it may be is difficult to project: "Oh! ne me demande pas de t'expliquer ce (bizarre? beau? triste?) sentiment." Clearly the fact that Jérôme felt compelled to delete this qualifier insinuates that at some level he feared it might compromise his reputation or the image of himself which he, as narrator, is seeking to convey to the reader.

The problematic fictive "je" (treated in depth by Sonnenfeld) which the narrator, using every possible trick of verisimilitude, attempts to pass off as "real" or nonfictional, provides an interesting variation on the Freudian dilemma: Freud's cast of characters is "real" but disguised with false names so as to protect anonymity; the details of the case are "true" but in their concatenation they have been smoothed over to give a more literary, hence more pedagogically facilitating flow; and, in a final overturning twist, Freud's authentic case history, with its literary trappings, will be destined, contrary to the analyst's intentions, for reading *as a novel* (albeit a "roman à clef "). "I am aware," he wrote,

> that — in this town, at least — there are many physicians who (revolting though it may seem) choose to read a case history of this kind not as a contribution to the psychopathology of neuroses, but as a "roman à clef " designed for their private delectation. I can assure readers of this species that every case history which I may have occasion to publish in the future will be secured against their perspicacity by similar guarantees of secrecy, even though this resolution is bound to put quite extraordinary restrictions upon my choice of material. (*D* 23)

Perhaps, like Freud, it was Jérôme/Gide's desire to protect the subject of his case history that led him to consign to secrecy those aspects of Alissa's discourse that might have guided the prurient sleuth towards discovery of her real identity (and after all, her physical and characterological resemblance to Madeleine Gide is impossible to ignore).[23] This benign motive notwithstanding, there rests the

[23] Many readers must have immediately assumed that Alissa's character was based on Madeleine's, for why else would Gide have felt compelled to expostulate in *Et nunc et manet in te* (85): "Mais quelle erreur celui qui croirait que j'ai tracé son portrait dans ma *Porte étroite*! Il n'y eut jamais rien forcé ni d'excessif dans sa vertu." His negation is uncannily denegated by Madeleine's Alissa-like behavior some ten years after the publication of *La Porte étroite*. In 1919, as a reprisal against Gide's

undeniable fact that the more "secrecy" is mentioned the more curiosity is provoked. Barthes's notion of "l'in-dicible," the forbidden utterance that proves an inducement to sexual fantasy, may be here appropriately contextualized, for Freud's protestations of professional discretion in regard to revelation of "the intimacies of the patients' psycho-sexual life" or the explication of "hysterical symptoms" that are "the expression of their most secret and repressed wishes" activate the erotic imagination all the more. So too does Jérôme's invitation to the reader to "imagine" his unspeakable thoughts and feelings as he read the *unexpurgated* version of Alissa's journal: "Vous imaginerez suffisamment les réflexions que je fis en les lisant et le bouleversement de mon coeur que je ne pourrais que trop imparfaitement indiquer" (*PE* 580).

Part of the reader's impetus to imagine a morbid, obsessive, even perverse sexual subtext when faced with censored pages and understated innuendos, derives from the fact that, as in *La Princesse de Clèves*, *La Porte étroite* contains one of the most protracted and frustrating accounts of sexual denial to be found in the history of literature. From the work's inception, the narrative, as a system of manipulative conventions, conspires against the fulfillment of reader expectations. Though it starts out with all the familiar scenes of an apprenticeship novel — Jérôme's fond reminiscence of childhood days spent playing with his cousin in the garden behind the house — and continues through their adolescence, charting pastoral trysts, this Romantic masterplot is continually brought up short, indeed travestied, by Alissa's irrational withdrawals and attacks of mutism. When the question of their engagement presses itself, Jérôme, whose sensitivity to Alissa's delicacy borders on the precious, resorts to a "périphrase": "Le mot: fiançailles me paraissant trop nu, trop brutal, j'employai je ne sais quelle périphrase à la place" (*PE* 521). Unable to tolerate even the merest allusion to the unspeakable subject, Alissa counters with what Freud identified as "aphonia" in relation to Dora. Alissa protests: "Ecoute, Jérôme, je ne puis te parler ce soir... Ne gâtons pas nos derniers instants... Non; non. Je t'aime autant que jamais; rassure-toi. Je t'écrirai; je t'expliqerai. Je te promets de t'écrire, dès demain..." thereby demonstrating her neurotic displacement of oral to written communication (*PE* 521). Freud noted precisely the same phenomenon during a phase of Dora's treatment:

trip to England with Marc Allegret, Madeleine burned all of Gide's letters to her. The profound anguish which this caused him is harrowingly recorded in *Et nunc* (84-87) and in *Les Cahiers de la Petite Dame*, CAG, IV, 9-11.

I remembered that long before, while I was working at Charcot's clinic, I had seen and heard how in cases of hysterical mutism writing operated vicariously in the place of speech. Such patients were able to write more fluently, quicker, and better than others did or than they themselves had done previously. The same thing had happened with Dora. In the first days of her attacks of aphonia "writing had always come specially easy to her." (*D* 56)

We have only to contrast Alissa's acute aphasia with the outpouring of feeling and thought in her letters to understand the extent to which this "substitutive function," as Freud calls it, is in operation. Reunited after a brief separation, during which Alissa has concocted the perverse plan of marrying her sister and her suitor, Jérôme confronts an Alissa incapable of speech: "Elle resta un instant devant moi comme interdite et les lèvres tremblantes; une telle angoisse m'étreignait que je n'osais pas l'interroger" (*PE* 535). But only a short time later, he receives a letter by Alissa to his aunt (which the latter has forwarded to her nephew having wisely construed the identity of the real destinataire), containing a fluent, indeed, positively garrulous account of sentiments that she was thoroughly unable to express verbally to Jérôme. Not surprisingly, the farther away he travels, the more intimate and bold she becomes in her missives. Freud noticed a somewhat similar occurrence with respect to Dora: "Herr K. used to write to her at length while he was travelling and to send her picture postcards. It used to happen that she alone was informed as to the date of his return, and that his arrival took his wife by surprise" (*D* 56). Like Dora, Alissa travels vicariously through the letters of her beloved: "Cher Jérôme, Je fonds de joie en te lisant. J'allais répondre à ta lettre d'Orvieto, quand, à la foie, celle de Pérouse et celle d'Assise sont arrivées. Ma pensée se fait voyageuse" (*PE* 548, italicized in text). She even goes so far as to regret her past silences when in his company, but the vague promise of renewed diaolgue that hovers tentatively in these pages is of course shattered at their next meeting, all the more grotesquely because of the vain efforts of Aunt Plantier to create a situation in which the lovers can be alone "to talk." It is at this point that the analogy to Dora's case begins to dissolve, for as Freud observed, the interpretation of Dora's aphonia was fairly straightforward: "When the person she loved was away she gave up speaking; speech had lost its value since she could not speak to *him*. On the other hand, writing gained in importance as being the only means of communication with the absent person" (*D* 56). Though for

Alissa, writing also "gains in importance as the only means of communicating," her mutism, by comparison to Dora's, appears far more "hysterical": Dora reverts to writing as a surrogate for spoken exchange with the *absent* lover whereas Alissa turns invincibly to writing as soon as the lover's *presence* becomes imminent. The neurotic reversal of presence and absence is, in fact, carried to such extremes that Alissa actually blames Jérôme's presence for spoiling her pleasure in letter-writing: "ainsi que notre correspondance naguère gâta notre revoir de l'automne, le souvenir de ta présence d'hier désenchante ma lettre aujourd'hui. Qu'est devenu ce ravissement que j'éprouvais à t'écrire?" (*PE* 565; italicized in text).

Without a doubt, Alissa's letters play a compensatory role for Alissa herself with respect to the physical and verbal relationship that she is unable to offer, but the more we read, the more we begin to suspect that despite his remonstrations, they may play a comparable role for Jérôme. After all, it is he, in the guise of intellectual mentor, who supervises her reading and encourages her textual expositions as part of her education. It is he who takes up precious hours in the early days of their courtship reading to her aloud, or, as Sonnenfeld has noted, reading over her shoulder (though unlike Paolo and Francesca, Alissa and Jérôme refrain from any embrace that literature might have fired them to risk). It is also he who inspires the sublimation of passion into writing with enthusiastic commentaries on his subjects of study; and finally, it is he who perhaps unwittingly, imprisons Alissa's living spirit — the "spirit of her letter" — in the margins of her books.

Sheepishly noting her misidentification of stanzas in Racine's fourth *Cantique spiritual* (she thinks they are by Corneille until Jérôme stages her detection of the error by sending her a copy of the Racine), Alissa writes: "Sans doute tu les connais déjà (des strophes) si j'en juge d'après les indiscrètes initiales que tu as mises en marge du volume" (italicized in the text). At this point in the transcript of the letter Jérôme permits himself an editorial clarification: "(j'avais pris l'habitude, en effet, de semer mes livres et ceux d'Alissa de la première lettre de son nom, en regard de chacun des passages que j'aimais et voulais lui faire connaître)" (*PE* 545). Jérôme's choice of the verb "semer" to indicate his interference with her text, reinforces the theme of writing as sexual sublimation, but even more striking is the trope of mastery and masculine domination implicit in his patronizing dictation of key passages and citations. By inscribing her "A" in the text, Jérôme, in a sense, entombs Alissa's letter, rendering it impossible, on the one hand, for her to interpret books for herself, and, on the other hand, to compose a text of her own that is free of his "instructive" influence. Perhaps then, we can begin to see Alissa's recalcitrant refusals of the spoken word as well as her literary machinations in the course of their correspondence not so much, in Sonnenfeld's words, as evidence of her "rhetorical dominance," but rather of her revolt against Jérôme's monopolization of the written word. In these terms his "master-reading" would be countered by the revenge of her "dead letter."[24]

It is possible, however, that we are being unfair to Jérôme by placing the onus of Alissa's snuffed-out monogram entirely on his shoulders, for there is another kind of letter, far more powerful in its paternalistic authority than the initials administered by Jérôme — that of the Biblical Word. Alissa's perversely literalized application of Scriptural teachings, particularly the Pauline doctrine of renunciation, is equally a determinant in the case history of her textual and sexual oppression. Certainly the story of her life provides ample psychological material for the development of such a neurosis: the adulterous exploits of her sensual mother, an adolescence devoted to the consolation of an abandoned and possessive father, and a motive (her younger sister's infatuation with Jérôme) for the "sacrifice" of her own marriage prospects. And so, misreading the spirit of the Biblical Letter (that is, divining in its doctrine only the most severe, constrictive and tyrannical of prescriptions for the life of the mind and the body), Alissa embarks on a project of abjection that will culminate in yet another kind of dead letter — her posthumous Journal.

Alissa's grim passage through the "narrow gate" of exaggerated virtue is marked by her divergence from the literary path previously forged for her by Jérôme. The medium of their sublimated passion — the love poetry of Baudelaire, Swinburne, Goethe, Dante and Shakespeare — is replaced with a collection of vulgar little prayerbooks, and the "de-aestheticization" of her reading is accompanied by the "dépoétisation" of her person and mien. ("Alissa! m'écriai-je le premier soir, presque épouvanté par la dépoétisation de ce visage qu'à peine pouvais-je reconnaître" [*PE* 568]). Attired in a severe frock which she refuses to change, coiffed in an unflattering manner, her movements ungraceful, her voice monotonous, and her daily occupations reduced to mending old socks for the poor, Alissa incarnates on a rhetorical level, the litotic figure of "more" diminished to "least." With cruel vigilance she routs out and destroys all sources of vanity. Her determination prompts

24 Sonnenfeld, p. 179.

her towards abasing the only remnant of self-indulgence which remains — her delight in "writing well." In the intimate journal enshrining her enduring love for Jérôme she confesses:

> Le mois dernier, en relisant quelques pages, j'y avais surpris un absurde, *un coupable souci de bien écrire...* que je "lui" dois...
>
> Comme si, dans ce cahier que je n'ai commencé que pour m'aider à me passer de "lui," je continuais à "lui" écrire.
>
> *J'ai déchiré toutes les pages qui m'ont paru "bien écrites."* (Je sais ce que j'entends par là.) J'aurais dû déchirer toutes celles où il est question de lui. J'aurais dû tout déchirer... Je n'ai pas pu.
>
> ...
>
> J'ai dû bannir de ma bibliothèque...
>
> *...Parfois je m'efforce d'écrire mal,* pour échapper au rythme de ses phrases; mais lutter contre lui, c'est encore m'occuper de lui. Je prends la résolution de ne plus lire pour un temps que la Bible (l'Imitation aussi, peut-être) et de ne plus écrire dans ce carnet que, chaque jour, le verset marquant de ma lecture. (*PE* 588, my emphases, italicized in the text)

The aesthetic of the "mal écrire," part and parcel of Alissa's twisted faith, produces a sordid model of "writing degree zero." The journal becomes populated with lifeless citations (contrasting sharply with the former quotations of celebrated literature) which Jérôme characterizes as "une sorte de 'pain quotidien,' où la date de chaque jour, à partir du premier juillet, était accompagnée d'un verset" (*PE* 588). Alissa's glosses on these homilies consist of desperate appeals to the "Seigneur" to aid her in the arduous task of salvation and deliverance from her persistent feminine longing for "jouissance." In the mediocre copybooks and defigured rhetoric of her last written testament, Alissa inadvertently retaliates against the unresponsive patriarch, for the journal of this rebellious nun represents the fruit of her union with the Sacred Word; it is a Scriptural travesty, a stillborn letter.

***

Retracing the trajectory of Alissa's case history, the evolution from speech to mutism becomes apparent. The sequence of her early loquacity, displaced to letters, and then displaced again to a journal that itself is quasi-aphasic or "sous-râture," affords a paradigm of textual penitence that, significantly enough, structurally reverses itself in the subsequent *récit* (*La Symphonie pastorale*, 1919). Without undertaking a lengthy explication of this work, it is worth noting how Gide's *récits* have a way of recapitulating each other from back to front, or folding into and out of each other as narrative paradigms. In *La Sym-phonie*, the "dead letter" is introduced at the very beginning, incar-nated in the character of the mute, unconscious Gertrude. Described as a barely human heap of living matter, "un être incertain," in-capable of sight and speech she finishes as the only *personnage* whose discourse carries the authority, the "mastery" of truth.

The theme of physical blindness, absent in *La Porte étroite*, serves to highlight the drama of the unspoken in *La Symphonie*, where mutism correlates to the absence of sight and complete articulation corresponds to total vision (in the moral as well as the physical sense). As a blind woman, for example, Gertrude, though highly sensitive to shades of expression in the tones and inflections of a voice (so that she com-prehends the pastor's affection for her) nonetheless fails to penetrate his ruse, the way in which he disguises his desire behind a rhetorical mask of Evangelistic love. As soon as Gertrude regains her vision, however, she realizes that she and her guardian have committed a sin — a sin of misreading, a "sin of omission" — in short, she is ignorant of words from the Bible which the pastor had withheld or rendered bankrupt with his false piety, self-deception and vaguely lecherous designs. The exact opposite of her counterpart, Alissa, Gertrude rescues the living word from the Scriptural text, thus reinscribing what Alissa had edited. Though it will also be her fate to die young and unfulfilled, she will at least, in her final hour, have her say, activating the living letter in a long, angry, passionate, and ruthlessly honest harangue against the pastor. In Gertrude's flood of language, Alissa's dead letter is redeemed.

Female Impersonations: L'Ecole des femmes, Robert, Geneviève

"Lesbianisme de Michelet." Pour Michelet, les rapports de l'homme et de la femme ne sont donc nullement fondés sur l'altérité des sexes; le mâle et la femelle, ce sont des figures morales, destinées à juger con-ventionnellement des faits ou des états historiques: l'Histoire est mâle, la Syrie est femelle. Mais, érotiquement, il n'y a qu'un spectateur et son spectacle; Michelet lui-même n'est plus ni homme ni femme, il n'est que Regard; son approche de la femme n'oblige à aucun caractère viril. Au contraire: puisque, d'ordinaire, c'est le mâle qui est le premier tenu éloigné, par une sorte de tabou génétique, de la crise sanguine de la Femme, Michelet s'efforce de dépouiller en lui le géniteur; et puisque cette même crise n'est livrée en spectacle qu'à d'autres femmes, à des compagnes, mères, soeurs, ou nourrices, Michelet se fait lui-même femme, mère, soeur, nourrice, compagne de l'épouse. Pour pouvoir mieux forcer le gynécée, non en ravisseur, mais en spectateur, le vieux lion revêt la jupe, il s'attache amoureusement à la Femme par un lesbianisme véritable et ne conçoit finalement le mariage que comme une sorte de couple sororal. (Roland Barthes, *Michelet*)

Speaking here of Michelet's writing persona as "femme," as "lesbian" voice and finally, as "language wet-nurse" ("langage-nourrice"), Barthes sets out the entire narratological problem of "female impersonations"—that is, the recitation by male authors of female roles.[25] What was the norm on the Greek and Elizabethan stage, emerges in both modern fiction and historiography, as a rather rare occurence. To be sure, illustrations abound of third-person or omniscient narrators who record the dialogue of women or, through either *style indirect libre,* or interior monologue succeed in simulating a woman's thoughts. But in French literature there exist relatively few cases of first-person narratives written by men that endeavor to authenticate themselves as replicas of the feminine "je."[26] Though epistolary examples may be identified (*Les Liaisons dangereuses, Julie ou La Nouvelle Héloïse,* Balzac's *Mémoires de deux jeunes mariées*), they lack the sustained psychological autonomy of a first-person diegesis. Indeed, in the

[25] In his "par lui-même" on Michelet, Barthes subverts the format of the series (as he does with his *RB par RB*) by using it as a vehicle for his own radical version of the historical carnival. Featuring the inversion of the sexes and the theme of the bisexual author, the book reaches a high point in the section on Michelet's "femmes." The typology includes "le sang," "Michelet-voyeur," "La Femme-fraise des bois," "L'Homme-femme de chambre," "Lesbianisme de Michelet" and "Le langage-nourrice." Under the section heading "Le langage-nourrice" Barthes offers a particularly provocative personification of the "Michelet-femme" which could easily stand in as a model for what we are referring to as the "Gide-femme":

Au fond, ici encore, rien d'étonnant: le parler bêtifiant des mères de famille était une volupté supplémentaire, parce qu'il constituait Michelet comme propriétaire officiel de la féminité. Pour se faire plus sûrement mâtrone, gardienne autorisée des secrets physiques de la femme, l'historien magistral, le vorateur énorme de toute l'histoire humaine, s'en remet voluptueusement au langage-nourrice. (Roland Barthes, *Michelet* [Paris: Seuil, 1975], p. 138)

[26] The fictive editor, "André Gide," introduces *Geneviève* as "le troisième volet d'un triptyque" (*Geneviève*, p. 1348). All references to the *récits* comprising this trilogy will be to the editions in *Romans, récits et sôties* and will appear in the text abbreviated respectively, *EF, R,* and *G*. With respect to the creation by a male writer of a feminine first-person narrative, see Stendhal's *Lamiel* and Gide's preface to same in *Préfaces* (Neuchâtel: Ides et Calendes, 1948).

transition within Gide's own oeuvre from epistolary dyad (*La Porte étroite*) to first-person triad, or to use Gide's term, to first-person "triptych" (*L'Ecole des femmes, Robert, Geneviève*), one observes Gide's attempt to perform what few writers before him had ever tried—the narrative transvestism of a woman's fictive "je." If Barthes's Michelet can be figured as a "Michelet-femme," ventriloquist for the mute statue of a far-off Joan of Arc, then so the author of this trilogy of *récits* may be figured as a "Gide-femme," singing the as yet unwritten song of some Nouvelle Nouvelle Héloïse.

Gide, in fact, signalled *La Nouvelle Héloïse* as an intertext of his *Geneviève* in response to Madame Théo Van Rysselberghe's inquiry as to whether this work would be a novel. "Oui et non, vous allez voir," he had replied: "ce sera autre chose, une manière de roman genre *Nouvelle Héloïse* avec de longues dissertations qui n'empêcheront pas le pathétique."[27] Referring here to *Geneviève's* bifurcated generic status as both tragi-comic family romance and *récit à thèse* (a problem to which we will return shortly), this seemingly casual reference to Rousseau's masterwork provides interesting grounds for speculation as to the origins of Gide's feminism, his possible sources of inspiration for the experiment of writing the feminine voice. On one side there emerges an obvious parallel to Rousseau insofar as *Geneviève* may be also read as a modern continuation of the Héloïse legend. A martyr to her passion (with passion later refined into courtly love, according to Denis de Rougemont) this medieval heroine motivated Rousseau's bourgeois rewriting of her story just as Rousseau's version prompted Gide's anti-bourgeois rewriting of a bourgeois rewriting. A rebel like Abélard's Héloïse, Gide's Geneviève (whose name recalls another medieval prototype of feminism, the enterprising patron saint of Paris), disregards the standards of conventional behavior to which women were subject at the end of the nineteenth century. Her only resemblance to her eighteenth-century model—Julie—lies in her crisis of sublimation, when, as a girl she is barred by her parents from pursuing a latent lesbian obsession with an exotic, alluring schoolmate. Implicitly posing Geneviève's homosexual longing for Sara against Julie's chaste veneration for Saint-Preux, Gide thus travesties the eighteenth-century bourgeois (Platonic) paradigm at the same time as he dramatizes a historic revolution in the mores of women in his own century.

[27] Mme Théo Van Rysselberghe, *Les Cahiers de la Petite Dame*, II in *CAG* 5 (Paris: Gallimard, 1974), 109.

But in its twentieth-century feminism *Geneviève* also seems to have derived its doctrine obliquely from Héloïse by way of a chain of personal relationships that joined Gide in the thirties to an Anglo-French circle of feminist writers and thinkers, including Dorothy Bussy, Gide's translator and the English historian Enid McLeod, author of an important biography of the original Héloïse and close friend of Elisabeth Van Rysselberghe, daughter of "la petite dame" and mother of Catherine Gide. The interlocking relationships between Gide, Elisabeth, Enid McLeod, and Ethel Whitehorn (called "Whity" in Madame Théo's *Cahiers*, and also an English schoolfriend of Elisabeth) have not yet been unravelled in detail, but it is clear that they are reflected on a number of levels in *Geneviève*.[28] After her parents withdraw her from school so as to break her infatuation with the artistic Sara, Geneviève, in recompense, receives English lessons from the mother of another schoolgirl, Gisèle Parmentier, who rivals Geneviève for the affections of Sara. Madame Parmentier, herself a highly educated English woman, provides the example of a moderated feminism to both daughter and pupil, who in turn recall Whity and Elisabeth. Further, the feminist Geneviève imitates Elisabeth's resolution to bear a child out of wedlock as a testimonial to the importance of women's independence. The substitution of a sororal support system for the nuclear family (in many ways the exact counterpart of the fraternal associations portrayed in *Paludes*, *L'Immoraliste* or *Les Faux-monnayeurs*), to which Geneviève commits herself as one of the founding members of the "Ligue pour l'indépendance féminine," reinforces the hypothesis that Gide's "gynotextuality" was profoundly influenced by the quasi-feminist ideology defined by Elisabeth and her friends. Like Enid McLeod, whose career was devoted to making the lost voices of women speak anew from Héloïse and Christine de Pisan to Colette, or Michelet's legendary "sorcières" who perished as victims of popular suspicion towards those of the weaker sex intrepid enough to take up the sword, Gide's Geneviève carries the suppressed chivalric heritage of women into modern middle-class society, leaving behind Rousseau as a kind of parenthical reminder of a Héloïse forever bound.

Though these intertexts for Gide's feminism are only possible to project rather than to verify (he himself left few clues either in his

[28] For a closer analysis of these relationships using Enid McLeod's memoirs (*Living Twice* [London: Huthinson Benham, 1982]), see my "La Nouvelle *Nouvelle Héloïse* d'André Gide: *Geneviève* et le féminisme anglais," in the Actes de Colloque: "Gide et l'Angleterre," Birkbeck College, University of London, 1986.

Journal or reported conversations), they nonetheless guide us towards the trilogy's generic status as a "*récit à thèse*," to its *thetic* (in the Greek sense of positioned or posed) rhetoric. Applied to the problem of gender-coding in relation to narrative voice, this thetic aspect focuses attention on the ideological identity of a homosexual voice that stands in for that of a lesbian. The model for such a substitution had perhaps been suggested to Gide by Proust, who, on receiving a copy of *Corydon*, had confided his unequivocal uranism and remarked on Baudelaire's successful adoption of a lesbian voice as proof that Baudelaire merited inclusion in the "Société des Tantes": "La manière dont il parle de Lesbos, et déjà le besoin d'en parler, suffiraient seuls à m'en convaincre." Recounting his conversations with Proust in his *Journal* (1921), Gide was preoccupied with Proust's avowed difficulty in "transposing" between the homosexual and the heterosexual. Proust, he noted, reproached himself for

> ...cette "indécision" qui l'a fait, pour nourrir la partie hétérosexuelle de son livre, transposer "à l'ombre des jeunes filles" tout ce que ses souvenirs homosexuels lui proposaient de gracieux, de tendre et de charmant, de sorte qu'il ne lui reste plus pour *Sodome* que du grotesque et de l'abject.[29]

It seemed to Gide, that in depleting his stock of positive homosexual experiences for his heterosexual episodes and in depicting the city of Sodom as ignoble, awkward or repellent, Proust was "stigmatizing uranism," a position directly opposed to that of *Corydon*. It was precisely the prospect of creating a lesbian feminist complement to *Corydon* that had initially aroused Gide's interest in *Geneviève*, as he confessed to "la petite dame":

> Je pense beaucoup à Geneviève... je voudrais faire dire à Geneviève des pensées extrêmes que je n'ai pas encore dites et auxquelles elle arrive à travers ses expériences:... Si j'arrive à dire tout ce que je veux ça pourrait être bien, je vous assure, bien plus hardi que *Corydon*, un vrai livre de combat comme je n'en ai, en somme, pas encore écrit, un livre qui serait à la fois vivant et plein de théorie...[30]

The difficulty of writing a "combat book," a work of theory animated by the life blood of fiction, became apparent to Gide as he began composing *Geneviève*, particularly when it came to the task of crafting a

[29] Gide, *Journal* (1889-1939), pp. 692, 694.
[30] Mme Théo Van Rysselberghe, p. 171.

feminine voice. Confessing in his *Journal* that he found it awkward and unrewarding to write "fémininement," he doggedly persevered only because he believed in the trilogy's value as exemplum in the ongoing political struggle for sexual freedom:

> Mais je n'éprouve aucune satisfaction à écrire fémininement, au courant de la plume, et tout ce que j'écris ainsi me déplaît. Je doûte que ce style sans densité puisse avoir quelque valeur et crains parfois de m'aventurer dans une entreprise désespérante indigne de tous les autres projets, que je me reproche dès lors de délaisser pour elle.[31]

Though the complaint here was of a primarily stylistic order— Geneviève's voice lacked density— Gide nonetheless refused to allow the thetic qualities of his normative program to predominate through simplistic, undigested polemics. As Albert W. Halsell, following Susan Suleiman's theory of the ideological novel has indicated, Gide's rhetorical strategies were consistently more refined. They included "des appels à l''autorité' du texte extradiégétique" (Molière's *Ecole des femmes*, *Jane Eyre*, *Clarissa Harlowe*, *Adam Bede*), the favoring in number and quality of female voices (Eveline, Geneviève) over male voices (Robert), and the use of preterition and antithesis ("Robert was wonderful/brilliant/perfect, etc., *but...*") as an understated means of casting Robert's words and gestures in a negative light.[32]

The last of these techniques is also particularly prevalent on what might be characterized as the *mimetic* level of discourse, the level on which Gide as male (rather than homosexual) voice tries to imitate directly the tones and cadences of a female narrator. Here we are led to investigate the presence, absence or distortion of what might be identified as classic feminine tropes.[33] Eveline's literary self-effacement, her silences, withheld inferences, and quotation of male

---

[31] Gide, *Journal* (1889-1939), p. 977.

[32] Albert W. Halsell, "Analyse rhétorique d'un discours gidien féministe: *L'Ecole des femmes, Robert, Geneviève*," *Bulletin des Amis d'André Gide* 9, no. 51 (July 1981), 305.

[33] Though there is as yet no consensus as to what these "classical feminine tropes" might be, recent work in feminist criticism by theorists too numerous to list here, has guided us towards the figuration of silence and blankness. As Susan Gubar, in her discussion of the "centrality of silence in women's literature" has noted: "While male writers like Mallarmé and Melville also explored their creative dilemmas through the trope of the blank page, female authors exploit it to expose how women have been defined symbolically in the patriarchy as a tabula rasa, a lack, a negation, an absence. But blankness here is an act of defiance, a dangerous and risky refusal to certify purity" (Susan Gubar, "The Blank Page and Female Creativity," *Critical Inquiry* 8 [Winter 1981], 259).

discourse all form a coherent pattern of figures conventionally attributed to the female voice. Alternatively, Geneviève's curious description of an Oedipal fixation in place of the expected Electra complex (as in Proust's *La Confession d'une jeune fille*), points to a lapse in the sustained mimesis attempted by the male author, a moment where psychological and textual verisimilitude predictably fail.

Intercalated almost imperceptibly within the structures of female impersonation, following the *thetic* and the *mimetic*, is a third level of *parody*, where questions of narrative transvestism most clearly emerge.[34] Is Eveline's voice comparable to an effeminate voice, that of a Gide in woman's costume? Or, to move in the opposite direction, do the pompous, histrionic, Tartuffian antics of Robert constitute a full-scale travesty of classic stereotypes of masculine behavior — vanity, domination and castration anxiety? On yet another plane is Gide, the homosexual male, masquerading as Geneviève, the homosexual female, and if so, can we detect an attitude of derision towards the feminist protagonist that also suggests a trace of auto-pastiche on Gide's part? Is finally the dissonance established between all three voices a parody of marital discord, secretly ensconcing a scathing indictment of the entire institution of marriage?

* * *

Though the three *récits* form a chronological sequence beginning with *L'Ecole des femmes* (1929) and ending with *Geneviève* (1936), their fictive frames establish the narratrice, Geneviève, as the proleptic reader of the entire trilogy. It is she who, acting as literary executor, forwards her mother's manuscripts to the editor, "Monsieur André Gide," as if anticipating that *L'Ecole des femmes* will prompt the counter-*récit* of her father, thereby creating a sympathetic climate for the reception of her autobiography. Mediator of the récits which precede hers, purveyor of a progressive social vision, and of the three narrators, the most firm in her convictions, Geneviève is naturally the most appropriate vehicle for the thetic dimension of the trilogy.

To a striking extent *Geneviève* illustrates the requisites of the paradigmatic *roman à thèse* as defined along general lines by Susan Suleiman. Positing the genre's "essentially teleological" nature — its reference to and resolution in "a doctrine that exists outside the novel,"

---

[34] In developing the theoretical framework of narrative transvestism, I found particularly suggestive Froma Zeitlin's article: "Travesties of Gender and Genre in Aristophanes' *Thesmophoriazousae*," *Critical Inquiry* (Winter 1981).

Suleiman prompts us not to underestimate the relationship between *Geneviève* as novel and *Corydon* as extra-textual credo, itself culled from writers as diverse as Hirshfeld, Krafft-Ebing, Bohn, Perrier, Ward, Plato, Goethe, Wilde, Whitman, Rémy de Gourmont, and Léon Blum. According to Suleiman, doctrine is textually transmitted through techniques that include "redundancy" (Barthes's "surplus of communication"), and the "reduction of ambiguity," with the latter frequently the result of "a dualistic system of values," as self-evident, incontrovertible "right" versus "wrong."[35] In *Geneviève*, the privileging of feminist values (right) over sexist values (wrong) is guaranteed (just as in *Corydon* homosexual values are privileged over antihomosexual attitudes) with the assistance of a dialogical model of apprenticeship. Corydon is to his recalcitrant pupil (the narrator) as Sara and Gisèle Parmentier are to Geneviève — the "donors" of enlightenment. As Suleiman, departing from Greimas, has observed, the apprenticeship dynamic often involves three actors or three roles, that of "donor," "helper" and "opponent." Following this model, Eveline and Madame Parmentier emerge as "helpers" who aid the donors (Sara and Gisèle) in positioning Geneviève against the "opponent" Robert. Here, however, we discover an interesting quirk resulting from the Gidean reversal of gender perspective, for if, as Suleiman argues, "the archetypal donor (or helper) is a paternal figure, then *Geneviève* furnishes the counter-example of donor-helper as *maternal* figure.

Eveline's journal, which goes only part way in outlining a feminist platform (it recounts the coming to consciousness of a woman formerly content to live in submission to her husband's volition), may be seen as a partial maternal donation, in need of supplementation by the more daring tenets of IF (the acronym, with pun on the English meaning intended, for the "Ligue pour l'indépendance féminine"). A number of IF's precepts appear to derive from *Corydon*: the idea that what society condemns as sexual aberration must be understood, defended with pride, and normalized within a protected, vanguard community, the belief that misogyny is culturally alleviated by homosexuality, or the commonplace that women are more practical, more down to earth, and thus better equipped to deal with material problems. Several of these ideas reveal a difficulty in conversion from the homotextual to the gynotextual code. The misogyny argument, for example, is carried over clumsily and inferred only implicitly. Corydon maintains that

[35] Susan Rubin Suleiman, *Authoritarian Fictions: The Ideological Novel as a Literary Genre* (New York: Columbia University Press, 1983), pp. 54-56.

la décadence d'Athènes commença lorsque les Grecs cessèrent de fré-
quenter les gymnases; et nous savons à présent ce qu'il faut entendre
par là. L'uranisme cède à l'hétérosexualité. C'est l'heure où nous la
voyons triompher également dans l'art d'Euripide et avec elle, comme
un complément naturel, la misogynie.[36]

The underlying logic, farfetched though it seemed to Gide's friend
Charles du Bos, is that the institution of pederasty in ancient Greece
enabled men to preserve an image of women as "pure," unbesmirched
by masculine desire, and thus worthy of the highest respect.[37] In
Geneviève this attitude finds its corollary in the heroine's commitment
to maintaining her distance from the male sex: "Quant à moi,"
Geneviève proclaims, "je ne puis accepter de me donner toute à quel-
qu'un. Je me révolte à l'idée de devoir soumettre ma vie à celui qui
me rendra mère") (*G* 1407). Her resolve to preserve self-respect by
remaining aloof from men is facilitated by the fact that her passion
is only aroused by women. When Gisèle asks her whether, if their
beloved Sara were born a man, Geneviève would wish him/her to
sire her children, Geneviève replies in the negative with, by way of
explanation, the admission that "physical attraction" is not sufficient
when choosing a mate. This exchange is significant not only because
it openly confirms Geneviève's hitherto unspoken lesbian proclivities,
but also because it indicates that father-figures constitute such a threat,
that to render them benign requires transforming them into female
surrogates, figuratively speaking, emasculating them.

[36] André Gide, *Corydon* (Paris: Gallimard, 1925), p. 128.
[37] Gide's friend Charles du Bos, who many critics consider to be the model for Robert,
was outraged by this argument which he read as an indication that Gide, having
lost his respect for literary history, had submitted his interpretation of Greek culture
to the dictates of his homosexual "passion":

> ...c'est ce que le faux pas concernant Euripide établit de façon irréfutable —
> cette "conviction" est toute "soumise" à la "passion" elle-même; et lorsqu'à la
> passion il échappe, moins que personne Gide n'ignore combien "d'admirables
> figures de femme et de jeunes filles" la littérature universelle comporte, que
> nul uranisme n'a suscitées: vis-à-vis du lecteur, je ne nous donnerai point ici,
> à lui et à moi, le ridicule de les devoir énumérer. — Mais, m'objectera peut-
> être Corydon — de celles-là, toutes ne sont pas de "pures images de femmes".
> — C'est bien là que je l'attends, car c'est là le point névralgique" du problème...
>
> C'est presque comme si, isolant sévèrement chez la femme le facteur "pureté",
> et se refusant à en prendre en considération aucun autre, le pédéraste visait
> à instituer la catégorie de la femme *Pure* au même titre que celle du roman
> *pur*... (Charles du Bos, *Le Dialogue avec André Gide* [Paris: Editions Corréa, 1947],
> p. 216)

On one level these subtexts allow Gide, as homosexual narrator, to be acknowledged as the courageous forerunner of a lesbian feminist "je," he who successfully translates a dualistic (albeit unconventional) set of values from one gender-code into the other. On another level, by implying that paternity sanctified by love and sanctioned by matrimony leads inevitably to some kind of symbolic castration for both sexes, the narrator of *Geneviève* may be suspected of eclipsing legitimate alternatives to the homosexual alliance. It is perhaps no accident that the only happy marriage of the entire trilogy — between Doctor Marchant and Yvonne, a close friend of Eveline's — is marred by her sterility and the existence of an unfulfilled yet undeniable sympathy between the Doctor and Eveline.

If infelicitous marital situations serve the thetic objectives of this gynotextual *récit*, they fail to facilitate the mimetic representation of a woman's authentic desire for a man. Eveline's rhetoric of esteem for Robert in the early days of their courtship is on all accounts unconvincing. With affirmations clouded by qualifiers, "mais, bien que, quoique, même" and so on, Eveline, as narrator of *L'Ecole des femmes* forfeits all semblance of genuine love for Robert: "Cette extraordinaire distinction de tout son être et de ses manières," she gloats, "je pense qu'il ne la doit qu'à lui-même, car il m'a laissé entendre que sa famille était assez vulgaire" (*EF* 1255). The false naiveté of her observation rings forth in the rhetorical antithesis, for what is offered to Robert by way of a compliment to his manner is immediately subtracted with the information that, despite allegations to the contrary, he is ashamed of his "vulgar" origins. In another context, Robert astonishes his fiancée, shortly after returning from his mother's funeral, with his "stoic" determination to settle the terms of the legacy:

> Je l'ai revu. Comme sa douleur est digne et belle! Je commence à le comprendre mieux. Je crois qu'il a horreur des phrases toutes faites, car il a pour me parler de son deuil la même réserve qu'il avait pour me déclarer son amour. Et même, par crainte de laisser paraître son emotion, il évite tout ce qui pourrait l'attendrir. Il n'a même été question entre nous que de questions matérielles, et avec maman que de règlement de succession et de la vente que Robert veut faire de la propriété qui lui revient. (*EF* 1262)

Here, Eveline plays the role of imperceptive narrator, fatuously asserting what we as readers see through effortlessly. As a narrator, she fails to communicate genuine erotic attraction to her future spouse, and her apparent unawareness of his opportunism and avarice is belied by repeated preterition. When, for example, Eveline remarks: "Je lui ai demandé de ne me présenter que ses amis véritables; mais il est difficile, dès qu'on le connaît un peu, de ne pas devenir son ami..." the covering phrase, "mais il est difficile," though intended to prevent the reader from discerning Robert's superficiality, is ultimately denegated by her own depictions of his comportment with others. Eventually such feeble excuses and efforts at rationalization induce reader disbelief towards her claim of happy marriage. In this respect, the attempt on the part of a male author to simulate the monological, confessional voice of a young girl in love emerges as fundamentally flawed.

More successful, though somewhat mechanical and stilted in construction and tone is the projection of lesbian desire in *Geneviève*, for, the difficulties of "transposition" notwithstanding, Gide as homosexual author clearly found it easier to produce a compelling facsimile of lesbian affection than its heterosexual analogue. In Geneviève's portrait of Sara there is an uncanny resemblance to Gide's description of Donatello's David (with the equivalent of his arresting gaze displaced to Sara's mesmerizing voice) or to Michel's rendering of Bachir and Moktir. Just as Michel, in the presence of these Arab youths, blushes with pleasure and shame as he seeks to overcome their indifference, so Geneviève, "rougissant beaucoup," endeavors to obtain the merest sign of recognition from her schoolmate. Here, in the first impression of Sara's "Oriental" beauty and strangely seductive mien, we discover the gynotextual body grafted onto the homotextual model as presented in *Les Nourritures terrestres* or *L'Immoraliste*:

> De peau brune, ses cheveux noirs bouclés, presque crépus, cachaient ses tempes et une partie de son front. On n'eût pu dire qu'elle était précisément belle, mais son charme étrange était pour moi beaucoup plus séduisant que la beauté. Elle s'appelait Sara et insistait pour qu'on ne mît pas d'h à son nom. Lorsque, un peu plus tard, je lus *Les Orientales*, c'est elle que j'imaginais, "belle d'indolence", se balancer dans le hamac. Elle était bizarrement vêtue, et l'échancrure de son corsage laissait voir une gorge formée. Ses mains rarement propres, aux ongles rongés, étaient extraordinairement fluettes. (*G* 1352)

Though there is nothing overtly incongruous in this ensemble, one discerns what seems almost to be an excess of metonymical symmetry in the substitution of feminine for masculine traits. From the darkness of complexion, to the "not quite pretty" overall effect of lazy, quizzical sensuality, the description is virtually androgynous, and when parts of the body are specifically noted it is as if their selection were based on their contiguity or opposition to corresponding parts of the male anatomy. Where the rounded shoulders and naked feet of young boys magnetize the erotic attention of Michel, it is the formed throat and graceful, if unkempt, hands that similarly function for the woman's body. Nor do the comparisons necessarily stop at the appreciation of physique. As Geneviève is careful to observe, Sara insists that her name be spelled in the biblical way, with the letter "h" suppressed. This mark of her "difference" can be interpreted as the badge of her Jewish identity (branding her as an exile and outcast, but also as "bohemian," sexually and artistically free), and as the sign of her destiny as a latter-day incarnation of Lot's wife, for like the biblical spouse she too has leanings towards Sodom, that "astral" city of inversion. Similar imprimaturs of difference had been even more developed in Gide's male gender code, with North Africa operating in the place of Israel as mytheme of cultural otherness and an Oscar Wilde prototype used to evoke aesthetic and erotic marginality.

Some feminist critics might argue that because the Sara figure is fundamentally entrenched in homoerotic stereotypes, her features broken into isolated fragments more characteristic of the fetishistic masculine gaze than the feminine (which tends perhaps more towards an organic, totalizing, sympathetic appraisal), she should be read as a parody rather than as a mimetic characterization of a woman's woman. This, of course, implies that a trade-off in gender investment has occurred: the feminization of the male narrator has dictated in return the masculinization of female characters. Undoubtedly, Geneviève, Sara, Gisèle, and to some extent Eveline, conform to caricatures of phallic women, those who, according to Sara Kofman's revisionist interpretation of Freud, surpass men in resolving the Oedipal complex. Whereas adolescent males relinquish their libidinal attachments to the mother as they gain confidence in the phallus (developing their super-egos as they overcome castration anxiety), women are "already castrated," and therefore must develop their egos through sheer determination. "...loin d'abandonner alors sa masculinité antérieure," Kofman says of the phallic woman, "elle s'y maintient obstinément, l'exagère même... cherche son salut dans une identification avec la mère ou le père: bref, cette voie est celle d'un 'puissant complexe de masculinité' où la fille fantasme qu'elle est malgré tout un homme."[38] Certainly Geneviève manifests a "masculinity complex"

---

[38] Sarah Kofman, *L'Enigme de la femme* (Paris: Editions Galilée, 1980), pp. 243-44.

as defined by Freud and ratified by a feminist theorist, especially in her strength of will and "identification with the mother." Moreover, her type, as analyzed by Kofman, is even more profoundly confirmed by a lesbianism that itself may be interpreted as surrogate homosexuality:

> Le choix d'objet homosexuel qui caractérise souvent ce type de femmes est pensé non comme le désir d'une femme pour une autre femme, mais bien comme le désir d'un homme pour un autre homme (pour une femme qu'elle pense, à son image, comme porteur de pénis, puisqu'elle-même s'identifie à la mère phallique ou au père). Son homosexualité serait simplement une conséquence de son complexe de virilité.[39]

If Gide's homoerotic portrayal of Geneviève's lesbianism and *maternal* surinvestment may be read in one sense as an Oedipal travesty (featuring Electra as patricidal Amazon), in another sense, it can be seen as an example of Freudian verisimilitude. In this respect it should be noted that Gide himself had become increasingly aware of Freud's work from the early 1920s. When, in 1922, he wrote in his *Journal*: "Freud, le freudisme... Depuis dix ans, quinze ans j'en fais sans le savoir," he articulated the striking predisposition of even his earliest writings towards psychoanalytical interpretations of sexual development.[40] Moreover, in *Geneviève*, he alludes directly to Freud through his heroine who attributes her illness to psychosexual neurosis: "Sitôt après ce que j'en ai dit, je tombai malade. La scarlatine où, comme dirait Freud, se réfugiait le désarroi de tout mon être" (*G* 1384-85). Here, the open recognition of Freud's impact would imply Gide's knowledge of the Freudian theory of female sexuality, as he seems to have based his typology of the masculine woman on research that was beginning to be popularized in the literature of the thirties. Seen in this light, the apparent satire of gender roles — feminine masquerading as masculine, lesbian masquerading as homosexual — emerges instead as psychoanalytical realism, a mimetic rather than parodic order of characterization.

But where, in this case, does mimesis end and parody begin? Certainly an element of high farce is injected into *L'Ecole des femmes* and *Robert* as Gide dons the costumes of beleaguered wife and injured husband, propelling a kind of Punch and Judy show into the narrative arena. Using similes such as "une comédie," "un tableau vivant," or

[39] Kofman, p. 245.
[40] Gide, *Journal*, p. 729.

the phrase: "Il me rappelle ces marionnettes à tête légère qui d'elles-mêmes se redressent toujours sur leurs pieds," to capture the hypocritical poses assumed by Robert, Eveline prepares the way for that consummate moment of grotesque inversion where she will appropriate Robert's role and he will be delegated her's (*EF* 1303). This gender reversal is presented from Eveline's perspective shortly after she avows that she no longer loves him:

> Alors il se passa quelque chose d'extraordinaire: je le vis brusquement prendre sa tête dans ses mains et éclater en sanglots. Il ne pouvait plus être question de feinte; c'étaient de vrais sanglots qui lui sécouaient tout le corps, de vraies larmes que je voyais mouiller ses doigts et couler sur ses joues, tandis qu'il répétait vingt fois d'une voix démente:
> "Ma femme ne m'aime plus! Ma femme ne m'aime plus!..." (*EF* 1305)

The spectacle of male tears, paralleling Arnophe's mask of outraged despair at the discovery of Agnès' unwitting infidelity in Molière's comedy, invites interpretation as a kind of mock castration scene.

In Robert's narrative, the fear of castration is parodied as he bemoans the maternal role that, due to her own laxity, his wife has forced him to play in the moral education of their children: "Que de fois j'ai senti que la position prise par Eveline retenait le vrai progrès de ma pensée en me forçant d'assumer dans notre ménage une fonction qui aurait dû être la sienne" (*R* 1324). But if the exchange of gender here provokes petty resentment and unease, later it precipitates full fledged paranoia as Eveline's visage becomes a "book" on which is printed the sign of the lost phallus—a "vertical, double bar": "Je lisais au pli de son front," Robert reveals, "à cette double barre verticale qui commençait de se dessiner entre ses sourcils, une obstination grandissante." As if to reinforce further the underlying graphic image of castration anxiety, Robert receives Eveline's penetrating gaze like the knife that is used in the ritual sacrifice of the phallus: "...ce regard opérait sur moi *à la manière d'un scalpel*, détachant de moi cette action, cette parole ou ce geste, de sorte qu'ils parussent non plus tant nés vraiment de moi qu'adoptés" (my emphasis). The surgical separation of self from self-image (diminshing the male ego as it emasculates the body) is unmitigated even by Robert's appeals for her salvation: "ma prière,... *pareille à la fumée d'un sacrifice non agrée*, retombait misérablement sur moi-même" (*EF* 1342; my emphasis). If before gender inversion was presented as the stuff of light comedy, it now gives way to the macabre carnivalization of what Lamartine, foreshadowing the tragic episode of Abélard's castration, said of the philosopher and his courageous lover Héloïse: "Ici, comme toujours, le coeur de la femme fut viril, le coeur de l'homme fut féminin."[41]

***

If one stands back to consider the interplay of the three levels of discourse hitherto discussed—the thetic, mimetic and parodic—there is certainly no single voice articulated in either gender or kinship role, that projects the dominant chord, thereby privileging one level over the other. In this sense the trilogy, taken as a medley of four fictive narrators (Eveline, Robert, Geneviève, and the "editor" André Gide) and at least six transsexual metanarrators: the male author as wife (Gide-Eveline), the patriarch as matriarch (Gide, father of Catherine-Eveline), the matriarch as patriarch (Eveline as object of Oedipal fixation and "masculine woman"), the homosexual as patriarch (Gide-Robert), the male sexist as woman (the emasculated Robert), and the homotextual voice as gynotextual voice (Gide alias Corydon-Geneviève), affords an example of what Barthes characterized as both "un neutre," or sexually indeterminate, and "le neutre," associated with "white writing" or writing without style (*P* 102). In *Roland Barthes* he defined "le neutre" through a now familiar chain of evocative figures:

> Figures du Neutre: l'écriture blanche, exemptée de tout théâtre littéraire—le langage adamique—l'insignifiance délectable—le lisse— le vide, le sans-couture—la Prose (catégorie politique décrite par Michelet)—la discrétion—la vacance de la "personne", sinon annulée, du moins rendue irréperable—l'absence d'*imago*—la suspension de jugement, de procès—le déplacement—le refus de "se donner une contenance" (le refus de toute contenance)—le principe de délicatesse—la dérive—la jouissance: tout ce qui esquive ou déjoue ou rend dérisoires la parade, la maîtrise, l'intimidation.[42]

Serving as intuitive index to an entire spectrum of derivations that range themselves behind the omnibus designation of "degree zero" or the rhetorical utopia of "neutrality," this entry commemorates the disappearance of a master-narrative—that supreme Romantic fiction anchoring history in the authoritative voice of its narrator. Not only has the modern narrator lost a fixed sexual identity, but his neutered, anonymous voice has been misplaced or displaced into a dystopia of

---

[41] Lamartine, *Héloïse et Abélard* (1864) as cited by Enid McLeod, *Héloïse: A Biography* (London: Chatto and Windus, 1938), p. 39.
[42] Barthes, *Roland Barthes*, p. 136.

conditional silence. Barthes's analogy: "La voix est, par rapport au silence, comme l'écriture (au sens graphique) sur le papier blanc," points to what remains of authorial identity after the post-Symbolist ascension to silence and white paper—it is, simply, "le grain de la voix,"—an expression that Gide himself, with his fondness for the music of the voice as well as for the image of the "grain" as inseminating particle and texture of wood, and floating, personal signifier, could have easily ceded to Barthes.[43] This ineffable, glottalized utterance, "un mixte érotique de timbre et de langage," is treated by Barthes as the originary sign of the subject, a carrier of the primordial "Ecoutez!" motivating the infant to its mother, the confessor to the priest, the patient to the analyst. "L'originalité de l'écoute psychanalytique," Barthes maintains, "tient à ceci: elle est ce mouvement de va-et-vient qui relie *la neutralité et l'engagement*, la suspension d'orientation et la théorie" (my emphasis).[44] On one level seen as the purest locutionary agent of mediation between the zero degree threshold of communication ("neutralité") and the point of spoken interaction with the Other, "le grain de la voix" is also conceived by Barthes as an "écriture"—a kind of "writing out loud." Defined in contradistinction to the "*actio*" of ancient rhetoric—the codes governing the physical exteriorization of expression in the art of oratory,—"l'écriture à haute voix," according to Barthes, articulates that "forgotten," "censored" part of speech that provides the essential liaison to the hidden, erotic source of expression:

> ..."l'écriture à haute voix" n'est pas phonologique, mais phonétique; son objectif n'est pas la clarté des messages, le théâtre des émotions; ce qu'elle cherche (dans une perspective de jouissance), ce sont les incidents pulsionnels, c'est le langage tapissé de peau, un texte où l'on puisse entendre le grain du gosier, la patine des consonnes, la volupté des voyelles, toute une stéréophonie de la chair profonde; l'articulation du corps, de la langue, non celle du sens, du langage.[45]

Barthes's alliterative rendering of this graphically invisible, incantatory, gutteral, phonetically abrasive, sexual vibrato recalls the abstract ideals of the Symbolist sign, particularly the emphasis placed by Baudelaire and Mallarmé on the imprecision of sense and corresponding refinement of musical tonality, respiration and stress. It

[43] Roland Barthes, *L'Obvie et l'obtus* (Paris: Seuil, 1982), p. 225.
[44] Barthes, *L'Obvie et l'obtus*, pp. 222, 225.
[45] Roland Barthes, *Le Plaisir du texte*, p. 105.

is this prelinguistic, proto-Symbolist instrumentation that, significantly enough, rings out in the voice of *Geneviève's* Sara, who, like her namesake Sarah Bernhardt, is gifted with the powers of transforming the *recit* (as genre of spoken writing) into a sensual, vocably self-referential *récitatif*. Not surprisingly, the literary intertext in the scene which stages Sara's "écriture à haute voix" is Baudelaire's sonnet, *La Mort des amants*. In the poem's second stanza, the motif of doubling — woman to woman, mirror to mirror, flame to flame, assonance to assonance — mimes the enunciation and echo of pure sound as it travels from the speaker to the enraptured auditor:

> Usant à l'envi leurs chaleurs dernières,
> Nos deux coeurs seront deux vastes flambeaux,
> Qui réfléchiront leurs doubles lumières
> Dans nos deux esprits, ces miroirs jumeaux.

This is the verse, with its Sapphic innuendos and sonoric repetitions "en abyme" that awakens in Geneviève (just as it had awakened in the young post-symbolist Gide whose *Traité du Narcisse* is "quoted" in Geneviève's response to the poem), the beginnings of a secret longing for "jouissance:"

> Je ne suis pas très sensible à la poésie, je l'avoue, et sans doute serais-je restée indifférente devant ces vers, si je les avais lus moi-même. Ainsi récités par Sara, ils pénétrèrent jusqu'à mon coeur. Les mots perdaient leur sens précis, que je ne cherchais qu'à peine à comprendre; chacun d'eux se faisait musique, subtilement évocateur d'un paradis dormant; et j'eus la soudaine révélation d'un autre monde dont le monde extérieur ne serait que le pâle et morne reflet. (*G* 1365)

In its evocation of a "dormant paradise," the brilliance of which reduces the real world to the status of a "pale and dull reflection," Sara's voice, like Narcissus' gaze, projects an object of desire that necessarily remains distant. But this strange, unearthly music of the human voice, as far as Sara is concerned, waits only to be translated into gestures by those whom it has sensually and spiritually stirred: "Mais il ne tient qu'à nous d'y vivre," she remonstrates to the dubious, romantically resigned Geneviève. In her confidence in the authenticity of "le grain de la voix," or what Barthes would also call "le bruissement de la langue," Sara acts as a cover for the counterfeit nature of the "Gide-femme," with its, at times, uncannily believable impersonation of the feminine voice.

SELECTED BIBLIOGRAPHY

Rhetoric, Stylistics, Narrative Theory

Bakhtin, Mikhail. *Problems of Dostoevsky's Poetics*. Tr. Caryl Emerson. Minncapolis: University of Minnesota Press, 1984.

_____. *Rabelais and His World*. Tr. Helene Iswolsky. Cambridge, Mass: MIT Press, 1968.

Barthes, Roland. *La Chambre claire*. Paris: Gallimard-Seuil, 1980.

_____. *Critique et vérité*. Paris: Seuil, 1966.

_____. *Le Degré zéro de l'écriture*. Paris: Seuil, 1972.

_____. *Essais critiques*. Paris: Seuil, 1981.

_____. *Fragments d'un discours amoureux*. Paris: Seuil, 1977.

_____. *Le Grain de la voix*. Paris: Seuil, 1981.

_____. *Michelet*. Paris: Seuil, 1975.

_____. *Mythologies*. Paris: Seuil, 1970.

_____. *L'Obvie et l'obtus*. Paris: Seuil, 1982.

_____. *Le Plaisir du texte*. Paris: Seuil, 1973.

_____. *Roland Barthes*. Paris: Seuil, 1975.

_____. *Sade, Fourier, Loyola*. Paris, Seuil, 1980.

_____. *Sollers écrivain*. Paris: Seuil, 1979.

_____. *Sur Racine*. Paris: Seuil, 1979.

Benveniste, Emile. *Problèmes de linguistique générale*. Paris: Gallimard, 1967.

Charles, Michel. *Rhétorique de la lecture*. Paris: Seuil, 1977.

Cohn, Dorrit. *Transparent Minds: Narrative Modes for Presenting Consciousness in Fiction*. Princeton: Princeton University Press, 1978.

Compagnon, Antoine. *La Seconde Main ou le travail de la citation*. Paris: Seuil, 1979.

Dällenbach, Lucien. *Le Récit spéculaire: essai sur la mise en abyme*. Paris: Seuil, 1977.

Dubois, J. et al. *Rhétorique générale*. Paris: Larousse, 1970.

Ducrot, O. and T. Todorov. *Dictionnaire des sciences du langage*. Paris: Seuil, 1972.

Dumarsais, C., Ch. *Des tropes*. Geneva: Slatkine Reprints, 1967.

Fontanier, Pierre. *Les Figures du discours*. Paris: Flammarion, 1977.

Frye, Northrop. *The Anatomy of Criticism: Four Essays*. Princeton: Princeton University Press, 1957.

Genette, Gérard. *Figures I*. Paris: Seuil, 1966.

_____. *Figures II*. Paris: Seuil, 1969.

_____. *Figures III*. Paris: Seuil, 1972.

Girard, René. *Deceit, Desire and the Novel*. Tr. Yvonne Freccero. Baltimore: John Hopkins University Press, 1965.

Greimas, V.A.J. *Sémantique structurale*. Paris: Larousse, 1966.

Guiraud, P. *Essais de stylistique*. Paris: Klincksieck, 1970.

Jakobson, Roman. "Two Aspects of Language and Two Types of Aphasic Disturbances." In *Fundamentals of Language*. The Hague: Mouton, 1956.

Jameson, Fredric. *The Prison-House of Language*. Princeton: Princeton University Press, 1972.

Jankélévitch, Vladimir. *L'Ironie*. Paris: Flammarion, 1966.

Kermode, Frank. *The Sense of an Ending: Studies in the Theory of Fiction*. New York: Oxford University Press, 1967.

Lanson, Gustave. *Histoire de la littérature française*. Paris: Hachette, 1895.

Morier, Henri. *Dictionnaire de poétique et de rhétorique*. Paris: PUF, 1961.

Ricoeur, Paul. *The Rule of Metaphor*. Tr. Robert Czerny. London: Routledge & Kegan Paul, 1978.

Riffaterre, Michael. *Essais de stylistique structurale*. Paris: Flammarion, 1971.

Said, Edward. *Beginnings: Intention and Method*. Baltimore: Johns Hopkins University Press, 1975.

Suleiman, Susan Rubin. *Authoritarian Fictions: The Ideological Novel as a Literary Genre*. New York: Columbia University Press, 1983.

Todorov, Tzvetan. *Littérature et signification*. Paris: Larousse, 1967.

_____. *Poétique de la prose*. Paris: Seuil, 1971.

Critical Theory, Psychoanalysis, Feminism

Blanchot, Maurice. *L'Entretien infini*. Paris: Gallimard, 1969.

_____. *L'Espace littéraire*. Paris: Gallimard, 1955.

Cixous, Hélène. *La Jeune née*. Paris: Editions 10/18, 1975.

_____. *Le Livre de Promothea*. Paris: Gallimard, 1983.

_____. *Portrait de Dora*. Paris: Editions des Femmes, 1976.

_____. *Vivre l'orange*. Paris: Editions des Femmes, 1979.

Deleuze, Gilles. *Différence et répétition*. Paris: PUF, 1969.

_____. *Logique du sens*. Paris: Editions de Minuit, 1969.

_____. *Nietzsche et la philosophie*. Paris: PUF, 1962.

_____. *Proust et les signes*. Paris: PUF, 1964.

De Man, Paul. *Allegories of Reading*. New Haven: Yale University Press, 1979.

Derrida, Jacques. *La Dissémination*. Paris: Seuil, 1972.

_____. *Marges de la philosophie*. Paris: Editions de Minuit, 1972.

_____. *Of Grammatology*. Tr. Gayatri Spivak. Baltimore: Johns Hopkins University Press, 1976. *De la grammatologie*. Paris: Editions de Minuit, 1967.

_____. *Writing and Difference*. Tr. Alan Bass. Chicago: University of Chicago Press, 1978. *L'Ecriture et la différance*. Paris: Seuil, 1967.

Foucault, Michel. *Histoire de la sexualité*: Vols. I, II, III. Paris: Gallimard, 1976, 1984, 1984.

_____. *Les Mots et les choses*. Paris: Gallimard, 1966.

Freud, Sigmund. *Dora: An Analysis of a Case of Hysteria*. Ed. Philip Rieff. New York: Macmillan, 1971.

_____. . *"Negation." Standard Edition of the Complete Works of Sigmund Freud*. 24 vols. Ed. James Strachey. 24 vols. London: Hogarth Press, 1953, vol XIX, pp. 234-36.

_____. *The Psychopathology of Everyday Life*. Tr. Alan Tyson. New York: Norton, 1965.

Hartman, Geoffrey. *Saving the Text*. Baltimore: Johns Hopkins University Press, 1981.

Jardine, Alice. *Gynesis*. Ithaca: Cornell University Press, 1985.

Johnson, Barbara. *The Critical Difference*. Baltimore: Johns Hopkins University Press, 1980.

Klein, Robert. *La Forme et l'intelligible*. Paris: Gallimard, 1970.

Kristeva, Julia. *Desire in Language: A Semiotic Approach to Literature and Art*. Tr. Thomas Gara, Alice Jardine, and Leon Roudiez. New York: Columbia University Press, 1980.

_____. *La Révolution du langage poétique*. Paris: Seuil, 1974.

Kofman, Sarah. *L'Enigme de la femme*. Paris: Galilée, 1980.

Lacan, Jacques. *Encore, Le Séminaire, livre II*. Paris: Seuil, 1975.

_____. "Introduction au commentaire de Jean Hippolyte sur la *Verneinung*." *La Psychanalyse* 1 (1956), 17-18. (Seminar of February 10, 1954).

_____. "Réponse au commentaire de Jean Hippolyte sur la *Verneinung* de Freud." *La Psychanalyse* 1 (1956), 41-58. (Seminar of February 10, 1954).

Lacoue-Labarthe, Philippe and Nancy, Jean-Luc. *L'Absolu littéraire*. Paris: Seuil, 1978.

Laplanche, J. and Pontalis, J.B. *The Language of Psychoanalysis*. Tr. D. Nicholson-Smith. New York: Norton, 1973.

Marin, Louis. *Détruire la peinture*. Paris: Galilée, 1977.

_____. *Etudes sémiologiques, écritures, peintures*. Paris: Klincksieck, 1971.

Works by Gide consulted which are not included in the Gallimard (Pléiade) edition

Ainsi soit-il ou les jeux sont faits. Paris: Gallimard, 1952.

Amyntas. Paris: Mercure de France, 1906.

"Considérations sur la mythologie grecque." In *Incidences*. Paris: Gallimard, 1924.

Corydon. Paris: Gallimard, 1924.

Eloges. Neuchâtel: Ides et Calendes, 1948.

Et nunc manet in te. Neuchâtel: Ides et Calendes, 1951.

"L'Evolution du théâtre." In *Nouveaux Prétextes*. Paris: Mercure de France, 1918.

Feuillets d'automne. Paris: Mercure de France, 1949.

L'Immoraliste. Ed. Elaine Marks and Richard Tedeschi. Toronto: Macmillan, 1963.

Incidences. Paris: Gallimard, 1924.

Interviews Imaginaires. New York: Pantheon, 1943.

Littérature engagée. Paris: Gallimard, 1950.

"Poussin." In *Feuillets d'automne*. Paris: Mercure de France, 1949, pp. 164-66.

Préfaces. Neuchâtel: Ides et Calendes, 1948.

Prétextes. Paris: Mercure de France, 1903.

"Réponse à une enquête sur le classicisme." In *Incidences*. Paris: Gallimard, 1924.

Si le grain ne meurt. Paris: Gallimard, 1942.

Théâtre. Paris: Gallimard, 1942.

Critical Studies of Gide and His Works

Angelet, Christian. *Symbolisme et invention formelle dans les premiers écrits d'André Gide*. Romanica Gandensia 19. Ghent: Romanica Gandensia, 1982.

Anglès, Auguste. *André Gide et le premier groupe de la Nouvelle Revue Française*. Paris: Gallimard, 1978.

Arland, Marcel, ed. *Entretiens sur André Gide*. Paris: Mouton, 1967.

Bastide, George. *Anatomie d'André Gide*. Paris: PUF, 1972.

Brée, Germaine. *L'Insaisissable Protée*. Paris: Les Belles Lettres, 1953.

Davet, Yvonne. *Autour des 'Nourritures terrestres': Histoire d'un livre*. Paris: Gallimard, 1948.

Delay, Jean, ed. *Correspondance: André Gide-Roger Marin du Gard 1913-1934*. Paris: Gallimard, 1968.

Delay, Jean. *La Jeunesse d'André Gide*. Vol. I: *André Gide avant André Walter (1869-1890)* and Vol. II: *D'André Walter à André Gide (1890-1895)*. Paris: Gallimard, 1956 and 1957.

Fillaudeau, Bertrand. *L'Univers ludique d'André Gide: les sôties*. Paris: Corti, 1985.

Freedman, Ralph. *The Lyrical Novel*. Princeton: Princeton University Press, 1963.

Freyburger, Henri. *L'Evolution de la disponibilité gidienne*. Paris: Nizet, 1970.

Goulet, Alain. *Les Caves du Vatican d'André Gide*. Paris: Larousse, 1972.

Goux, Jean-Joseph. *Les Monnayeurs du langage*. Paris: Galilée, 1984.

Guerard, Albert J. *André Gide*. Cambridge, Mass.: Harvard University Press, 1951.

Holdheim, Wolfgang W. *Theory and Practice of the Novel: A Study on André Gide*. Geneva: Droz, 1968.

Hytier, Jean. *André Gide*. Paris: Charlot, 1945.

Ireland, G.W. *Gide*. London: Oliver and Boyd, 1963.

Lang, Renée. *André Gide et la pensée allemande*. Paris: Egloff, 1949.

Lehman. A.G. *The Symbolist Aesthetic in France*. Oxford: Blackwell, 1968.

Lejeune, Philippe. *Lecture de "Si le grain ne meurt.": exercices d'ambiguïté*. Paris: Lettres Modernes, 1974.

————. *Le Pacte autobiographique*. Paris: Seuil, 1975.

Magny, Claude C. *Histoire du roman français depuis 1918*. Paris: Seuil, 1950.

Maisani-Léonard, Martine. *André Gide ou l'ironie de l'écriture*. Montréal: Les Presses de l'Université de Montréal, 1976.

Mallet, Robert, ed. *Correspondance: D'André Gide et de Paul Valéry*. Paris: Gallimard, 1955.

Martin, Claude. *André Gide par lui-même*. Paris: Seuil, 1963.

————. *La Maturité d'André Gide: De Paludes à L'Immoraliste*. Paris: Klincksieck, 1977.

Martin du Gard, Roger. *Notes sur André Gide*. Paris: Gallimard, 1915.

Marty, Eric. *L'Ecriture du jour: le Journal d'André Gide*. Paris: Seuil, 1985.

McLaren, James. *The Theatre of André Gide: Evolution of a Moral Philosopher*. New York: Octagon Books, 1971.

Moutote, Daniel. *Les Images végétales dans l'oeuvre d'André Gide*. Paris: PUF, 1970.

————. *Le Journal de Gide et les problèmes du moi*. Paris: PUF, 1968.

O'Brien, Justin. *'Les Nourritures terrestres' d'André Gide et 'Les Bucoliques' de Virgile*. Boulogne sur-Seine: Prétextes, 1953.

————. *Portrait of André Gide: A Critical Biography*. New York: Knopf, 1953.

Painter, George. *André Gide: A Critical and Biographical Study*. New York: Roy, 1951.

Peters, Arthur King. *Jean Cocteau and André Gide: An Abrasive Friendship*. New Brunswick, N.J.: Rutgers University Press, 1973.

Raimond, Michel. *Les Critiques de notre temps et André Gide*. Paris: Garnier, 1971.

Rivière, Jacques. *Etudes*. Paris: Gallimard, 1924.

Robidoux, Réjean. *Le Traité du Narcisse (Théorie du Symbole) d'André Gide*. Ottawa: Editions de l'Université d'Ottawa, 1978.

Rossi, Vinio. *André Gide: The Evolution of an Aesthetic*. New Brunswick, N.J. Rutgers University Press, 1967.

Teppe, J. *Sur le "purisme" d'André Gide*. Paris: Clairac, 1950.

Veyrenc, Marie-Thèrese. *Genèse d'un style: la phrase d'André Gide dans 'Les Nourritures terrestres.'* Paris: Nizet, 1976.

Watson-Williams, Helen. *André Gide and the Greek Myth*. Oxford: Clarendon Press, 1967.

Weinberg, Kurt. *On Gide's Prométhée*. Princeton: Princeton University Press, 1972.

Articles on Gide

Albouy, Pierre. "Paludes et le mythe de l'écrivain." *Cahiers André Gide* 3 (1972), 241-51.

Angelet, C. "Ambiguïtés du discours dans *Paludes*." *La Revue des Lettres Modernes, Cahiers André Gide* 3, nos. 331-35 (1972), pp. 85-96.

Apter, Emily. "Writing without Style: the Role of Litotes in Gide's Concept of Modern Classicism." *French Review* (October 1983).

_____. "Gide's *Traité du Narcisse*: A Theory of the Post-Symbolist Sign?" *Stanford French Review* 9, no. 2 (Summer 1985), 189-99.

_____. "Homotextual Counter-Codes: Gide and the Poetics of Engagement." *Michigan Romance Studies*, no. 4 (1986).

_____. "Female Impersonations: Gender and Narrative Voice in Gide's *L'Ecole des femmes, Robert* and *Geneviève. Romanic Review*, no. 3 (May 1986).

_____. "*Stigma Indelible*: Gide's Parodies of Zola and the Displacement of Realism." *Modern Language Notes*, no. 4 (September 1986).

_____. "Le Mythe de degré zéro." *Critique*, no. 473 (October 1986).

_____. "La Nouvelle *Nouvelle Héloïse* d'André Gide: *Geneviève* et le féminisme anglais." *André Gide et L'Angleterre* (1986).

Beaujour, Michel. "Is Less More?" In *Intertextuality* II. New York: New York Literary Forum, 1978, 237-43.

Benjamin, Walter. "Oedipe ou le mythe raisonnable." In *Oeuvres* II. Tr. Maurice de Gandillac. Paris: Denoël, 1971.

Blanchot, Maurice. "Gide et la littérature d'expérience." *L'Arche*, no. 23 (1947), pp. 87-98.

Blum, Léon. "André Gide: *Les Nourritures terrestres*." *La Revue Blanche* (1897), pp. 77-79.

Brigaud, Jacque. "Gide entre Benda et Sartre." *Archives des Lettres Modernes*, no. 134 (1972), pp. 30-42.

Brosman, Catherine Savage. "Le Monde fermé de *Paludes*." *La Revue des Lettres Modernes, André Gide* 6 (March 1979), 134-49.

Cahiers André Gide 1. Paris: Gallimard, 1969.

_____. 3. Paris: Gallimard, 1972.

_____. 4-7. "Les Cahiers de la Petite Dame: Notes pour l'histoire authentique d'André Gide." Paris: Gallimard, 1973.

Fokkema, D.W. "A Semiotic Definition of Aesthetic Experience and the Period Code of Modernism." *Poetics Today* 3, no. 1 (1982).

Freedman, Ralph. "Imagination and Form in André Gide: *La Porte étroite* and *La Symphonie pastorale,*" *Accent* 18, no. 4 (1957), 217-28.

Goulet, Alain. "La Figuration du procès littéraire dans l'écriture de *La Symphonie pastorale.*" *Revue des Lettres Modernes*, nos. 331-35, (1972), pp. 27-55.

Halsell, Albert W. "Analyse rhétorique d'un discours gidien féministe." *Bulletin des Amis d'André Gide* 9, no. 51 (July 1981), 293-317.

Holdheim, Wolfgang W. "The Dual Structure of *Le Promethée mal enchaîné.*" *MLN* (1959).

_____. "Gide's *Paludes*: the Humor of Falsity." *French Review* (April 1959).

Hoog, Armand. "Gide ou les sexes de l'esprit." *Nef* 3, no. 22 (1946), 129-31.

_____. "André Gide et l'acte gratuit." *Nef* 3, no. 18 (1946), 130-32.

Klinkenberg, J.M. "L'Archaïsme et ses fonctions stylistiques." *Le Français Moderne* (July 1970), pp. 10-34.

Lacan, Jacques. "Jeunesse de Gide ou la lettre et le désir." *Critique*, no. 131 (April 1958), pp. 291-312.

Lioure, M. "*Le Journal* d'Alissa dans *La Porte étroite.*" *L'Information Littéraire* (January 1964), pp. 39-45.

O'Brien, Justin. "Gide's Fictional Techniques." *Yale French Studies*, no. 7 (1951), pp. 81-90.

_____. "*Paludes* et le *Potomak.*" *Cahiers André Gide* 1 (1969), 265-82.

O'Reilly, Robert F. "The Emergence of Gide's Art Form in *Paludes.*" *Symposium* 19, no. 3 (1965), 235-48.

Peyre, Henri. "Gide in His Journals." *Yale Review* 18, no. 1 (Autumn 1948), 162-64.

Riffaterre, Michael. "Un Singulier d'André Gide." *Le Français Moderne* 23 (1955), 39-44.

Sartre, Jean-Paul. "Gide vivant." *Les Temps Modernes* 65 (March 1951), 85-89.

Sonnenfeld, Albert. "On Readers and Reading in *La Porte étroite* and *L'Immoraliste.*" *Romanic Review* 67 (1976), 172-86.

_____. "Strait Is the Gate: Byroads in Gide's Labyrinth." *Novel* (Winter 1968), pp. 118-32.

Sontag, Susan. "Writing Itself: On Roland Barthes." *The New Yorker*, April 26, 1982, pp. 122-41.

Sypher, Wylie. "Gide's Cubist Novel." *Kenyon Review* 2, no. 2 (Spring 1949), 291-309.

Viart, Denis. "Paludes e(s)t son double." *Communications* 19 (1972), 51-59.

Watson, G. "Gide's Construction 'en abyme.'" *Australian Journal of French Studies* 7 (January-August 1970), 224-33.

Whartenby, H.A. "Precursors of the Gidean *Récit.*" *Romanic Review* (April 1969), pp. 104-14.
York, Ruth B. "Circular Patterns in Gide's *Sôties.*" *French Review* 34 (1961), 336-43.

INDEX

l'art pour l'art   4
Abélard, Pierre   136, 147, 148
Adam   23, 29-32, 36-38, 139
Allegret, Marc   129
Alpers, Paul   56
Angelet, Christian   2, 36, 39, 56, 64, 78
Anglès, Auguste   11, 75, 119
aphasia   129-33
archaism   85
Aristotle   9, 21, 22
askesis   83, 90, 103
autobiography   6, 103, 140
autoeroticism   90

Bakhtin, Mikhail   11, 46, 53
Balzac, Honoré de   135
   Mémoires de deux jeunes mariées   135
Barbey d'Aurevilly, Jules   15
Barrès, Maurice   50, 51
Barthes, Roland   3, 5-9, 19, 28, 30, 40,
      43, 44, 59, 62, 72, 73, 81-83, 102,
      103, 105, 107, 108, 113, 121, 129,
      135, 136, 141, 148, 149
   Le Bruissement de la langue   14
   Le Degré zéro   5, 7, 43, 108
   Existences   5
   Fragments d'un discours amoureux   30,
      43, 44, 62, 73, 81, 82, 103, 107
   Le Grain de la voix   v, 149, 150

Michelet   135
   L'Obvie et l'obtus   149
   Le Plaisir du texte   40, 59, 107, 149
   Roland Barthes par Roland Barthes   6,
      107
Baudelaire, Charles   13, 38, 47, 132,
   149, 150
Beaver, Harold   98, 99
Benjamin, Walter   32, 110-112
Bernhardt, Sarah   150
bisexuality   109
Blanchot, Maurice   vii, 3, 80, 81
blason   20-22, 78
Blum, Léon   79, 83, 84, 141
Boethius   93
Bourget, Paul   2, 41, 42
Brée, Germaine   1
Brosman, Catherine Savage   62
Butor, Michel   72

Carlyle, Thomas   36
carnivalesque   4, 53, 54, 147
Carpenter, Edward   viii
castration anxiety   63, 140, 145, 147
Cixous, Hélène   125
classicism   4, 5, 9-11, 15, 41-43, 91, 93,
   103, 110
Cocteau, Jean   11, 69
Cohn, Robert Greer   16, 38

159

D'Annunzio, Gabriele   77
Dante   132
Davet, Yvonne   75
deconstruction   vii, 8
degree zero   35, 39, 47, 103, 133, 148, 149
Delay, Jean   1, 2, 34, 35, 58-60, 79, 90
Deleuze, Gilles   vii, 117, 119, 120
dénégation   61, 63, 73, 108, 112
Dermée, Paul   79, 91, 92
Derrida, Jacques   vii
desire   6, 23, 26, 29-31, 33, 56, 59, 61, 63, 72, 82, 87, 89, 90, 96, 109, 110, 128, 134, 142-44, 150
difference   12, 31, 32, 38, 39, 44, 61, 63, 64, 66, 70, 82, 94, 99, 100, 103, 124, 145
disfiguration   121-23
displacement   vi, 60, 86, 103, 112, 123, 129
Douglas, Lord Alfred   103
Du Bos, Charles   142
Dumont, Jean-Paul   64
Duras, Marguerite   72

ellipsis   11, 114, 118, 127
Ellis, Havelock   90
emblem   20, 21, 49, 97
Eve   30

feminine voice   139, 150
feminism   110, 124, 126, 136-41, 143, 146
fetishism   17, 63, 122, 145
Fillaudeau, Bertrand   49, 51
Flaubert, Gustave   9, 49
Fontanier, Pierre   9, 10, 80
Foucault, Michel   46, 48, 104
fragmentation   6, 94
framing   23, 72, 124
Freedman, Ralph   79
Freud, Sigmund   52, 61, 105, 106, 111, 112, 116, 122, 125-30, 145, 146
   Dora: Fragment of an Analysis of a Case of Hysteria   125-26, 129-31
   The Psychopathology of Everyday Life   105
Freudian slip   105, 106, 112, 113, 121, 124

Gautier, Théophile   4
gaze   21, 33, 96, 103, 116, 122, 123, 144, 145, 147, 150
gender   64, 105, 109, 110, 120, 135, 138, 140, 141, 143, 145-48
Genette, Gérard   84
Gide, André
   Les Cahiers d'André Walter   vi, 3, 24, 42
   Les Caves du Vatican   4, 49, 53, 54, 69, 70
   Corydon   viii, 32, 82, 138, 141, 142, 148
   L'Ecole des femmes   vi, 12, 107, 110, 134, 136, 139, 140, 143-48
   Et nunc manet in te   109
   Les Faux-Monnayeurs   vi, 137
   Feuillets d'automne   41
   Geneviève   vi, 110, 134-46, 148, 150
   L'Immoraliste   12, 26, 45, 79, 89, 105, 106, 110, 113-20, 122-25, 127, 137, 144
   Incidences   4, 41, 113
   Journal   v-vi, 5, 78, 95, 96, 127, 139
   Les Nourritures terrestres   vi, viii, 2, 11-12, 18, 34, 54, 55, 74-79, 81-85, 89, 91-92, 94-97, 99, 100, 102, 144
   Oedipe   110, 111
   Paludes   v-vi, 2, 4, 11, 12, 43-62, 64-70, 72-75, 77-79, 84, 92, 100, 137
   La Porte étroite   vi, 12, 27, 107, 124-34, 136
   Le Prométhée mal enchaîné   4
   Robert   vi, 16, 20-22, 34, 38, 90, 134, 136, 139-44, 146-48
   Si le grain ne meurt   44, 89, 103
   La Symphonie pastorale   12, 107, 133-34
   La Tentative amoureuse   1
   Thésée   111-14
   Le Traité du Narcisse   1, 3, 11-44, 55-56, 74, 150
   Le Voyage d'Urien   1, 39, 56
Gide, Catherine   137
Girard, René   63
Goethe, Johann Wolfgang   77, 82, 91, 93, 132, 141
Goncourt, Jules and Edmond   49
Goulet, Alain   70
Gourmont, Rémy de   141

Greimas, V.A.J. 141
grotesque 4, 30, 48, 53, 54, 61, 114, 123, 147
Gubar, Susan 139
gynotextuality 110, 137, 141, 144, 145, 148

Halsell, Albert 139
Hartman, Geoffrey 52
Héloïse 135-37, 147, 148
hermeneutics 66
Hertz, Neil 126
heteroglossia 11, 46
hieroglyphs 17, 35, 36
Holdheim, Wolfgang 48, 49, 67, 68
homoeroticism 2, 64, 115, 145, 146
homosexuality 30, 32, 64, 74, 95-98, 102, 103, 108-10, 114, 136, 138, 139-41, 143, 146, 148
homotextuality viii, 98-103, 110, 123, 141, 144, 145, 148
Huysmans, J.-K. 3, 15, 45, 49, 50, 52
hyperbole 4, 43, 79, 81-88, 90, 103, 104, 124
Hyppolite, Jean 61
Hytier, Jean 79, 85, 86, 92

imprese 21
irony 5, 8, 10-12, 20, 39, 45, 53, 55, 72, 74, 81

Jameson, Fredric 118
Jammes, Francis 75, 76
Jankélévitch 10
Jardine, Alice 117
Jones, Ernest 106
jouissance 99, 107-09, 124, 133, 148-150

Klein, Robert 21, 22
Kofman, Sarah 145, 146
Krafft-Ebing 141
La Nouvelle Revue Française 11, 100
Lacan, Jacques 61, 107, 108
Lacoue-Labarthe, Philippe 93
Laclos, Choderlos de 135
Lamartine, Alphonse de 147
Lanson, Gustave 53
Laplanche, Jean 105
lapsus 105, 110, 112, 113, 116

Le Corbusier 91
Leconte de Lisle 36
Lehmann, A.G. 1
lesbian 135, 136, 138, 142-144
lesbianism 146
litotes 4, 5, 9-11, 19, 60, 61, 67, 79-81, 83, 84, 132
Loti, Pierre 108
Louÿs, Pierre 15, 52

Maeterlinck, Maurice 15
Mallarmé, Stéphanie 1, 2, 4, 12, 13, 15-18, 33, 34, 37-39, 47, 51, 55, 57, 75, 139, 149
Mallet, Robert 34
Man, Paul de vii
marginality 97, 103, 110, 145
Martin, Claude 45, 54, 64, 76, 77
Martin du Gard, Roger 76, 77
Marty, Eric 26
Marxism 100-02
Maupassant, Guy de 3, 49
maxim 12, 92-95
McLeod, Enid 137
Meredith, George 57
metaphor 7, 40, 62, 66, 67, 94, 95, 97, 115, 121, 124
metonymy 94-96, 113
Michelet, Jules 134-37, 148
mimesis 140, 146
mise en abyme 12, 20, 23, 42, 67, 78, 121, 123
misogyny 110, 123, 141
misreading 105, 132, 134
modernism 1, 5, 52, 79, 92
myth 2, 11, 14, 15, 17-20, 23, 28-30, 32-36, 43, 47, 67, 102, 108, 110, 111-13, 118

Nancy, Jean-Luc 93
Narcissism 23, 26, 30, 34
Narcissus 2, 13-15, 17-20, 28, 29, 31-34, 36, 43, 56, 150
narrative voice 79, 109, 138
naturalism 3, 46, 92
Naturism 75, 76
negation 5, 7, 11, 13, 27, 29, 40, 44, 61, 65, 70, 71, 83, 105, 110, 120, 121, 122, 124, 128, 139

negative writing   5, 8, 12, 69, 74, 106
neoplatonism   2, 22, 24
Nietzsche, Friedrich   7
nihilism   12, 35, 40
North Africa   27, 103, 113, 145

O'Brien, Justin   91
onanism   2, 30, 88-90

paradise   14, 23, 29-31, 38, 41, 42, 150
parody   3, 30, 39, 44, 46, 47, 49, 52,
   53, 57, 64, 72, 74, 140, 145, 146
pastiche   1, 2, 4, 6, 20, 45-47, 49, 51,
   78, 94
Plato   9, 15, 30, 36, 54, 64, 82, 136, 141
polyphony   54
Pontalis   J.-B.   105
postmodernism   2, 14, 117
poststructuralism   5
Proust, Marcel   49, 50, 72, 73, 98, 99,
   119, 120, 140

Rabelais, François   53
realism   3, 4, 45, 46, 52-54, 146
récit   5, 75, 77, 79, 103, 105-07, 111,
   113, 123-25, 133, 136, 138, 140, 143,
   150
repetition   16, 23, 31, 35, 39, 40, 65, 66,
   79, 82, 88, 89, 121
repression   27, 61, 74, 79, 90, 106, 108,
   111, 112, 129
rhetoric   2, 7-9, 13, 15, 29, 33, 39, 42,
   46, 87, 116, 133, 138, 143, 148, 149
Riffaterre, Michael   85
Rimbaud, Arthur   77
Rivière, Jacques   32, 79, 81, 86-89
Robbe-Grillet, Alain   72
Robidoux, Réjean   19, 24, 34
romanticism   4, 35, 93, 94
Rondeaux, Madeleine   26, 35, 42, 109,
   124, 128
Rossi, Vinio   67
Rougemont, Denis de   136
Rousseau, Jean-Jacques   45, 135, 136,
   137

Sarraute, Nathalie   72
Sartre, Jean-Paul   79-81, 118

satire   50, 52, 72, 146
Schlegel, Friedrich   93
Schmidt, Albert-Marie   24
Schopenhauer, Arthur   24
Schwob, Marcel   75
semiotics   viii, 8, 85, 98
Seneca   93
sexual nomadism   101
Shakespeare, William   132
Simon, Claude   72
simulacrum   117
Socrates   54
Sonnenfeld, Albert   127, 128, 131, 132
sôtie   3, 4, 49, 50, 52-54, 56, 72, 78
Spivak, Gayatry   7
Stendhal   3, 135
Suleiman, Susan   139-41
Swinburne, Algernon Charles   132
symbolism   1-4, 11-13, 15, 25, 34,
   44-50, 52, 53, 72, 74, 75

Tacitus   93
Taine, Hippolyte   36, 78
textual impotence   46, 68
textual reflexivity   20
thetic   138-40, 143, 148

Valéry, Paul   9, 20, 33, 34, 57, 77
Van Rysselberghe, Elisabeth   137
Van Rysselberghe, Madame Théo   90,
   136-38
Veyrenc, Marie-Thérèse   85, 86, 92
Virgil   50, 51, 56-58, 66, 77, 78, 91, 93
voyeurism   63, 118

Weinberg, Kurt   50, 52-54, 57
Whitehorn, Ethel   137
Whitman, Walt   77, 141
Wilde, Oscar   27, 45, 103, 141, 145
Winckelmann, Johann Joachim   95

Ygdrasil   18, 35
Yourcenar, Marguerite   110

Zeitlin, Froma   140
Zola, Emile   49, 52, 54